TRANSACTIONS

OF THE

AMERICAN PHILOSOPHICAL SOCIETY

HELD AT PHILADELPHIA
FOR PROMOTING USEFUL KNOWLEDGE

NEW SERIES—VOLUME 65, PART 1
1975

THE CZECHOSLOVAK HERESY AND SCHISM
The Emergence of a National Czechoslovak Church

LUDVIK NEMEC
Professor of Humanities, Rosemont College; Visiting Professor of Church History, Chestnut Hill College

THE AMERICAN PHILOSOPHICAL SOCIETY
INDEPENDENCE SQUARE
PHILADELPHIA

March, 1975

Copyright © 1975 by The American Philosophical Society

Library of Congress Catalog
Card Number 75-2606
International Standard Book Number 0-87169-651-7
US ISSN 0065-9746

THE CZECHOSLOVAK HERESY AND SCHISM

The Emergence of a National Czechoslovak Church

Ludvik Nemec

CONTENTS

	PAGE
Introduction	3
Abbreviations	8
I. The seeds of schism	9
II. The emergence of the Czechoslovak Church	21
III. Czechoslovak-Orthodox schism	40
IV. An independent and national church	59
Index	76

INTRODUCTION

1. MEANING OF HERESY AND SCHISM

To the academic community of the Western World, the words "heresy" and "schism" are subjects which connote unpleasant situations and personalities. With the international political detente of the 1970's and its substitution of pragmatic accommodation for ideological constants, such uncongenial words are increasingly avoided.

In the ecclesiastical and theological circles of organized religions, there is even greater reluctance to employ such language, especially in the aftermath of Vatican II. Despite the current tendency to diplomatic niceties or ecumenical evasion, the historian cannot easily escape the fact that words like "heresy" or "schism" have had an objectival content for centuries. Although not always interrelated, schism[1] and heresy[2] are, nevertheless, frequent companions of the Ecclesia Semper Reformanda;[3] and, as such, appear as puzzling phenomena in the history of mankind.

In view of the variety and frequency of heresies, the question about the meaning of schisms poses a real problem.

Biblical expressions vary in their indirect and direct connotations to single out their meaning. Earlier (c. 50 A.D.) there were "factions and dissensions" (1 Cor. 1:10–:3:3; 11:19; Gal. 5:19–21' Col. 2:8) with possible connotations of heresy. The reality we now call heresy, became prominent at the end of the first century and was spoken of under the terminology of novel doctrine (1 Tim 1:3–4), doctrines of devils (1 Tim. 4:1), fables (2 Tim. 4:4), fierce wolves (Acts 20:29), deceivers (Tit. 1:10–11), false prophets (1 Jn. 4:1–6); 2 Pet. 2:1–3), unbelief (Jn. 3:19, 5:44, 8:37, 47) etc. These were not meant to attach positive significance to heresies, in the sense that they promote the knowledge and manifestation of truth, but rather as advance warning of heresy's terrible threat to salvation—a threat not only to the individual, but even more so to the Church, which heresy would tend to divert from her true goal.[4]

Initially, "heresies" meant only widely divergent Christian theologies which differed either as to the interpretation of content, or as to what was originally "given."[5] Gradually, the idea of an orthodox (universally accepted) doctrine took hold, especially when the teaching office became an instrument for preserving a sociologically oriented unity—a unity which the Church was encouraged to build in imitation of the successful organizational structures of the Roman Empire.[6] In fact, this idea of orthodox expression emerged relatively late in the history of theology, and began to take form only in the third and fourth centuries.[7] The Church's teaching function was understood to include a practical verbal expression of doctrinal belief. The teaching, once formulated, was then assumed to be also the basic expression of that faith. However, this development of unity did not go unchallenged through the centuries; various chapters in the history of theology poignantly

---

[1] E. Maguire, *Is Schism Lawful? A Study in Primitive Ecclesiology with Special Reference to the Question of Schism* (Dublin, 1915, *passim*; Derek Baker, *Heresy, Schism and Religious Protest* (Amsterdam, Holland 1972).

[2] Leon Cristiani, *Heresies and Heretics* (New York, 1959); Jean Guiton, *Great Heresies and Church Councils* (London, 1965); M. L. Cozens, *A Handbook of Heresies* (London, 1928).

[3] This is a traditional *dictum*, frequently used by Church Fathers, that the Church is in need of continuous reforms all the time, as coming of age with the times. Derek Baker, ed., *Schism, Heresy and Religious Protest* vol. IX in *Studies in Church History* (Cambridge Univ. Press, 1972).

[4] August Frazen and John P. Dolan, *A History of the Church*, (New York, Herder and Herder, 1969), p. 43.

[5] John Charlot, *New Testament Disunity*, (New York, E. P. Dutton, 1970), *passim*; Hans Dieter Betz, "Orthodoxy and Heresy in Primitive Christianity: Some Critical Remarks on George Strecker's republication of Walter Bauer's Rechtgläubigkeit und Ketzerei in ältesten Christentum," *Interpretation* 19 (1965): pp. 299–311; Helmut Koester, "Häretiker ine Urchristentum als Theologisches Problem," *Zeit und Geschichte Dankesgabe an Rudolph Bultmann zum 80 Geburtstag*, ed. E. Dinkler (Tubingen: 1964), p. 61.

[6] Francis Dvornik, *The Idea of Apostolicity in Byzantium and The Legend of the Apostle Andrew* (Cambridge, Mass., Harvard Univ. Press, 1958), pp. 3–38.

[7] W. Bauer, *Rechtgläubigkeit und Ketzerei im ältesten Christentum* (Tübingen, 1964), *passim*. H. E. W. Turner, *The Pattern of Christian Truth: A Study in the Relations between Orthodoxy and Heresy in the Early Church* (London, Mowbray 1954).

illustrate the attempt to steer the teaching office from its uncompromising course.[8] With the passing of time, especially since Vatican I, the Church seemed to crown her striving for preponderant doctrinal influence with a seemingly unshakable capstone[9] (papal infallibility).

In retrospect, one can see that the Biblical "heresy" is applicable either (a) to a body of persons who adhered to their own tenets and followed their own way of life,[10] or (b) to the unconforming dogmatic and moral dissent itself, which was stubbornly defended.[11] The follower of such false doctrine was called a heretic (Tit. 3:10). It is of the nature of religion to be polarizing, and there are many dissenters; so that the history of Christianity includes also a history of heresies. Thus, a history of Christianity includes the Church's attitude towards heresy and, a fortiori, a history of the very concept of heresy itself.[12] All religions which have anything like a well-defined doctrine experience differences of opinion about their teachings and about the agreement of the religio-sociological structures with the different doctrinal tenets. To this extent, it might be said that the "eidos" of heresy is to be found in all highly developed religions, but that only Christianity provides the presupposition for a specific understanding of heresy, viz., a radical, quite defined ethos of truth.

Thus, it is clear that the real nature of heresy is to be found only within the framework of truth.[13] Two factors probably specify the ethos of truth: the recognition that a divine revelation of truth exists; and that this truth is significant for salvation. For the Christian of earlier periods, the person who professed heresy was not simply the holder of a different opinion about which one could have a quiet chat, but someone whose views were directly and mortally dangerous to eternal salvation. The antiheretical "ethos" of Christianity was directed primarily against the error which was being aggressively welcomed into the very core of a person's existence; and, more importantly, the religious error was regarded as a danger to salvation.

Furthermore, it was to be understood that heresy was a species of unbelief. Heresy by its very nature destroys the virtue of faith and is incompatible with the general will to believe the whole of God's revealed word, with the will to accept all that God has revealed.

In the juridical realm of the Church, a heretic is defined as someone who, after baptism, and while retaining the name Christian, pertinaciously denies or doubts any one of the truths of Catholic faith.[14] Hence, to be a heretic in the meaning intended by the "magisterium,"[15] one must first be baptized. This means that heresy is an event within Christianity itself; it is an opposition from within, not from without. Nowadays, however, the whole outlook of man has become pluralistic; and this has brought about a change in the form of heresy, which Rahner calls "cryptogamic" heresy.[16] This type of heresy has an essential tendency to remain unsystemized, a fact which accounts for its peculiar and extraordinarily dangerous character.[17] The man of today lives in a spiritual, existential environment which, as an individual, he is unable to measure fully, and for which he cannot assume complete responsibility. However, this existential environment, replete as it is with pluralistic views, undoubtedly colors, and in turn is colored by, his attitudes, his doctrines, and his tendencies; so that these, too, must be regarded as heretical and contradictory to the teaching of the gospel.

The fact that the Church is "the throng of the faithful" themselves, and not a substantial something over and above the Christian community, does not prejudice our claim that this "people of God" constitutes a sacred society, governed by the officeholders, and led by the Holy Spirit. Understood in this way, the Church is the mass of the faithful, living in a pluralistic world of technology and propaganda, which is at the same time a heretical, or at least a crypto-heretically structured, world. Hence, her members, unknowingly, cannot help being infected. The Church is a church of sinners, where mutually contradictory principles can co-exist in the same person, especially if the true principles are not explicitly formulated. This unformulated cryptogamic heresy is not necessarily formal and culpable, although the Church, with greater or less success, still defends herself against it. Thus, it may be seen that there can be "practiced" heresy as well as unintentional heresy parading under the appearance of orthodoxy.

The implicit nature of this kind of heresy in today's church member finds a strange ally in modern man's reluctance to let himself be tied down to concepts in

---

[8] Gary Lease, *Witness to the Faith*, (Pittsburgh, Pa., Duquesne Univ. Press, 1971), p. 131.

[9] J. Neumann, "Die Rechtsprinzipien des zweiten vatikanischen Konzils als Kritik an der traditionellen Kanonistic," *Tübinger Quartalschrift* 147 (1967): pp. 251–8.

[10] Like Sudducees (Acts: 5: 17) or Pharisees (Acts 15: 5; 26: 5) and in the opinion of the Jews, the Nazarenes or Christians (Acts 24: 5; 14: 28: 22).

[11] (I Cor. 11: 19; Gal. 5: 20; 2 Pet. 2: 1).

[12] Karl Rahner, "What is Heresy?" *Theological Investigations* 5 (Baltimore, Helicon Press, 1966): pp. 468–512.

[13] Karl Rahner, 1966: p. 470.

[14] *CIC*, can. 1325, par. 2.

[15] John A. Abbo and Jerome B. Hannon, *The Sacred Canons. A Concise Presentation of the Current Disciplinary Norms of the Church* (2 v., St. Louis, B. Herder Book Co., 1952), pp. 557–584.

[16] *Cryptogamic* is English transl. of German *kryptogame*. The term is used of a plant having no stamens or pistils and therefore, no proper flowers. *Rahner*, 1966: p. 981.

[17] K. Rahner, *Gefahren im heutigen Katholizismus* (Einsiedeln, 1955), pp. 63–80.

religious matters.[18] Nowadays, a person's heretical view need not become theoretically expressed and exactly formulated, as would have been the case in the past. Today, one can live in heresy but shrink from formulating it as a "system of doctrine" and, in this case, the matter would never come before the Church for discussion.

This new-found heresy adopts various tactics to remain hidden. It may be a heresy of false emphasis, of exaggeration, of one-sidedness, which can be proved only with difficulty and which, consequently, cannot be branded by the Church's magisterium as heresy. The situation is made even more difficult because of certain ambiguities, ambivalences, half-truths, evasions, mental reservations, very "undialectic" and stilted formulations. The epidemic has become so widespread that, as St. Paul warned (Rom. 12:2), only the man with conscience and who is in grace, can resist "being conformed to this world." While this personal heresy is dangerous and difficult to cope with, the present essay is more concerned with traditional heresy and its sociological impact. Here is where there is a real clash between the individual and the Church.

The Church's stand is firm, and clearly stated in the sacred canons[19] which are so all-embracing that not much room is left for any opposition. Thus, under an obligation of Catholic faith, all those matters must be believed which are contained in the written word of God or in tradition, and which, thus, as divinely revealed truths, are proposed for belief by the Church's authority, either through a solemn pronouncement or through her ordinary and universal magisterium (teaching authority).[20] However, if before the Church's proposal of a doctrine as divinely revealed, anyone were individually to know of its divine origin, he would be gravely obligated to accept it; but, then, the obligation would be of divine faith, and its rejection would not render him a heretic in the juridic sense. Nor is one a heretic who violates the obligation of accepting those truths which the Church declares only to be "intimately connected with" revealed truth.[21]

Yet the mere avoidance of heresy is not enough; it is also necessary to be diligently on guard against those errors which are more or less akin to it.[22] If one pertinaciously denies or doubts any of the truths which are of obligation by Catholic faith, he is a heretic; if he gives up the Christian faith entirely, he is an apostate; finally, if he refuses submission to the pope, or if he rejects the community of faith with those who are subject to the pope, he is a schismatic.[23] If the doubting or denying of a truth results from crass ignorance, the act is not pertinacious and, consequently, not formally heretical. To be formally heretical, the doubt or denial must be both internal and external although, if it is externally manifested, the internal assent is presumed, as far as the external forum (juridic court) is concerned. If the heresy is only material, and the internal assent has occurred through ignorance, it is not blameworthy although, as far as the external forum is concerned, culpability must be presumed. These principles apply also to acts of apostasy and schism.[24]

Schism does not arise from an aloofness based on merely personal grounds, but only when it repudiates the bond of ecclesiastical union with the pope *as the head of the Church*. Ignorance may prevent the schismatic's act from being a pertinacious repudiation of the pope; thus, while outwardly committing an act of schism by deliberately cutting himself off from the pope, he might still be saved from the stigma of heresy. However, in the external forum, schism should be considered heretical.[25]

The canonical framework concerning schism and heresy has undergone some change since the recent emphasis on religious freedom[26] which permits a broader scope for dissent so as to facilitate dialog.[27] The former rigorous form of protective defense against all heretical inroads has been changed into a more open encounter to deal with them as ideologies or theories which might possibly be interpreted in a new light, perhaps eventually be compromised, maybe even accepted. The sharp white-black coloring of the Church's stand has been replaced by the many-shaded stand of tolerance toward practically everything. The former antithesis, polarization, and antagonism may disappear, and a synthetic convergence of ideas come to take its course, as a result of which, a kind of modification might occur as to

---

[18] James Hitchcock, *The Decline and Fall of Radical Catholicism* (New York, Herder and Herder, 1971), pp. 225–228 and *passim*.
[19] John A. Abbo and Jerome D. Hannon, 1952: pp. 557–564.
[20] *CIC*, can. 1323.
[21] *CIC*, can. 1324. On August 12, 1950, Pius XII issued an encyclical, Humani Generis (*AAS* 42 (1950): p. 561, setting forth anew the fundamental principles governing the teaching office of the Church, and the duty of the latter to protect divine revelation against all inroads from falsehood and error.
[22] Whether calling on its prerogative of infallibility or not, the Church discerns various degrees of error, which are characterized by a distinctive terminology, e.g. *haeresi proxima*, very close to heresy; *erronea*, contrary to the truth; *errori proxima*, very close to erroneous; *temeraria*, recklessly proposed; *scandalosa*, giving scandal or *piis auribus offensiva*, offending pious ears. In some cases, the doctrine is condemned, not as false, but as leading to false conclusions.
[23] *CIC*, 1325, par. 2. Coronata, *Institutiones iuris canonici*, (5 v., Turin-Rome, Marietti, 1935-1939) 2, 911.
[24] John A. Abbo and Jerome B. Hannon 1952: **2**: p. 562.
[25] J. Chelodi, *Jus poenale et ordo procedenti in indiciis criminalibus inxta codicem Iuris Canonici* (3rd ed., Trent, A. Ardesi & Co. 1933), p. 57.
[26] Walter M. Abbott, *The Documents of Vatican II*, (translated by Joseph Gallagher, (New York, the America Press, 1966), pp. 675–696, concerning *Declaration on Religious Freedom* of Dec. 7, 1965.
[27] Walter M. Abbott, 1966: pp. 341–366, concerning *Decree on Ecumenism* of Nov. 21, 1964.

the meaning of a particular schism or heresy. In this view, a heresy of yesterday might not be one of today; and a reappraisal of values might be in order. But, as Rahner[28] points out, this reappraisal of values does not take away the material objectivity of yesterday's schism and heresy, but only changes their modes of modern relevancy. The reappraisal may make a heresy antiquated but not entirely devaluated. This would seem to be the case with the Czechoslovak Schism and Heresy.

2. MEANING AS APPLIED TO THE CZECHOSLOVAK CHURCH

Since Vatican II there is a reluctance to use the word "heresy" but, from what follows, it will become clear that the national Czechoslovak Church represents both a schism and a heresy.

The outstanding churchman of the Czechoslovak Church, Professor F. M. Hník, himself singles out "heretical authenticity" (*Kacířská opravdovost*)[29] as one of the most important characteristics of this new church.

"A special characteristic," he says

of the first theoretical [ie., dogmatic and moral] formation of the Czechoslovak Church is her heretical authenticity against the much exaggerated orthodoxy of the historical churches. The formulation of her doctrine was intended to express the optimal Czech aspirations toward God and people so as to be acceptable to a maximal number of the faithful. This functional concern was the most decisive work of her doctrinal council because at stake was the unconditional truthfulness of the Czech relationship to God. In this regard, the new church generously offered her membership a religious freedom which was happily appreciated and utilized.

The internal honesty by which the doctrine of the Christian religion was elaborated, has brought anathema to the Czechoslovak Church not only from Orthodox Christians, but also from those who are not involved. The Czechoslovak Church was not interested in a heretical radicalism, or in novelty as such; she was trying to preserve the religious content of the early Christian credal formulas in her doctrines, putting aside only the antiquated verbiage which seemed to be unsuited to modern times. The Czechoslovak Church does not consider Divine Revelation to have been finished by the tragedy on Golgatha. Instead, she is interested in the valuable contributions offered by the most recent religious experiences of the Christian and non-Christian atmosphere, as far as is consonant with the spirit of the gospel.

The Czechoslovak Church was influenced in her heretical, dogmatic iconoclasm by the principle of evolution, transferring the application of the general evolutionary law which was valid for biology, into the realm of psychical phenomena and, concretely, into the evolution of Christian dogma. This application of the evolutionary theory encouraged the reformers of the new church to accept Christian dogma in the manner recommended by that outstanding historian, Adolph Harnack, as "Christian thought, gradually conditioned by the unfolding of time."

The most fundamental revision undertaken by the theological thinkers of the Czechoslovak Church was in the realm of Christology; while the problem of God, his essence, his qualities and his relationship to the world has been solved in accordance with Biblical theism. The Czechoslovak Church did not accept the doctrine of the Holy Trinity as presented by the orthodox dogmatists of the historical Christian churches. Instead, she proclaimed her faith in the Trinity, as independent divine persons, as hidden triune divinities; and she refrained from any metaphysical speculation concerning Christ as Logos, or Word, eternally concomitant, yet existing independently in time. Furthermore, while preserving her own religious content as to the dogma of the Trinity, she emphasized a moral sense of divine sonship in Christ. Here she simply mirrors the early Christian faith, the rich and perfect divine hope in his Essence, as well as his relationship to the Light, which is expressed in the article about the triune activity of God, as that of Creator, Savior, and Sanctifier. The Czechoslovak Church is convinced that, in this concept of the triune problem, she is closer to the historical meaning of the New Testament sources, as found in the early Christian credal formulas.

The courageous reform in the Czechoslovak Church is further evident from her critical acceptance of the proper content of God's revelation. According to her teaching, God's word is in the Bible, but not everything in the Bible represents the essence of God's will. The Bible is the book of religious experiences, whose binding power must be measured by the supreme religious experience, i.e., by Divine Revelation in Jesus Christ.

I think it would have been the beginning of the end for religious creativity if our Church were to be content with blind acceptance of a static doctrine of the Christian religion, since creativity is the basis of the first formative work which needed to be done. The doctrinal development is healthy so far and, in a certain measure, logically sequential. If we continue the ideological work so promisingly initiated, it will remain for us in the Czechoslovak Church, to prepare a correct formulation of the religiously creative factors of Christian piety, and of the ideological structure of the Catholic Churches from the church fathers, down through scholasticism, to the Renaissance, to the Counter-reformation, and to modernism. Only in this religious way will the Czechoslovak Church be able to overcome [Roman] Catholicity. At the same time it will be necessary to study the Protestant theologies of Hus, Chelčický, Luther, Calvin, Zwingli, Barth, Brunner, and Hromádka, so that we can understand the spiritual essence of the Czech Reformation, as well as that of the world, of which we are an organic part.

In rejecting old-time views which seemed foreign and unintelligible, the weakness and sterility of human thought became manifest. The religious strength of the new development will appear when we are able, in the domain of Christian truth, to evaluate correctly, according to their dynamic potential, and not according to the views of people, the internal value, the binding nature of spiritual ideals, which originate in the soil of the gospel. . . .[30]

---

[28] Karl Rahner, "What is Heresy?" *Theological Investigations* 5 (Baltimore, Helicon Press 1966): p. 508. Richard P. McBrien, *Do We Need the Church?* (New York, Harper & Row, 1969), pp. 223–227.

[29] Dr. Frant M. Hník, *Duchovní Ideály Československé Církve* (Spiritual Ideals of Czechoslovak Church, the Contribution Toward the Analysis of her Social Christian Structure) (Prague, Blahoslav, 1939), pp. 160–165.

[30] This is author's translation of Czech text given by F. M. Hník, 1939: p. 92 ff.

From the testimony of this Czech theologian[31] speaking on behalf of his Church, it seems clear that our title "Czechoslovak Heresy and Schism" is not only appropriate, but just and conceptually adequate. Heresy and schism, in both the traditional and modern sense, seem evident here, for we have a deviation from the Catholic point of view, as well as an expression of modern thought which has recourse to what is called a *Religionswissenschaft*,[32] rather than to theology. We have an attempt to express views in a framework of completely unrestricted religious freedom. Substantiation and clarification of this will come to light as we unfold the historical make-up and doctrinal development of the Czechoslovak Church.

Moreover, the title "Czechoslovak [instead of Czech] Heresy and Schism" should be explained. The movement originated, developed, and was realized in the countries of the Czech crown, i.e., in Bohemia, Moravia, and Silesia; where all the propagandizing for the schism was done, and where all the proponents of the schism were living. Only later was the "Czech Schism" extended to Slovakia where, in the beginning, there was no following at all. The importation came later through Czech officials who had been transferred there to take over government jobs. The title "Czechoslovak Heresy and Schism" was eventually accepted for convenience, to describe the National Church, rather than to suggest any kind of balanced proportionate distribution among its followers. The fact that there has never been any ardent apostleship for the Czechslovak Church in Slovakia, shows that Slovakia never was inclined towards the schism. Instead, she was forced to witness the Czech Schism spreading through her territory by the newly arriving immigrants. Eventually, through these immigrants, Slovakia came to inherit the schism. In reality the Slovaks were victimized rather than overjoyed by it. The fact that the new church was later extended also to Ruthenia, only confirms the statement that the name Czechoslovak Church was meant to be synonymous with "national church" in the Czechoslovak Republic.

One peculiarity of heresy and schism is their emphasis on dissent and protest, no matter what course of reasoning they may employ in their defense. National churches may be understood as an expression of dissent or protest in accidentals, even though they mean to continue essentially on the same spiritual mission, and share the same heritage as the universal church. They differ from the universal church in their conditioning. The difficulty of accommodating the Church of Christ to varying conditions is further aggravated by theological difficulties in understanding the Church in her divine mission.[33] This is so because of various false interpretations; and they, in turn, have established a justification for differing. National churches share a sense of righteousness in fulfilling the Church's mission, but in their own way. However, the very rise of national churches was not purely accidental, but was the consequence of a growing antithesis between nationalism and internationalism.[34] In part, this can be traced to dialectical ideology which by the year 1900 had matured sufficiently to change the political thought of Western culture and, thereby, certain attitudes towards Christianity.

It is customary to associate Marx and Lenin with dialectical thinking, but the idea of reducing everything in the world to the interaction of opposites, is almost as ancient as philosophy. The first dialectician of renown in the Western world was the Greek Heraclitus (500 B.C.) who said that it was a law of nature for everything to be determined by opposites. For him, the constant and inevitable conflict itself was effective in producing a sort of balance or harmony in the universe. "War is the father and king of all," he taught; "everything is generated by strife." He had little direct influence before our time and, except for men like Hegel in philosophy and Marx in political theory, he would scarcely be remembered.

Three forms of dialectical thinking have left their imprint on the contemporary church-state relationship, each with its own history: nationalism, patriotism, and intellectualism. Nationalism, as developed in recent decades, became an advocate of national interests and, when assuming a dialectical approach, took on an aura of myth, and went far beyond concrete facts, to become a form of belief; it was not religious in the traditional sense but, perhaps precisely because of this divorcement, was extremely effective as a motivating force. Nationalism,[35] from the word nation, means a certain unit of territory, with people of a certain past, and with

---

[31] One will find more evidence of the theological direction of this Church in Frant M. Hník, *Církve v čase rozhodování K základům sociálně theoriché orientace v Československe církvi* (Churches at the time of Decision, Concerning the Foundations of the Social Theological Orientation in the Czechoslovak Church) (Praha, 1956). Ludvik Nemec, "Czechoslovak Schism: The Appearance of the Czechoslovak Church," *Program of the Sixth Congress of Czechoslovak Society of Arts and Sciences in America* (Washington, D.C., George Washington University, Nov. 10-12, 1972), pp. 17-18.

[32] Joachim Wach, *Religionswissenschaft: Prolegomena zū ihre Grundlegung* (Leipzig, J. C. Hinrichs, 1924).

[33] Henri de Lubac, *The Church: Paradox and Mystery* (Staten Island, N.Y., Alba House 1969), pp. 1-30; Francis A. Cegielka, *Handbook of Ecclesiology and Christology* (Staten Island, N.Y. Alba House, 1971), pp. 21-41.

[34] Luigi Sturzo, *Nationalism and Internationalism* (New York, Roy, 1946), *passim*.

[35] Joseph F. Zacek, "Nationalism in Czechoslovakia," in: *Nationalism in Eastern Europe*, ed. by Peter F. Sugar and Ivo J. Lederer (Seattle, Univ. of Washington Press, 1969), pp. 166-206; it is detailed analysis, including extensive and well-selected bibliography.

certain characteristics, such as a common language and government. One's devotion to this nation and its characteristics, is called patriotism; and patriotism was an indispensable part of being nationalistic.

Especially its moderate tone, as opposed to nationalism with its extreme tone, was beneficiary to Czechs. It was due to this patriotism that Czechs and Slovaks emerged as an independent nation in 1918 and were not lost in international political intrigues of that time nor were taken over by the propaganda of Panslavistic utopia. Furthermore, it was a patriotism of Czech Catholic priests, which reconciled the Catholic Church with an emerging nation and kept church-state relationship in a balance, while extreme nationalism greatly conditioned a creation of this Czechoslovak heresy and schism.

Another form of dialectical thinking was intellectualism, an attitude which gives absolute priority to thinking rather than to moral conduct or virtues. It cultivates the intellect as the main way to happiness; it respects intellectual ability and activity above every other human possession and achievement. Once the mind's intellectual values became normative, a series of conflicting opposites was created: intellectual versus ignorant, literate versus illiterate, rational versus emotional. Another series of pejorative contrasts was suggested: reason versus religion, open versus closed mind, science versus faith, evidence versus myth, demonstration versus dogmatic assumption.

This was conditioned by the legacy of the past Hussite experience which had a profound, galvanizing effect upon the growth of Czech national consciousness. In view of this heritage the Czechs began also to liberate their mentality by following liberal modes, modern ideas, and progressivist tendencies with the emphasis on reason and national speculation.

Because of this dialectical thinking, modern man has been so affected by ideals of nationalism, patriotism, and intellectualism, that he has learned to balance himself precariously between the opposites. As Veblen writes, "Born in iniquity and conceived in sin, the spirit of nationalism has never ceased to bend human institutions to the service of dissension and distress."[36] It would seem that Czech nationalism has profoundly affected the Czech in his thinking and, as a result, he has come to express his dissent and protest so frequently and vehemently, that he seems to find himself in religious schism whenever he tries to set up a reform; revolt seems to eventuate from his encounters with new ideas. It was because of this balancing between the opposites of ideals that the "Czech Church" was in a constant tension with the universal church, and that national churches appeared so often in Czech history in one form or another. The conditioning antecedents and the history of the national Czechoslovak Church of A.D. 1920 will be detailed in the following pages.

The peculiarity of this Czechoslovak Schism is that it is so truly a product of the times, and so much the result of all the components of modern secular Czech mentality, that it represents a most advanced type of progressive rebellion against a whole theological school of thought and ecclesiastical practice. Within the framework of dialectic ideology, as mentioned earlier, the Czechoslovak Schism represents an antithesis of practically everything Rome and the Orthodox Churches in general stand for. The dichotomy may be indicated by saying that, as Vatican II tried to put the Church into the modern world,[37] the Czechoslovak Church attempted to bring the modern world into the Church. To elucidate all this, we will follow the movement, in its gradual transition from reform to revolt.

ABBREVIATIONS

AAS—Acta Apostolical Sedis.
ACV—Acta Conventus Velehradensis.
ASS—Acta Sanctae Sedis.
BKV—Bibliothek der Kirchenvater.
CIC—Codex juris canonici
Club of Reformistic Priests—Separatis part of the Union of Czech Clergy.
ČČH—Bohemian historical periodical O Český časopis historický (Prague).
Coll.—Collection of the laws and regulations of the Czechoslovak Republic.
ČKD—*Journal of Catholic clergy*—*Časopis Katolického Duchovenstva*
Cz. Ch.—Czechoslovak Church.
Č. C.—Československá Církev.
Czech. Rep.—Czechoslovak Republic.
DTC—Dictionnaire de la theologie catholique.
ES—Denzinger-Bonnwart-Umberg: Enchiridon Symdolorum (Friburgi Brisgoviae: Herder and Co., 1931).
Jednota—Union of Czech Clergy; Central Organ of the Union of Czech Clergy.
KA—Katolická Akce (Catholic Action).
LaDC—La Documentation Catholique.
NCFE—National Committee for a Free Europe, New York.
NCWC—NCWC News Service, Archives in Washington, D.C. (News service issued by the Press Department of the National Catholic Welfare Conference).
NŽ—Novy Zivot (New Life). Organ of the SS Cyril and Methodius League, London, 1949–1953; Rome, 1954–.
RBi—Revue biblique.

---

[36] Thorstein Veblen, *Absentee Ownership* (New York, Huelach, 1923); John A. Hardon, *Christianity in the Twentieth Century* (Garden City, New York, Doubleday & Comp., 1971), pp. 348–398.

[37] *Pastoral Constitution on the Church in the Modern World* (Gaudium et Spes) of Pope Paul VI—of November 21, 1969. Walter M. Abbott, *The Documents of Vatican II* (New York, Guild Press, 1966), pp. 14–96.

I. THE SEEDS OF SCHISM

The Union of Czech Clergy (Jednota)[1] was the *avant garde* of modern clerical progressivism and unionism. Its only aim had been to effect reform but it resulted in revolt (schism) as soon as heresy gained its foothold. Originally, its program was proposed for the larger dioceses where the Czech clergy considered the pressures of the predominant Germany hierarchy unfair. Back in 1895, a Union of Catholic Clergy, (*Jednota Katolického Duchovenstva*) had come into existence as an important vehicle for carrying out reforms among the Czech clergy. The success of this Union had become so great that bishops had to take it seriously. Some twenty years later, with the establishment of the Czechoslovak Republic on October 28, 1918, events began to change rapidly and, especially in the light of anti-Catholic propaganda, a revival of the Jednota seemed called for. Accordingly, ten days later, on November 7, 1918, the council of the Jednota convoked a general assembly of Czech clergy and formed a new organization, the Union of Czechoslovak Clergy in Prague (*Jednota Československého Duchovenstva v Praze*). Five months later, on April 9 and 10, 1919, the Jednota issued a 66-page official memorandum under the title of "Proposal of the Czechoslovak Clergy on the Renewal of the Catholic Church in the Czechoslovak Republic" (*Návrh Českoslovanského Duchovenstva Na Obnovu Církve Katolické v Československé Republice*).

All things considered, the Jednota now became regarded as a sign of the times,[2] a call to "reform and revolt," sounding an alarm which the universal Church could not ignore. Although some proposals in the Jednota's program were ahead of their time, most of the priests did not intend to compromise their loyalty to the Roman Catholic Church, but only to express more clearly their identification with the newly established Czech nation. To balance national and ecclesiastical sentiments was not easy for a Czech Catholic priest in those troubled times, especially since the priest's patriotism was under constant malicious attack from the "progressives."

On July 1, 1919, Rome notified the Jednota delegation that some of its demands were excessive and went too far beyond tradition. As a result, there was a three-way split among the Jednota members: (1) the conservatives, who favored an ecclesiastical *status quo* while yet remaining responsive to national issues, were led by the Rev. F. X. Novák, champion of total loyalty to the Church; (2) the moderates, who were in the majority, called for conciliation, and were under the leadership of Dean F. Krojher; (3) the die-hard radicals, who were for *de facto* revolutionary procedures, and were led by Rev. Dr. Karel Farský, who always favored opposition to ecclesiastical authority, and was especially hostile to Rome.

On September 9, 1919, Monsignor Francis Kordač, professor of philosophy at Charles IV University, was appointed archbishop of Prague and immediately there was a regrouping of the Jednota members. The conservatives rejoiced at his nomination, and the moderates expressed their loyalty and support on principle. The die-hard radicals, however, under the name *Ohnisko* (Fireplace), and with help from the Jednota Central Committee, now initiated the "double standard" policy: on the one hand they pressed for a maximum of reform, and on the other hand, by alliances and the progressive press inside and outside the country, began to exert pressure to gain their demands. Six days after the archbishop's appointment to Prague (September 15, 1919) the radicals decided to reorganize for a still more radical program under the name of Club of Reformist Priests of the Union of Czechoslovak Clergy (*Klub Reformnich Kněží Jednoty Československého Duchovenstva*).

Further trouble began to brew. Father Farský, professor of religion at Pilsen and long-time enemy of the new archbishop, now began to encourage radical reforms and attracted some alienated priests who said they did not feel at home in the Catholic Church. Frustration, confusion, secularization, liberalism, modernism, nationalism, and free thinking, along with the double standard, of thinking one way and living another, became accumulating pressures which these priests claimed they could no longer handle. In one sense these priests were products of their times although their alienation was influenced by numerous earlier hostile movements of the nineteenth and early twentieth centuries.

Since the days of John Hus (1369–1415), there had always been a progressive and scholarly element among the Czech clergy working for ecclesiastical and social reforms, always with nationalistic overtones, and often at variance with the official stand of the Church. Over the centuries we find priest reformers working zealously and with dedication, nearly all of them within the Church, although sometimes even they became idealistic rebels who, unfortunately, sided with conspiratorial heretics or schismatics. Prominent names in the Czech tradition would include Sts. Cyril and Methodius,[3] St. Wenceslas,[4]

---

[1] Ludvik Nemec, "The Czech Jednota, the Avant-Garde of Modern Clerical Progressivism and Unionism" *Proc. Amer. Philos. Soc.* 112, 1 (1968): pp. 74–100.

[2] Franz Böchle, ed., *Understanding the Signs of the Times*, vol. 25 of the *Concilium* (New York, Paulist Press 1967); see especially the chapter "Signs of the Times" by M. C. Vanhengel and J. Peters, pp. 143–152.

[3] Frant, Dvornik, *Byzantske Misie u Slovanů* (Prague, Vyšehrad 1970), idem, *Les legèndes de Constantin et de Constantin et de Méthode vues de Byzance* (Prague, 1933); L. Nemec, "Cyrillo methodian sources and their basic problems" *Czechoslovakia: Past and the Present*, ed. by M. Rechcigl, Jr. (2 v., The Hague, Mounton 1964), pp. 1151–1174 and *passim*; F. Dvornik, *The Making of Central and Eastern Europe* (London, 1949), *passim*.

[4] F. Dvornik, *The Life of Saint Wenceslas, Duke of Bohemia*

St. Adalbert,[5] St. Procopius,[6] Blessed Agnes,[7] Ernest of Pardubic,[8] John of Jenstein, archbishop of Prague,[9] who revived the Czech *devotio moderna*,[10] St. John Nepomucene[11] its reorientation in the Counter-reformation,[12] in the awakening of the patriot priests[13] in the eighteenth century, and the present century's Jednota.

These names and titles are connected with reform within the Catholic Church. Other movements, Hussitism, the Reformation, Josephinism, Febronianism, Rationalism, Enlightenment, Liberalism, Away from Rome (*Los von Rom*), Modernism, and the Czechoslovak Heresy and Schism, all represented, in some form or other, an antipathy to Rome. Yet these currents, both from within and from without the Church, while divergent in their orientations and methods, were agreed upon the need for reform; *in capite et in membris*, they were concerned about religious freedom, yet stressing nationalism in their endeavors.[14] Nationalism is closely associated with the modern tendency toward political and social democracy. When people become more literate and ambitious, they aspire to decision-making in matters they consider to their interests. As they become more democratically inclined, they discover that they can best operate the machinery of democracy within linguistic frontiers, within nationalities. In the case of Slavic peoples generally, and of the Czechs especially, this national awareness has been increasing since the ninth century so that nowhere else can there be found a nationalistic dynamism equal to theirs.

While it may be that the rise and fall of nationalism is related to an underlying tendency of modern times, it should not be overlooked that the eighteenth and nineteenth-century skepticism regarding the supernatural must have created an unnatural, disturbing mental void, especially among the intellectual and middle classes. For them it would seem preferable to supply for the deficiency with native national gods and fervent national cults, rather than with far-off cosmopolitan deities and some vague humanitarianism. At any rate, from the very outset, modern nationalism assumed a religious complection, as did also traditional and liberal nationalism. Integral, total, nationalism, however, came to surpass all its predecessors in rites and ceremonies, in mysticism and devotion, but likewise in intolerance.[15] Furthermore, Czech nationalism had a special mystique, in view of the fact that it was surrounded by Germans, always ready to control, to dominate.

Still another "underlying tendency" was a growing belief that the state, particularly a national state, could and should promote human progress. The eighteenth- and nineteenth-century era, when systematic nationalism was first formulated, was a time of eager faith in the "progress" and perfectibility of man and his society. It was the time, too, of sharp reaction against wordy debates and wars over religious dogmas; it was a time of deep yearning to substitute for words, a friendly rivalry in good works. However, it was also a time of criticism—not merely destructive criticism of existing institutions and practices, but constructive criticism to the end that institutions might be reorganized, and practices

---

(Prague, 1929); August Naegele, *Kirchengeschichte Boehmeus* (2 v., Wien and Leipzig, 1915), *passim*; Josef Pekař, *Die Wenzels und Ludmila Legenden und die Echtheit Christians* (Prague, 1906), *passim*; Josef Vajs and J. Vašica, *Literární památsy o sv. Václavu a sv. Ludmile* (Prague, 1929), *passim*; T. X. Stejskal, *Sv, Václav* (Prague, 1925), and others.

[5] F. Dvornik, *Sv. Vojtěch, II biskup pražský* (Chicago, Bohemian Benedictine Press, 1950); H. G. Voigt, *Adalbert von Prag* (Berlin, 1898); Frant.Krásl, *Sv. Vojtěch* (Prague, 1898); ed. Sittler & A. Podlaha, *Album Svatovojtěšské* (Prague, 1897); L. Nemec, "The New Historical Portrait of St. Adalbert," *Polish Review* 7 (New York, 1962): pp. 41–64.

[6] Frant Krásl, *Sv. Prokop, jeho klášter a úcta u lidu* (Prague, 1895).

[7] J. K. Vyskočil, *Legenda blahoslavené Anežky a čtyři listy sv. Kláry* (Prague, 1932); Bela Dlouha, *Blahoslavená Anežka Přemyslovna* (Prague, 1928) and others.

[8] F. Tadra, *Kanceláře a písaň v zemích českých za králů z rodu lucembarského Jana, Karla a Václava IV* (Prague, 1892), *passim*. A Frind, *Geschichte der Bischöfe und Erzbischöfe von Prag* (Prague, 1873), *passim*.

[9] R. Holinka, *Církevní politika archbiskupa Jana z Jenštejna za pontificata Urbana VI.* (Bratislava, 1933); J. V. Polc, *De origine Festi Visitationis BM.V.* (Rome, Univ. of Lateran Press, 1967), *passim*.

[10] Albert F. Hyma, *The Christian Renaissance. A History of the Devotio moderna*" (2nd ed., Hamden, Archon Books, 1965); *cf.* its review by L. Nemec, *Theological Studies* 27 (1966): pp. 122–124; Ed. Winter, "Die europaische Bedeutung des Fruehhumanismus in Böhmen," *Zeitschrift für deutsche Geistesgeschichte* 1 (Salzburg, 1938): pp. 175–185; R. Schreiber, "Böhmens religiose Bewegung im 14 Jahrhundert," *Vok and Glaube* 1 (1936): pp. 84 ff.; M. A. Lucker, "Meister Eckhard und die Devotio Moderna," *Studien und Texte zur Geistesgeschichte des Mittelalters* 1 (Leiden, 1950); F. M. Bartoš, *Ze Zápasu české reformace* (From the struggles of the Czech Reformation) (Prague, 1959); Paul de Vooght, *Les Sources de la doctrine chrêtienne d'âpres les theologiens du XIV siècle et du debut du XV* (Bruges, 1954); V. Novotný, *Náboženské hnutí česke v 14 a 15 stoletî* (The Czech religious movement in the fourteenth and fifteenth centuries) (Prague, 1920). There is a great need for a systematic work on the Czech *devotio moderna*, although the singular monographs written by Czech scholars about the precursors of Hus have rich material about it. There is an abundance of evidence for determined efforts toward needed reforms under church auspices before and during the Hussite period.

[11] Josef Pekař, *Tři kapitoly v sv. Janu Nepomuckén* (Prague, 1921); F. X. Stejskal, *Sv. Jan Nepomucký* (2 v., Prague, 1921–1922); Ed. Sittler and A. Podlaha, *Album Svatojánské* (Prague, 1896). Jaroslav V. Polc and Václav Ryneš, *Svatý Jan Nepomucký* (2 v., Rome, Křest, Akademie, 1972), *passim*.

[12] Václav Oliva, *Stručné dějiny katolické reformace v zemích československých* (Short History of Catholic Reformation in Czechoslovak lands) (2 v., Prague, Vlast, 1922).

[13] Jan Strakoš, *Počátky obrozenského historicismu a Mikuláš Adaukt* (Prague, 1929), *passim*, and others.

[14] D. Perman, *The Shaping of the Czechoslovak State, Diplomatic History of the Boundaries of Czechoslovakia* 1914–1920 (Leiden, E. J. Brill, 1962), pp. 9–27.

[15] Carlton J. H. Hayes, *The Historical Evolution of Modern Nationalism* (New York, Macmillan, 1931), pp. 298–305.

reformed so as to provide an ambience most conducive to human progress. Intellectuals looked for the practical fruition of their ideas, not in the supernatural realm, but in the realm of human reason and human effort, and hence they turned away from the Church and toward the state. It was the state, their respective states, which they would reorganize and reform and which, thereupon, would assure "progress" to them and their fellows.

In such an atmosphere, the growth of national consciousness naturally stimulated efforts to achieve greater independence from Austrian rule, and political autonomy for the lands of the Czech crown. Traditionally, the Czech nobility had based its claims for political autonomy on territorial loyalty, as expressed in their provisional constitution.[16] The rising Czech middle class, on the other hand, based its patriotism on romantic nationalism, yet still emphasizing the right of national self-determination.[17] Its demands for constitutionalism and democracy were interwoven with demands for national autonomy[18] and when, in 1918, disintegration of the Austrian Empire became imminent, the idea of a nation-state appeared to make it imperative for Czechs and Slovaks to take the administration of their affairs into their own hands. This was looked upon as fulfillment of people's expectations.

As a result, the newborn Czechoslovak Republic, a new national state, was regarded as the political antithesis to the old Austrian Empire; as a democratic republic, it was taken as the antithesis to the Habsburg monarchy. In the minds of the Czech and Slovak people, there was an aversion to everything that was closely related to Austria, including the Catholic Church, which came to be resented because of her close connection to the Catholic Habsburg dynasty. Consequently, religious liberation also came to be regarded as an urgent national need.

To handle this problem properly and conveniently, the *Union of Czech Clergy* (Jednota) undertook many activities. The times were rapidly changing and, with the cessation of World War I, a new political structure had arrived on the Central European scene. While conservatives and moderates of the Jednota tried to institute an orderly transition of the Catholic Church from the old Austrian environment to the changed atmosphere of the Czechoslovak Republic, the radicals insisted that, if the Catholic Church were to continue to be relevant for them, she too would have to be changed radically to conform to the radically secular atmosphere of a new Czechoslovak state. The radical minority, dissatisfied with the reform proposals accepted by the majority, and disturbed by the nomination of Mons. F. Kordač as archbishop of Prague, began to launch a new revolt so as to achieve their church's complete independence from Rome.

Perhaps the most interesting early aspect of the whole matter was the obvious lack of interest on the part of the Czechoslovak government itself, whose help these radicals had solicited, and had fondly hoped to secure. Prime Minister Vlastimil Tusar, a Social Democrat, recognized religion as a private matter, and Minister Antonín Švehla displayed such a disinterest in the nomination of the archbishop of Prague, that he told his colleagues in the Agrarian Parliament Club: "This is not a matter of importance to us!" The minister of foreign affairs, Dr. Eduard Beneš, made every effort to avoid any possible conflict with Rome, because he preferred to maintain a good relationship with it.[19] To young Dr. Beneš, the Catholic Church represented a world power and, skillful diplomat that he was, he knew well that it would not be profitable for the young republic to initiate a fight which could hardly be won. These facts should be kept in mind since at the beginning of the republic, one of the points included in the program of the republic had been the principle of separation of church and state. This was expressed in the so-called *Declaration of Washington* of October 18, 1918;[20] that it reflected T. G. Masaryk's thoughts on the Austrian debacle, can be seen clearly from his words:

> I am for the separation of state and church, but I do not encourage this separation because of any antipathy towards religion but, contrariwise, for the benefit of religion. The recent fall of Austria must teach a lesson to every thinking man: the long and close association of the state and the Church, and especially the subordination of the church to the political interests, did not serve well either the Church or religion; on the other hand, neither could the Church save Austria from its fall. . . .[21]

His attitude evidently was based upon the American church-state separation,[22] which had been intended

---

[16] Jaroslav Prokeš, *Základní problémy českých dějin* (Prague, 1925), p. 259, ff. 283; S. Harrison Thomson, "Czech and German: Action, Reaction and Interaction," *Jour. Central European Affairs* 1 (1941): pp. 318–322.

[17] Karel Stloukal, "Idea československého státu u Františka Palackého," *Idea Československeho státu* (Prague, 1936) 1; Josef Fisher, *Myšlenka a dílo Františka Palackého* (Prague, cin. 1926–1927) 1: *passim*: Otakar Odložilik, "A Czech Plan for a Danubian Federation—1848," *Jour. Central European Affairs* 1 (1941): pp. 274 ff.

[18] Otakar Odložilik, *Nástin československých dějin* (Prague, 1946), pp. 85–105.

[19] Ferdinand Prášek, *Vznik československé církve a patriarcha G. A. Procházka* (Prague, 1922), pp. 46–50.

[20] This *Declaration* was signed by T. G. Masaryk, R. F. Štefanik, and E. Beneš in Paris. The Declaration had twelve principal chapters, the third of which was titled: "The Church will be Separated from the State."

[21] Reinhard Steffler, *Die Neuen National Kirchen der Tschecho-Slowakei* (Leipzig, 1931), pp. 33 34.

[22] John Courtney Murray, "Separation of Church and State," *America* **76** (Dec. 7, 1946): pp. 261 ff. *Idem*, *We Hold These Truths* (New York, Newman, 1960); *idem*, "On Religious Freedom," *Theological Studies* 10 (Sept. 1949), pp. 22–23; Joseph C. Fenton, "Principles underlying Traditional Church-

for adaptation in the Czechoslovak Republic; only later was the relationship changed into a traditional church-state cooperation. The fact that Dr. Eduard Beneš, a close collaborator of T. G. Masaryk, was later instrumental in getting the opposite policy, is clear indication that Masaryk, as well as the radical minority of the Jednota priests, misunderstood the role of the Catholic Church and misjudged her vitality. Even they did not include strict separation of state and church in their reform program.

For the purpose of delineating a tentative program of this radical minority, Father Matěj Pavlík published on August 1, 1919, a special appeal to the Czech clergy titled "What We Want"[23] which reads as follows:

1. Introduction of the Czech and Slovak language into a liturgy for the Czechoslovak nation.
2. Establishment within the Catholic Church, of a Czechoslovak patriarchate which would be not merely a titular one, but one endowed with certain jurisdiction, as was the custom in the first Christian centuries.
3. Freedom of religion in the state for all, as well as for us.
4. Fostering of a truly religious and moral life and good education.
5. Abolishment of compulsory celibacy of Catholic priests and making it totally optional as was the case in the early Church, so that clerical life would become freed from the terrible burden of internal suffering.
6. Widening of responsibility of the faithful in the Church so that they will have not only obligations, but also certain rights, as was true in the early Church.
7. Amelioration of the study and education of seminarians.
8. A new adaptation of the Breviary, so that it would not be a book for mechanical recitation, but an inspirational tool for the religious uplift of men to God.
9. We desire that church ownership should not be concentrated in a few hands (Olomouc and Prague archbishoprics); and that properties of some richly endowed monasteries should be used for the benefit of all.
10. As long as the religious orders and congregations serve their proper functions and deserve to continue their existence in this territory, they should have their mother houses and major superiors in this country and not abroad.

In all this we want to liberate ecclesiastical life from absolutism and from unbearable and undesirable centralization; we want to be filled with the spirit of the first Christians; we want to eliminate those foreign elements which have been found unsuited to the organism of this nation; we want to insure development of religious life and the use of all positive resources of the Czechoslovak nation for the benefit of mankind and the growth of our country. Whoever is good, let him join us![24]

As anyone may see, at that time there was no suggestion for church-state separation, or for a schismatic church, but there was a strong determination to nationalize the Catholic Church in an acceptable and reasonable manner. There was no intent, originally, to break away from Rome, but only to adapt the Catholic Church to a new environment. The fact that the national schism happened later, reveals how much emotion was displayed at a time when there should have been restraint, moderation and patience.

Failure of the Jednota's delegation to Rome, especially the lack of generous understanding on the part of Rome for the Jednota's demands concerning the question of celibacy; and then, mainly Rome's nomination of Kordač as archbishop of Prague, were aggravating issues that caused an imbalance between reform and open revolt. Irritation now flared beyond control. Glowing optimism and angry pessimism made for mixed feeling among the Czech clergy, and the leader of the radicals, Father Karel Farský, took advantage of the situation. He viciously attacked the newly nominated Archbishop Kordač, blaming him for everything, especially for his failure to stand fast for the Jednota's demands, and for his supposed lack of interest in the contemporary church's problems, especially the needed reforms.

According to some observers[25] of the situation, this hostile and tense Kordač-Farský rivalry may have been motivated by Farsky's personal ambition for the Prague archbishopric. To gain this promotion, he had expected support from the leader of the National Democrats, the then prime minister, Dr. Karel Kramář, with whom he had been in cordial relationship, but whose looked-for help never materialized. In July, 1919, Dr. Kramář was replaced by Social Democrat Mr. Tusar, and with that, of course, the great hopes of the ambitious, despotic, and power-hungry Father Farský, faded away. In retrospect, this clash seems to have been inevitable, since both Kordač and Farský were strong-minded personalities, and were always serious contenders in mutually displaying their influence in public. However, both of them were great patriots, nationals,

---

State Doctrine," *Amer. Ecclesiastical Rev.* 126 (June, 1952): pp. 452–462; Donald J. Wolf, "American Catholic Theories of Church-State Relationship," in: *Current Trends in Theology*, ed. D. J. Wolf (New York, Doubleday, 1965), pp. 197–220; for their historical perspective, see E. A. Goerner, *Peter and Caesar: Political Authority and the Catholic Church* (New York, Herder and Herder, 1965); *cf.* its critical review by Patricia Barrett in *Theological Studies* 27 (March, 1966): pp. 138–141. Alaphridus Ottaviani, *Institutiones Juris Publici Ecclesiastici* (2 v., Rome, 1925) 2: pp. 81–116.

[23] *Právo Národa* (The Right of Nation) of August 1, 1919 (No. 13), p. 217

[24] This is translated from German text taken from Rudolf Urban, *Die Slavischnationalkirchlichen Bestrebungen in der Tschechoslowakei* (Leipzig, 1938), pp. 29–30.

[25] This observer was Father A. Havelka, who knew Father Farský personally since both (the former became archdean to Pilsen, the latter was professor there) worked in the same city for a longer period of time. His views are expressed in *Český deník* of July 30, 1931.

democrats, impressive orators, successful organizers, ambitious personalities, and scholars. A biographical sketch of these two men should include an account of why, with so much in common, they eventually became violent antagonists. In broad outline, the facts are these.

Francis Kordač (1852–1934)[26] was born into a poor farming family in northeast Bohemia, and raised under the influence of pious parents. Because of extraordinary talent, he was sent to a gymnasium in Bohosudov; later for theology, he went to the Roman Gregorian University, where he gained doctorates in philosphy and theology. He was ordained to the priesthood in 1878 for the diocese of Litoměřice (Leitmeritz). After several years as Chaplain in Liberec, he became a professor of New Testament, then rector of the diocesan seminary in Litoměřice. In 1922 he became successor to Professor Eugene J. Kadeřávek whose chair of Christian philosophy at Charles IV University he took over. During this period he was active in contributing philosophical items for the Czech theological dictionary.

Later he published independent monographs like *Bohosloví* (1915), *Bůh*, (1916), *Církev* (1916), and *Člověk* (1922), in addition to other articles and studies, in various papers and journals. Besides his scholarly attainments, he was a great organizer and builder. Along with other prominent persons, he is credited with establishing the college in Mladá Boleslav, and finishing the Pontifical College Nepomucenum in Rome. Thereupon, he was elected by the Christian Democrats as deputy to parliament in 1918, where he excelled impressively as a defender of Christian causes. On September 9, 1919, he became the archbishop of Prague. During his first ten years as archbishop, he normalized the greatly turbulent religious situation in the Czechoslovak Republic and was highly regarded by the whole nation as a social-minded, democratic, and Christian philosopher, a well-respected scholar-churchman, and he was no less highly esteemed by President Masaryk. Always ready for the defense of the Catholic Church, he was its influential protector in the newly established republic, so that his tenure as Prague's archbishop was a great blessing for the whole country. Towards the end, some tension was created between him and the nuncio Ciriaci, so that in 1932, to the great regret of the public, he was forced to resign.[27] He retired gracefully to his residence in Dolní Břežany, thereby increasing his stature, and until his death on April 25, 1934, he was respected by all at home and abroad.

Karel Farský (1880–1927) born on July 26, 1880, was the third son of a small Czech farmer in the little village of Škodějov near Rupertice near Vysoké Mýto in Bohemia. (By this time, Francis Kordač was already two years a priest.) His father, Francis Farský, led a strict Catholic family life, was always on guard against all innovations, and did not participate even in national affairs.. When Karel was twelve years old, with the support of his uncle, Msgr. Josef Farský, canon at Vyšehrad, he entered the Academic Gymnasium in Prague, where he studied in the years 1892–1900. Then he entered the priestly seminary in Prague and in 1904, was ordained for the archdiocese of Prague. He worked as chaplain in the parish of Schlackenwerth near Karlovy Vary (Carlsbad) in 1905 and, in 1906, as parish administrator on Barringen near St. Joachimsthal. Until 1909 he was lector in the theological faculty in Prague, and was then promoted to doctor of theology.

Later, he substituted as lecturer in the chair of New Testament for Professor Jan Ladislav Sýkora (1852–1928). Evidently, he did not succeed in this position because, in 1910, he became a teacher of religion in the (non-classical) Real Schools in Vršovice and Vinohrady in Prague. In 1914 he was appointed professor of religion in the (semi-classical) Real Gymnasium in Pilsen where he began to be active in politics. While here, during the years of 1914–1918, he contributed to a local Catholic paper called *Český Západ* (Czech West), and dedicated himself to the struggle for Czech ideas. Later, he contributed to the *Český Deník* and *Národní Listy*. During the war years, his political views collided with those of Father Kordač and their differences later developed into open hostility. Farský had been active in Cyrillomethodian unionism and participated in the early union congresses at Velehrad, especially in the second and third ones, in 1909 and 1911. Later, he became a member of the Jednota and, when this was dissolved, joined the Club of Reformist Priests of the Jednota of Czechoslovak Clergy. On September 15, 1919, Father Karel Farský was elected its chairman. He was also one of the candidates nominated for the Prague archbishopric in 1919, but his nomination was rejected. After the establishment of the Czechoslovak Republic, he aspired to political office, becoming chairman of the Club of National Democratic Clergy, and chairman of the National Democratic Party in the district of Pilsen. He was always on friendly terms with the national leader Dr. Karel Kramář.

On January 8, 1920, when the new Czechoslovak Church was organized, Farský became a member of its church council and its principal spokesman.

---

[26] Josef Hronek, *Přehled katalicke theologie české* (Prague, Kropač & Kucharský, 1935), pp. 9–10; Edward Winter, *Tausend Jahre Geisteskampf im Sudetenrauns* (2nd ed., Salzburg-Leipzig: Otto Müller, 1938), p. 386 and *passim*: RŠ "Prázdninová vzpomímka na archbiskupa Kordače," *Nový Život* **21** (Rome, 1969): pp. 101–111.

[27] *AAS* XXIII: p. 442: letter of Pope Pius XI to archbishop Kordač on the occasion of his resignation: Dr. F. Kordač, "Nuntius Ciciaci und meine Resignation" and "Micara und Marmaggi," *Prager-Tagblatt* (Prague) no. 9/10 of 12–13 Jan., 1934.

In August, 1921, he was chosen to be Bishop of Prague for the "new" Czechoslovak Church, and thereby also metropolitan of the entire new Czechoslovak Church. After some months, upon failing to secure episcopal consecration from a church with apostolic succession, he had himself (in 1924) consecrated "presbyterially" (in Presbyterian fashion) and, thereupon assumed the title of bishop, later receiving also the title of Patriarch of the Church, which he held until his death in 1927. As one observes his gradually expanding career, one can see how Dr. Farský must have been a skilled pragmatician, operator and architect of great ambitions.[28] His writings were prolific.

Although he was rather a popularizer, his writings represent a wide area of interest but always with reference to contemporary problems and issues. Perhaps, for this reason, he was widely read and known. His books covered so wide a spectrum of topics, that it is difficult to single out any of special interest.[29] One has but to glance at the multitude of articles, appearing in various newspapers and journals, to gain a perspective of Dr. Farsky's busy literary activities. His published materials cover church history, Czech history, contemporary political problems as well as liturgical and organizational matters concerning the Czechoslovak Church, but they do not evidence any great intellectual depth. A fair criticism of his genius, would be to say "multa, non multum."[30] In spite of all this, there are evidences of admirable qualities, such as decisiveness, determination, responsiveness to situations, ability to communicate, organize, and express himself, as well as an undoubted ability for leadership. In one way, it would seem that Dr. Farsky was the right man at the right time: a man of action in time of action; and that he acted with force as occasion presented itself.

So swift was the course of central European events that a clash between the archbishop and Farsky seemed inevitable. The radical position taken by the Club of Reform Priests was implemented by several acts of protest after the Jednota meeting of September 15, 1919. Aggravated by Rome's nomination of Kordač as archbishop of Prague, the Club publicly showed its displeasure by offering as its own candidates: Professor Xaver Dvořák, Father Jindřich Baar, Dr. Karel Farský, University Professor Dr. Adalbert Šanda, Benedictine Abbot P. Šup. of Abbey of Rajhrad in Moravia, and Father Th. Perutka, pastor of Silesia. For some time, the names of the above-mentioned candidates had been under consideration, but the matter had not been pressed publicly, since the general feeling prevailed that Rome usually moves slowly. Needless to say, all were taken by surprise this time by Rome's quick action. Publication of this list now could have had only one purpose: to discredit Rome in the eyes of the Czech public.

Another radical move was concentrated on the problem of priestly celibacy. A well-prepared campaign was waged through various Czech newspapers, e.g., *Národní Listy*, when on August 20, 1919, a proposal of the same club was publicized requesting that "the rapid purification and democratization of our religion be accomplished." The proposal continued to focus on its central issue: "We invite the Reformist clergy to start contracting church marriages. At the same time, we exhort any priest who feels in conscience that he ought to get married, to do so without delay and, by so doing, publicly purify his conscience."[31]

As if to exemplify this advice, the well-known pastor, writer, and, at that time, consultor at the Ministry of Schools, Fr. Bohumil Zahradník-Brodský, contracted a civil marriage on September 18, 1919, and encouraged other priests to do the same. When he was criticized for so doing, he explained that he had been secretly married in church[32] in 1908, hoping always that his action would be recognized as right sooner or later. However, since church recognition seemed as far away as ever, he felt he should have his marriage approved at least by civil authority. Since the Czechoslovak government had facilitated the marriage of Catholic priests through a special law, promulgated on May 22, 1919, he and other priests were taking advantage of it.

This unilateral action of the Czechoslovak government was certainly strange in view of the fact that there was, as yet, no constitution, so that the existence of this governmental provision indicates how much pressure the Club and Dr. Farsky were able to exert. By this new law, priests would still be recognized by the government as clergy in good

---

[28] Rudolf Urban, *op. cit.*, pp. 31-34 and *passim*; F. Pokorný, *Sborník Dra Karla Farského, kniha vzpomínek, dojmů a úryvků z díla a života zakladatele církve československé* (Prague, 1928), *passim*. This whole book is dedicated to the memory of Fr. K. Farský. Here one can find all data concerning his life and activity.

[29] Among his published material, the following score significantly. (1) *Stvoření. Výklad k Biblickému líčení Světa v Duchu Církve Československé* (Prague, 1920); (2) *Z Pode Jha. Vznik Československé Církve* (Prague, 1920); (3) *Zápas o Svobodu Ducha v Církvi Československé* (Pilsen, 1920); (4) *Přelom. Vzpomínkové Feuilletony k Dějinám ČCS* (Prague, 1924); (5) *Československý Katechism. Učebnice pro Mládež a Věřící Čsl. Církve* (Příbram, 1922); (6) *Stát a Církev. Poměr Státu Českeho k Církvi Římské od Prvopočátku až do Roku 1924* (Prague, 1924); (7) *Náboženství v Národě Československém* (Prague, 1924); (8) *Liturgie (Mše) pro Církev Československou* (Prague, 1925); (9) *Naše Postyla. Sbírka Prostých Výkladu a Úvah k Evanděliu Ježíšovu* (Prague, 1925); (10) *Stručné Informace v Náboženských Názorech, Úkolech a Organisaci Církve Československé* (Prague, 1929); *Zpěvník Písní Duchovních se Stručným Přídavkem Věroučné Nauky a Modliteb* (Prague, 1922), and others.

[30] Frant. Cinek, *K náboženské otázce v prvních letech naší samostatnosti 1918-1925* (Olomouc, 1926) pp. 1-3 and *passim*. R. Urban, *op. cit.*, p. 319.

[31] Dr. Josef Doležal, *Český kněz* (Prague, 1931), pp. 67-69.
[32] Rudolf Urban, *op. cit.* p. 35.

standing despite their married status. It was, of course, direct state interference in the ecclesiastical discipline of the Catholic Church, and an obvious violation of her freedom. Father Ferdinand Stibor,[23] pastor in Radvanice in Silesia, was married on September 25, 1919, in his own parish church and in the presence of priest colleagues. Some others followed suit, while still others, like Rev. Dr. Isidor Zahradnik (brother of Zahradnik-Brodsky), after his departure from the Order of Norbertine Fathers in Prague and his subsequent apostasy, was married before a justice of the peace without bothering to obtain a dispensation from the Church. He later became minister of railroads.

These canonical anomalies reveal the grave extent of the celibacy situation. Matters were further aggravated by scandalmongering conducted by (among others) the wives of these former priests. For instance, Mrs. Plesingerova-Zahradnikova, wife of B. Zahradnik-Brodsky, speaking of her entry "into the struggle for human rights,"[34] advocated priestly marriage in the name of human rights, and with emotional and sentimental demagoguery denounced priestly celibacy as nonsense. With the help of "free thinking" movements, and some non-Catholic churches, slanders against priestly life were fabricated, rumored, or so exaggerated that Catholic priests came to be ridiculed publicly, and sometimes their activities hindered entirely. Suspicion, insinuation, and innuendo were interspersed, in public accounts, to humiliate Catholic priests and to create an atmosphere of distrust among the people, thus isolating priests from the influence they had previously enjoyed. For some priests, the result was frustration, confusion, and discouragement, for others it meant greater determination to exemplify true Catholic priestly authenticity. Thus a "who's who" division began among the priests. The vast majority expressed their indignation at such dishonest tactics and reaffirmed their priestly celibacy, which now became the big issue of the day.

Another controversial issue which concerned liturgy, and was a central point of the reform proposals by Jednota, was solved by the "via facti" method (use of force). On Easter, 1919, without any ecclesiastical authorization, Father Karel Farský introduced the entire Mass in the Czech language. Using his own translation, he celebrated this liturgy in his native parish church of Rupperdorf. This was regarded as a daring novelty, although the use of the vernacular for certain parts of the Mass, had been customary for a long time. Other priests followed his example, despite the warning of Archbishop Kordač on November 15, 1919, which forbade any priest *sub gravi* (under the penalty of grave sin) to celebrate a Czech liturgy without legitimate authorization.[35] This disregard of ecclesiastical authority alarmed conscientious priests, many of whom now dissociated themselves from the Jednota. Some five weeks earlier, on October 7, 1919, the episcopal chancery office of the diocese of Brno, in Moravia, had prohibited membership in the organization, claiming it was being used for liberal abuses alien to its original purpose. Perhaps this was a reaction to Dr. Farsky's article titled "Česká Liturgie" published on October 1, in *Právo Národa*, in which he vehemently defended the practice of having the entire Mass in Czech, since the people would be benefited by their public participation. Archbishop Kordač acted quickly in an effort to cope with the continually worsening situation and, to avoid open conflict, on November 27, 1919, invited Father Karel Farský, as leader of the Club, for a conference. Father Farský described this meeting in great detail,[36] so that we have a full picture of how it went. Farsky appeared in secular clothing and shook the hand of the archbishop in greeting, omitting the usual courtesy and etiquette of kissing his episcopal ring. The archbishop overlooked this arrogance, and began a discussion on ecclesiastical reforms, the chaotic situation in general, and the problems of the laity. The archbishop outlined his reform program concerning priestly education and moral discipline. He also communicated to Father Farsky the pope's views on celibacy and the election of bishops, by point out that these traditional practices would have to be retained, although other reforms might well be adapted to modern times. He emphasized that reform must be within the Church, and that reformers must strive for what can be legitimately accomplished in accord with Rome. Archbishop Kordač begged Father Farský to reconsider the stand he had taken, and promised to compensate him for the injustices supposedly done to him by Archbishop Skrbenský and Huyn. Should he, however, refuse to follow this advice and moderate his activities, the archbishop would be forced, in the interest of Church unity, to take drastic measures to crush his opposition. Father Farsky replied that he had no faith in such promises, that it was too late to hope for the fulfillment of any promises made by the Church. The conference lasted from 11:00 A.M. until 12:48 P.M. and, by Farsky's admission, was conducted in a friendly manner with the archbishop showing extreme concern to preserve church unity. To avoid any possible breakup, the archbishop made an offer of reconciliation and forgiveness of the past, so that even Father Farsky should have been touched. Nevertheless, pride did

---

[33] Rudolf Urban, *op cit*. pp. 35–36.

[34] *Kostnicke jiskry* (Prague) of October 19, 1919. J. Doležal, *op. cit.*, p. 68; Frant Žilka, "Zum Zölibat," *Das Schwarze Korps* 27, 8 (July, 1937): p. 11 ff.

[35] F. M. Hnik, *Za lepší církvi* (Prague, 1930), n. 28 ff. *Právo Národa* 2, 17 (Prague, 1919); p. 287.

[36] Dr. Karel Farský, *Přelom, Vzpomínkové feuilletony k dějinám církve československé* (Prague, 1921), p. 10 ff.

not allow him to accept this generous offer. Antagonism and resentment were too strong to be set aside by the sympathy of Archbishop Kordač, whom he regarded as a victorious rival only trying to be nice to him. With the excuse that it was too late, Father Farsky left, embittered and without even looking back, and more strongly than ever determined to continue on his course.

That very same day, Father Farsky presided over a meeting of the General Assembly of the *Club of Reformist Priests* in Smíchov, where he related his conversation with Kordač. Now, instead of the moderation so earnestly sought by the archbishop, a still more radical course was decided upon. The Assembly agreed that, beginning with Christmas of 1919 (only a month away), they would use a Czech liturgy publicly in all their churches. That this determined action to celebrate a Czech liturgy was well planned and organized, can be judged from the fact that shortly before Christmas the *Czech Misale*[37] was published and distributed to the churches.

The real tone of the movement came to be felt in an article titled, "Historické Vánoce" (Historical Christmas), published in the Czech paper *Právo Národa* of December 15, 1919, where an appeal was made to the entire clergy to carry out this part of liturgical reform. It assured them that the Holy See would certainly understand and eventually give its approval, because a similar matter had been confirmed twice by popes "for all time," in what is known as "Cyrillomethodian Heritage." The article went on:

"Therefore, we recommend that every priest eager for reform, should begin by celebrating the Midnight Mass this coming Christmas in the Czech and Slovak language. For this reason, an announcement should be made to the people on the fourth Sunday of Advent, that on Christmas the Divine Liturgy will be in Czech; and they all should be instructed to support it because of its importance. We urgently request that *Redaction* of *Právo Národa* in Prague, Štěpánská ul. 26, be informed where the Czech Divine Liturgy will be introduced, and how faithfully this first legacy of Cyrillomethodian heritage is accepted."[38]

It must be said that connecting the new Czech liturgy with the old "Cyrillomethodian Heritage" was a skillful piece of propaganda; and it certainly influenced many by its patriotic tone. While it is true that the liturgy in the vernacular had been a privilege in the Slavic nations since the ninth century, defiance of ecclesiastical authority was always alien to "Cyrillomethodian Heritage." In themselves, such radical and illicit reforms did not seem to widen the gap immediately between the Reform Priests and those who were determined to remain loyal to the Catholic Church; but division soon began to appear, encouraged by the progressive Czech public which, by now, relished every defiance against the priests. On January 1, 1920, a public appeal was made to the clergy which said, in effect that, if "all reforms are to be conclusive, the democratization of the Church must be the next step to offset the Church's absolutism, which has now reached unprecedented heights. As the Czech nation has liberated itself from the tyranny of the past, so the Church, too, must be freed, if she is to fulfill the hopes of the Czech people."[39] The dissension among the priests associated with the Jednota had discredited the organization, not only in the eyes of dedicated local clergy, but of those abroad, especially at Rome. On January 3, 1920, Pope Benedict XV sent a letter[40] to the archbishop of Prague asking him to convoke the bishops of Bohemia and Moravia to hear their suggestions on the matter. The pope characterized the demands of the Jednota as unwise, and gave the following directives: "It is impossible to cancel the regulations and provisions concerning celibacy; the demands for a democratic constitution and the election of bishops are not in accord with the principles of canon law, which depend on papal jurisdiction."[41]

With this firm stand of the pope, who expressed great understanding for liturgical reform, but excluded the question of celibacy and a change in church structure, the Czech clergy became divided into three camps: the vast majority were consoled by it; the hesitant and weak were encouraged; and the tiny minority which, in spirit, were already lost to the Church, became bitterly aggravated.

In this tense atmosphere, the Club convoked a general assembly on January 8, 1920 at the *Národní Dům* (National House) in Smíchov, Prague, at which there was an attendance of 300 persons. Of these, 211 were priest members, some were wives of already married priests, and some were guests. In front,

---

[37] *Český Misál* (Czech Missal) published by the Club of Reformistic Priests in Prague, 1919–1920; it followed in seven booklets; Part I: for Christmas, 1919, Part II: for after the Epiphany and Lent, Part III: for Easter, 1920, Part IV: for Pentecost, Part V: Summer, Part VI: Fall, and Part VII: Fall of 1920. It received wide publicity in all progressive media and was financed by various progressive Czech circles, especially *Volná Myšlenka* (Free Thinkers). It must be said however that it was the first completely Czech rendition designed for liturgical use, and its translation for the most part was good.

[38] This is author's transl. from German text, found in Urban, *op. cit.*, p. 37, which appeared originally in *Právo Národa* 2, 22: p. 361.

[39] *Právo Národa* (Prague) of January 1, 1920; the entire appeal is to be found in Urban, *op. cit.*, pp. 38–39. This ominous "liberation of the Church" was soon to become a fact. This would reveal that the Club of Reformistic Priests had entertained the idea of schism from the very beginning, counting on the help of the progressive public, rather than on that of the priests themselves.

[40] *AAS* 11 (1920): pp. 33–37. This papal letter is marked by a determined tone and deals with every point of the reformistic proposals of the Jednota as outlined in the memorandum of the Jednota's delegation to Rome and as stressed repeatedly in public media. This papal letter clearly states the position of the Vatican.

[41] *AAS* 11 (1920): p. 34.

among others, sat the wife of Father Zahradník-Brodský, who with other ladies made a great commotion. It was the purpose of this general assembly to establish an independent national Czechoslovak church, an idea abhorrent even to some of the most radical priests.[42]

The possibility of schism was always a frightening thought to the Jednota priests, and when it actually occurred, only a few could accept it. Even those who had vehemently insisted on the *via facti* reforms, i.e., to proceed with the whole reform program without ecclesiastical authorization, spoke out adamantly at the last minute against schism. Among them were Dr. Josef Hoc, Father Holba, and Frank Ševčík, well-known catechetist and later dean in Mladá Boleslav. On the other hand, those priests who did not have much opportunity to return, like the already married Father F. Stibor of Radvanice, or the excommunicated priest and later apostate, Father Emil Dlouhý-Pokorný, were in favor of schism because for them there was no other choice left; yet even some of them felt a great reluctance. For instance, Father Pokorný expressed this thought: "If the merciful God tolerates 460 million Buddhists, 250 million Mohammedans, 200 million Evangelicals and 150 million Orthodox, then he can also save thousands of Czechoslovak Catholics...."[43] It sounded like hopeless surrender.

This stormy January 8 meeting, presided over by Father Farský, was officially described by Mr. Staněk, post minister of the Czechoslovak government and member of the Agrarian party, as "an important contribution to the progressive cause."[44] The most radical proponent was Father Zahradník-Brodský, the then ecclesiastical adviser in the Ministerium of Education who, in a spirited diatribe against the Catholic hierarchy, exhorted priests to seize the opportunity now presented to them. To the hesitant he said, "We have nothing against dogma, but only against the Church's discipline; and when the whole nation favors a change, its will must be accepted."[45] Another radical speaker, Father G. A. Procházka, pastor of Jenišovice, called for a vote to decide on a schismatic church. Some priests left the meeting at this point, and of those remaining only about 140 priests voted in the affirmative; 66 voted against the schism, and 5 votes were invalid. In this way, a new Czechoslovak Church came into existence with a newly elected board of 12 trustees, 6 clerics, and 6 laymen. The clerics elected were: Fathers Farský, B. Zahradník-Brodský, G. A. Procházka, F. Stibor, Tichý, and Smrček, although the last two declined. Many of the priests who had voted in the affirmative later revoked their consent, so that in the end only about sixty priests remained defiant.

In view of the fact that so few priests were in favor of the schism, its advocates made a strong appeal for popular support in all Czech dailies on January 10, 1920. Under the title "To the Czechoslovak Nation," there was a spirited exhortation to the people to leave the Catholic Church and join the Czechoslovak Church, for the sake of freedom and conscience, for the moral rejuvenation of the nation, and for the sake of the democratization of religious life.[46] The appeal was so extreme that most priests felt betrayed by it. Because the protagonists of the new church still retained a minority membership in the Jednota, a hurried meeting of that Society was called, at which, on January 13, 1920, a letter was composed for public circulation protesting the establishment of a separate church.[47] Thereby the majority dissociated themselves from the aims of the new sect, and in restating the real Jednota aims, affirmed its capacity to serve the needs of priests. They also published an appeal to "The Catholic Clergy and the Czechoslovak People," which appeared in the Czech dailies to warn both clergy and laity of the dangers inherent in such a new church.

The establishment of a Czechoslovak Church sounded the alarm for speedy action on the part of the Catholic bishops. In accord with the wishes of the pope, the Czech and Moravian bishops met in Prague on January 17, 1920, and came to grips with the developing issues. They published a joint pastoral letter[48] wherein they gave notice that the present Jednota was to disband; they restated the area of the legitimate reforms, condemned the Czech Schism, and put any future reorganization of the Jednota under direct diocesan control so that its officers and any public communications would require prior ecclesiastical approval.

By this strongly worded pastoral letter, two things became clear: (1) the majority of the priests of the

---

[42] Blažej Ráček, *Československé dějiny* (Czechoslovak History) (2d ed., Prague, 1933), pp. 693–695; Josef Doležal, *Český knéz* (Prague, 1930), p. 68; it is noteworthy, how tiny minority of priests was represented in the Club of Reformistic Priests (Ohnisko), in contrast membership of the Jednota was around 4,000 or more.

[43] Urban, *op. cit.*, p. 40.

[44] J. Kubalík, "Nejnovější sekty po světové válce v naší vlasti" (The Newest Sects in Our Country After the World War), *ČKD* 80 (1940): pp. 276–284; 372–376; *idem*, "Náboženská společnost českomoravská cirkví Husovou?" (Is the Czechomoravian Religious Society the Hus Church?), *ČKD* 81 (1941): pp. 217–223; *idem*, "Věrouka náboženské společnosti českomoravské" (The Doctrine of the Czechomoravian Religious Society), *ČKD* 82 (1942): pp. 292–298.

[45] For details, see Urban, *op. cit.*, p. 40. This statement is a typical example of the demagoguery by which the radicals attempted to seduce those priests of "good faith."

[46] The entire text may be found in Urban, *op. cit.*, pp. 41–42.

[47] The entire text may be found in the periodical *Jednota* of January 13, 1920; its German text appears also in Urban, *op. cit.*, pp. 43–44.

[48] The entire text may be found in Urban, *op. cit.*, pp. 45–48. Karel Farský, *Z pode jha. Vznik československé církve* (Prague, 1920), p. 48.

Jednota did not support the idea of the Czech Schism, and (2) Jednota's well-intended program had been exploited by a minority, who sought to force their drastic illicit reforms on the rest; and they, in turn, were determined to resist the pressure. Unfortunately, it was too late to avert the schism. That it developed despite the efforts against it, reveals the strong influence exerted by the "progressive" Czech public, whose patriotic acceptance of the tenets proposed by the Club contributed greatly to the formation of a schismatic ediface. To a certain extent, the blame must be shared by some Protestant churches, which encouraged the radicals in the Jednota toward an open split. One example may be seen in the proclamation of the Evangelical Church of the Czech Brethren, Free Thinkers, and Czechoslovak Church, published on March 1, 1920: "After five centuries of colorful history, in which Rome was always a destructive power, our generation of liberated Czechs must now emancipate itself from the yoke of the Catholic Church with which we were once forcibly reunited. Away with the name Catholicism. After de-Austrianization, de-Romanization must follow!"[49] Such appeals had a telling effect on priestly defections. Statistics of 1921 reveal the following (the first number represents the number of defections to the new church; the second number, those who were laicized): Prague Archdiocese, 29,17; Budějovice Diocese, 4,30; Hradec Králové Diocese, 11,31; Litoměřice Diocese, 10,10; Olomouc Archdiocese, 7,7; Brno Diocese, 0,3. Thus, only 61 defected to the Czechoslovak Church although 108 chose to return to the lay state.

These figures show that the Czech Schism found little favor even among the apostate priests, who preferred a return to the lay state rather than be associated clerically with the new church. Historically, the real harm in these priestly defections was in influencing, directly or indirectly, the subsequent defection of the laity. Lay defection followed quickly upon that of the priests, and soon the resulting struggle for church buildings erupted into such disorder that some Catholic churches were taken over forcibly for use by the new church. It required considerable legal effort on the part of Catholics to have them restored through the courts. Small wonder that the Catholic bishops of Bohemia and Moravia took such a firm stand, and that they ordered the Jednota to be disbanded. However, some Jednota representatives still felt that a great injustice had been done them, and that rather than be blamed for the schism, they should be praised for trying to correct what was a bad situation. Great indignation was expressed by Father Jindřich Baar, who wrote in answer to the bishops' pastoral letter:

For me there is only one answer:

1. As citizens we have the right to organize.
2. As priests, we already have a diocesan organization in vicariates, which is sufficient.
3. Professional questions of the priest do not merely concern those of one diocese, but are of universal interest.
4. There is no reason to crush an organization which was established with such great difficulty and which has proved its value.
5. It is unreasonable to aggravate the priests with such harsh conditions in such difficult times.
6. The newly imposed conditions for organizing Diocesan Union are a travesty on the freedom to organize at all.[50]

The creation of the Czechoslovak Church on January 8, 1920, spread a cloud of blame over the Jednota, although Rome seemed to understand the precariousness of the situation and was very careful not to extend blame beyond the Club of Reformist Priests. Thus, a decree of the Congregation of the Holy Office was issued under date of January 15, 1920, in virtue of which *schismatica nonnullorum e clero Bohemo sacerdotum coalitio damnatur*. All priests taking part in the schism were excommunicated under provisions of Canon 2384. The text of this decree reads as follows:

It has been brought to the attention of the Holy See that certain priests of the Bohemian clergy, whose actions have even before this caused protests to be presented to the same Holy See, have lately assembled in defiance of law and, in an attempt at schism, have announced their separation from the Roman Church, the mother and teacher of all other churches, and the center of Catholic unity, and have banded together in what they call a "national" church. This august body of the Sacred Congregation of the Holy Office, to whom is entrusted the task of guarding faith and morals, now deeply scorned though it be, recognizes that the said church or schismatic group falls within the scope of its jurisdiction, and forthwith reproves, condemns, and anathematizes this monstrous crime, and by this present decree, in the name of and by the authority of His Holiness Benedict XV, reproves, condemns, and anathematizes the aforementioned priests, adjudicating them, whatsoever be their status, position, and condition, to have already incurred *ipso facto* excommunication reserved by Canon 2384 *speciali modo* to the Holy See, and sentencing them to be subjected, without delay, to all attendant penalties and restrictions laid down in the Sacred Canons if—which God forbid!—they persist contumaciously in this state of excommunication. The venerable bishops of the Czechs shall, as part of their duty, take steps in as effective a manner as they, in God's sight, see fit, to make this decree known to the faithful under their charge, and to restrain them from associating in any way with this schismatic group lest they also incur the same condemnation.[51]

This action of the Holy See supported the procedure mentioned in the bishops' pastoral letter of

---

[49] This *manifesto*, published in Czech dailies, was a commentary on the 550th anniversary of the proclamation of the Crusade against the Czech heretics made by Pope Martin V; Doležal, *op. cit.*, p. 70.

[50] This reaction to the bishop's pastoral letter was published in the organization's publication *Jednota*, No. 5 (1920): pp. 12–15.

[51] *AAS* 12 (1920): p. 37. This decree of the Holy Office was signed by its secretary, Aloysius Castelano. K. Farsky, *op. cit.*, pp. 48–49.

January 17, 1920, but which the Jednota was declared dissolved, but could be reorganized on the diocesan level. Since some priests continued to be members of the disbanded Jednota, the bishops issued another pastoral letter on February 20, 1920, by which all priests were ordered *sub oboedientia* to leave the organization. However, even now the Board of Directors of the ecclesiastically disbanded Jednota made one last attempt to save it when, on March 9, 1920, the chairman of the organization, Father Krojher, sent a special petition to the Holy See requesting reconsideration of the decision of dissolution. In reply, a letter of May 6, from Cardinal Gaspari affirmed the decision of the Czech bishops as final, and said there was no need for further appeal. Archbishop Kordač of Prague then pressed the Jednota to accept the decision of the Holy See without further delay.

One may assume that the Holy See's awareness of the steadily worsening situation in Czechoslovakia would result finally in a serious consideration of the Jednota's demand for reform. Papal recognition of some suggested reforms had become all the more urgent in view of the aggravations and tensions under which loyal Catholic priests were laboring. Accordingly, although it seemed too late to avert the Czech Schism, the decree of Pope Benedict XV, May 20, 1920, revealed papal concessions regarding approved reforms. These can be summarized as follows:

1. At High Mass the singing of the Epistle and Gospel in the vernacular may be retained.
2. At baptisms and weddings, all liturgical forms and prescribed prayers may be retained in the vernacular.
3. At funerals all prayers may be said in the vernacular.
4. Litanies and the various customary prayers used at processions on the feast of St. Mark, and on the prayer day for the faithful, may be said in the vernacular whenever circumstances indicate its propriety.
5. The entire High Mass in the Old Slavonic language, written in the Glagolitic alphabet, and from canonically approved books, may be said on the feasts of Sts. Cyril and Methodius, St. Wenceslaus, St. Ludmilla, St. Procopius, and St. John Nepomucene, as well as in the following sacred places: Velehrad in Moravia; Sazava, Vysehrad in Prague; at St. Wenceslaus' chapel in the monastery of Emaus in Prague; at the grave of St. John Nepomucene at St. Vitus's Cathedral, at the grave of St. Ludmilla in St. George's in Hradčany; in the Church at Stará Boleslav, the place of St. Wenceslaus' murder; and in the shrine at Holy Berg in Pribram.[52]

That the content of this papal decree came as a great disappointment to the Czech clergy appears obvious. It merely confirmed the old privileges but conferred nothing new. In fact, it offered even less than had been sought by the Czechoslovak bishops before this time of tumult. As Father Krojher pointed out, "This decree offers really less than our episcopate had in 1872; even then our bishops demanded more than was granted to them by Pope Pius IX."[53]

Aggravated by this decree, the members of the Jednota gathered in a General Assembly on August 9, 1920, in Prague. This meeting was attended by 1,595 members, 1,528 of whom voted for continuance of the old national Jednota. Only 49 members voted for a diocesan Jednota, as suggested by the bishops. The blame for the schism, generally attributed to the Jednota, was repudiated by 1,394 and accepted by only 103 members. Such an unfortunate state of affairs was, of course, dangerous to the authority of the bishops, who made a great effort to handle the situation patiently. To achieve some kind of understanding, a special General Assembly of the Jednota was convoked eleven weeks later, on October 26, 1920, in Prague. The very popular Msgr. Antonín Cyril Stojan, vicar general of Olomouc, and Msgr. Jan Šrámek, chairman of the People's party, obviously sent by their bishops, begged the members of the Jednota to make a sacrifice for the sake of church unity, and dissociate themselves from the Jednota. In spite of their appeals, 345 members still voted for continuation of the old Jednota, while only 60 voted for its dissolution. In the meantime, Archbishop Kordač of Prague tried to settle the question by persuasion; but it was all in vain.

Unfortunately, before the earnest efforts of both the bishops and Jednota leaders could achieve accord, the Vatican acted. One can easily understand how its patience had been tried by the continued and stubborn stand of the Jednota for what its members considered relevant reforms. Nevertheless, the action taken by the Vatican now appears as ill-timed and precipitate. In a private session of the cardinals, held December 16, 1920, Pope Benedict XV delivered an allocution by which the liquidation of the Jednota was approved and its principal reform proposals rejected:

While numerous problems preoccupy our minds, two great worries sadden us. The first concerns a part of the Czech clergy, which behaves as if it has forgotten the honor of the priestly profession. You are witnesses of the effort made to bring these misguided priests to the right path. Many of them have reached the point where they even denounce their church. The majority of the Czech priests, however, have remained faithful to the Catholic Church. The Czech episcopate certainly has discharged its obligation in encouraging priestly fidelity. In a conference of the Czech and Moravian bishops, it was decided that the Czech clerical organization, the Jednota, should be liquidated and replaced by a diocesan organization under the auspices of its bishop. By the end of February, 1920, we approved this decision of the Czech episcopate through a letter sent to the archbishop of Prague.

---

[52] This decree may be found in Urban, *op. cit.*, p. 64. *AAS* 12 (1920): pp. 302–304.

[53] This criticism was publicly stated in the General Assembly of the Jednota on August 9, 1920. Pope Pius IX was generous in granting privileges to various nations in an effort to lessen the strongly antagonistic spirit which followed upon Vatican I.

However, the Jednota resisted the bishops' decision under the pretext that the clergy had not been heard. The Jednota seriously violated ecclesiastical discipline, and it was the obligation of the episcopate to intervene for the defense of the Church's discipline. The episcopate's decision announcing the liquidation of the Jednota was an act of church administration, and not that of a court. Although all this was known to the Jednota's committee, its members, nevertheless, appealed in order that their opposition might be prolonged. What is more, some priests appeared in the Jednota, and spread rumors that the Vatican intended to modify celibacy, and that it would give the necessary dispensations to priests who request it. There is no need to prove the fallacy of such statements. If and when the Catholic Church flourished in any age, it was because of priestly celibacy. For this reason, celibacy should be preserved in the Catholic Church, by all means and in all circumstances. Especially so in these difficult times when temptations to the sinful life are so many, when wild passions and lusts are so powerful that it might seem we are living only for such things.

It is greatly to be desired that the Catholic priest be a leader by his own example of self-discipline, according to the advice of Pope Siricius, who reminded us that at ordination the priest promises to dedicate his heart and life to chastity and abnegation. Therefore, we here emphatically proclaim that the Apostolic See never intended the ecclesiastical law of celibacy to be abrogated or relaxed. In our letter to Prague we have already stated that all the so-called democratic demands toward the relaxation of the Church's discipline must be rejected. We insist that the decision of the Czech episcopate concerning the liquidation of the Jednota be observed, and we again confirm it. It pleases us that the German clergy of the Czech state submitted itself through obedience to the episcopate, and that many priests of Czech nationality have already left the Jednota. It is necessary that all the rest do the same.[54]

This papal allocution was the final verdict upon the Czech reform movement. Although delivered in a rather brusque tone, it showed Rome's patience to the end, if we keep in mind that its previous warnings had gone almost unnoticed by the Jednota. The allocution was also characterized by a lack of diplomatic tone—"*sit venia verbo*." An especially bitter pill for the Czechoslovak clergy to swallow was the mention of the exemplary action of the German clergy, since the Jednota had been established precisely for protection against the German bishops. The latter had cared little for the Czech nation, frequently not even bothering to learn the language of the people, and thus alienating them from the Church. Needless to say, this papal allocution was received even by loyal Czech Catholics with mixed feelings. For the progressives, it became another weapon in their recriminations against Catholics.

One cannot but notice the difference between the harsh tone of this papal allocution as compared with all the previous ones, in which the leading motif had been the pope's rather paternal anxiety. To understand this, one has to keep in mind that agitation, turmoil, chaos, and revolt had increased so much that the pope had to express his sternness accordingly.

Interim factual and legal status of the new Czechoslovak Church was a predominant factor in all this. A proclamation to the Czechoslovak nation of January 10, 1920, noted that "until its own order can be established, the Czechoslovak Church will continue with the religious rules of the Roman Catholic Church, but renewed in the spirit of democracy." This proviso with ambivalent policies created disorder and confusion, which made the transition period more difficult both for those who were concerned about, and for those who were involved in, the schism. Since there existed no legal provision, forcible methods were used to gain possession of some rectories, churches, and buildings, to compel propaganda on behalf of the new church, to exercise undue influence on government authorities, and to exploit different enemies of the old church to the advantage of a new. As a result, staunch Catholics became more adamant in their manner, while progressives were more daring in pressing their demands; and the moderates attempted, unsuccessfully, to build some bridges to unite the already irreconcilably polarized blocs. Among the zealous "bridge builders" were some priests of the old Jednota, who had defied all orders from Rome and continued to keep this association alive with a new chairman, Father F. Xaver Dvořák, until 1923, when they were silenced by the Pius XI decree of excommunication.[55]

This was the end of the Jednota, and with it, the end of the Czech reform movement. A summary of the many and varied factors involved in the Czech reform movement shows that a vast majority of priests remained faithful to their priesthood when they realized that the tragic end of some schismatic priests was due to their extremist attitudes. While everybody had been convinced of the need for reform, the extremist views provided a facile way to heresy. The radicals continued to confiscate or vandalize Catholic Churches, thirty-six of which they seized by force, expelling the loyal Catholic priests. Through propaganda, they soon had established forty-one of their own parishes in Bohemia, seven in Moravia, five in Silesia (none in Slovakia), having 150,000 adherents, mostly former members of the socialistic and free-thinking organization. The conservatives displayed such heroism for the defense of the Catholic Church that their equal can hardly be found in annals elsewhere. It is a pity that such a worthwhile reformist organization as the Jednota should have become unwittingly a seed of schism. Yet, it is interesting to note that the founders of the Czechoslovak new church reaped what they had

---

[54] *AAS* 12 (1920): pp. 583–588, translation by the author. Only a fragment of the allocution is rendered here to illustrate the final act of Papal dissolution of the Jednota.

[55] *AAS* 14 (1923): pp. 379–330; whole decree may be in L. Nemec, "The Czech Jednota," 1968: p. 96.

sowed. They came from chaos, and they continued to live in a chaos of thought, action and following.

There is one more interesting detail to be noticed here, the relation of heresy and schism is now in reverse order. The development is marked by the schism first, to be followed by the development of heresy later, so that the final make-up of the Czechoslovak Church is a component of both. As a result, our title "Czechoslovak Heresy and Schism" is fully justified, formally and materially, by the appearance of today's Czechoslovak Church.

II. THE EMERGENCE OF THE CZECHOSLOVAK CHURCH

Having brought about the Jednota's dissolution, the militant, radical Club of Reformist Priests, proceeded to complete their revolt by separating themselves unequivocally from the Catholic Church. Unsuccessful in their effort at internal reform they now fell into the abyss of real heresy, in the eyes of the orthodox faction, by setting up a new National Czechoslovak Church on January 8, 1920. Throughout Czechoslovakia many were hoping that the forthcoming national Constitution would somehow reduce religious animosity and stabilize amicable relations but, in the final draft of late February, the proposal to separate state and church was abandoned. Opposition to the separation had been voiced simultaneously by Dr. Eduard Beneš, minister of foreign affairs, the Roman Catholic hierarchy, and Dr. Jan Šrámek, chairman of the People's party.

The Czechoslovak government had been in the process of emendation since 1918 when Prime Ministers Karel Kramář and Vlastimil Tuzar, together with President T. G. Masaryk, had first prepared a provisional Constitution of the Republic. With acceptance of the final draft on February 29, 1920, the old constitutional assembly ceased to exist.[1] While the new Constitution was accepted by the Slovak deputies and the Slovak People's party, other Slovaks under the leadership of Monsignor Andrej Hlinka, insisted upon fidelity to the so-called agreement of Pittsburgh and demanded self-rule for Slovakia, although within the framework of the Czechoslovak Republic.[2] After 1921, this unresolved dispute would become the basis of Slovak opposition. According to the new Constitution of February 29, 1920, No. 121 Coll., the main rights of religion were protected by certain provisions which advanced the principle of tolerance and freedom of conscience:

Section 117:

1) Every person may, within the limits of the law, express his or her opinion on religious matters by word, in writing, in print, in pictures, etc.
2) The same applies to legal entities within the limits of their competence.
3) No one shall suffer in the sphere of his work or employment for exercising this right.

Section 121:

All inhabitants of the Czechoslovak Republic enjoy, to the same degree as citizens of the republic, the right to profess and exercise publicly and privately any creed, religion, or faith whatsoever, insofar as the exercise of same is not in conflict with public law and order or with morality.

Section 123:

No one shall be compelled either directly or indirectly to take part in any religious rite or ceremony whatsoever; rights pertaining to paternal or guardian authority being nevertheless respected.

Section 124:

All religious confessions (denominations) shall be equal before the law.

Section 125:

The performance of specific religious rights may be prohibited if they are in conflict with public morals.

As an additional protection to the Church's position, the following laws were added later:

Law of April 15, 1920, n. 277 Coll.

Sec. 1, art. 1: "Parents shall be entitled to specify the religion of the child within 14 days from birth, or to leave the child without denomination."

Law of April 23, 1925, n. 96 Coll.

Sec. 15: "The status 'without denomination' shall also be considered a religious denomination within the meaning of the present law."[3]

Finally, the Czechoslovak laws declared the right of every adult citizen not only to choose a denomination, but also to be registered officially as having no religious denomination (*bezvyznání*). By these provisions, all religious rights were seemingly protected, legal equality guaranteed, complete religious freedom realized, and the relationship between the various churches safeguarded. All in all, we can say that democratization of religious life (to use the reformers' terms) was certainly attempted.

By a special government Law, No. 542, on September 15, 1920, the new national Czechoslovak Church was recognized also in the territory of Bo-

---

[1] The constitution was compiled by Alfred Meisner, Social Democrat. See: *The Constitution of the Czechoslovak Republic*, a reprint of the English version published in Prague in 1920 by the Société de l'effort de la Tchecoslovaquie, with an introduction by Jiri Hoelzel and V. Joachim (New York, Czechoslovak Government Information Office Service, 1947).

[2] The Pittsburgh Agreement was dated May 30, 1918. A photocopy of the text may be seen in Gottfried Zarnow, *Masaryk-Benesch, Philosophen, Absenteurer Staatsgrunder* (Berlin, 1939), p. 182.

[3] The English texts of these laws are in "Czechoslovakia: Church and Religion," compiled by Stephen Kočvara and Henry Nosek, and edited by Vladimir Gsovski; *cf. Digest-Index of Eastern European Law* (Washington, D.C., Library of Congress, National Committee for Free Europe, 1951), pp. 5–8.

hemia and Moravia-Silesia,[4] and incorporated among the nationally recognized churches. (Later, by the Law of 1925, No. 123, the Czechoslovak Church in Slovakia and Ruthenia[5] was also recognized. Perhaps the delay in extending the laws to these regions was due to the lack, until some Czechs moved in, of parishes of the new church. Naturally, before this government recognition was obtained, representatives of the Czechoslovak Church in the new territory had first to fulfill all the requirements.)

After that noisy and turbulent General Assembly of January 8, 1920, when the national church had been set up, the original membership of 140 priests who had voted in favor of schism, was gradually reduced until it stabilized at about fifty three priests actually functioning. This was partly due to the Catholic bishops' conciliatory pastoral letter calling for the return of the separated brethren, and partly to unforeseen internal difficulties which soon left only about forty priests avowedly working on behalf of the new church.

Dr. Karel Farsky moved to Prague and lived temporarily with the Brothers of Mercy who were in charge of the hospital. Here the first meetings were held and the first arrangements made for the new church in Bohemia.

The newspaper, *Právo Naroda* (The Right of a Nation), which until now had been the organ of the Club of Reformist Priests under the editorship of Father Matthias Pavlík, was easily taken over by the new Czechoslovak Church because Father Pavlík always had been a great enthusiast for a new church; and the other former members were not interested in a club which seemed about to be liquidated. Moreover, this paper had often been used for promoting the progressive cause. Later its title would be changed to *Český Zápas* (Czech Fight) to fit it into the new atmosphere and new purpose; and a former priest, Rev. Emil Dlouhý-Pokorný (1867–1936), who for his scandalous conduct[6] had been previously sentenced and suspended by the ecclesiastical court in Prague, became its editor. Thereafter, *Český Zápas* was characterized by a highly critical, often insulting, attitude toward Roman Catholicism.

The search for an appropriate location for divine worship was solved through Dr. Farsky's contacts with officials of Prague; and St. Nicholas Church[7] in Staroměstské Square near the City Hall, was turned over by the city authorities for the use of the new church. This octagonal baroque-style edifice, with chapels in its corners, had been built between 1727 and 1737 by the famed architect, Kilian Ignatius Dietzenhofer (1690–1751), under contract to the Benedictines. Vandalized in the reign of Joseph II, and later degraded to become a municipal warehouse, it was not reinstated for ecclesiastical functions until 1870, when a request was made by the Slavic Charitable Association of Petrograd,[8] Russia, for use by the Orthodox Church. Located at one corner of the Old City Square, the traditional site for all Hussite celebrations, the Church of St. Nicholas was strategically located for Farsky's purposes.

To serve the public legitimately, a special clerical committee had been elected on January 22, 1920, to petition the government formally for official recognition of the new Church as a legal entity. Members of this committee were: Dr. K. Farsky, Zahradník-Brodský, F. Tichý, Hoffer, J. R. Stejskal, Kysilka and E. Dlouhý-Pokorný. After a week's deliberation, the committee agreed to formulate the statutes which, on January 29, became the framework for the ideological basis of the Czechoslovak Church. They were published as "A Preliminary Order of the Czechoslovak Church" and read as follows:

1) The followers of this Christian religious belief who insist on the principle of freedom of conscience and of religious conviction, and who attempt to adapt their religious lives to the spirit of brotherly love, constitute the Czechoslovak Church. The ideological foundation of the Czechoslovak Church is to further the Gospel of Christ. For the Czechoslovak Church, after the Apostles, the guiding lights to interpret the Gospel in accord with contemporary spiritual needs, are the Slavic apostles Cyril and Methodius, Master John Hus and the Czech brethren.
2) With regard to centuries-old tradition, which was built up in the Czechoslovak nation by the Roman Catholic Church, and whose development and inheritance is now taken over by the Czechoslovak Church, the Czechoslovak Church will follow the religious customs of the Roman Catholic Church but with pertinent changes.
3) The Czechoslovak Church is indeed a universal or Catholic Church in the pure sense of the word. Its liturgical language is the native language.
4) The members of the Czechoslovak Church constitute the religious community within the borders of the former Roman Catholic parishes. Small communities will fuse together.
5) Each religious community will elect its own council for a period of three years on the basis of a simple majority of voters in the Assembly. Communities of up to 5,000 members will elect a council of 9; those with up to 20,000 members a council of 13; and those with over 20,000 members will elect a council of 25 elders without regard to sex. Persons to be elected must be twenty six years old, and of moral and civil integrity. The spiritual administrator of the community is an *ex officio* member and head of the council. The number of clergymen in the council should not

---

[4] Vratislav Bušek and Nicolas Spulber, ed. *Czechoslovakia* (New York, Frederick A. Praeger, 1957), p. 138.

[5] Vratislav Bušek (1957) *ibid*.

[6] Fr. Emil was living in an open-marriage-like household outside of the rectory. All parish priests, except professors in higher institutions, had an obligation to reside in an appointed rectory or any kind of spiritual house, monasteries, convents and retreat homes. Only exceptions were given to those priests who had an opportunity to live in their parents' home.

[7] Zdeněk Wirth, ed. *Dějepis Výtvarných Umění v Československu* (Prague: Sfunx B. Janda, 1935), p. 130. Antonín Pedlaha, *Posvátná Místa Království Českého* (Prague, 1907–1913) 1.

[8] This is to be found in Urban, *op. cit.*, p. 60, see note.

exceed one half the total. The other half is to be composed of elders; with this provision a complete election can be accomplished within one month.[9]

Some twenty-seven statutes followed, defining preliminary fields for religious communities and ecclesiastical offices. Statutes numbered two and three, above, are of particular interest for, clearly, they were intended to give the new church a purely national character. To say that a "native language" is a "liturgical language" does not mean that the Czech language alone was so considered; German, too was acceptable. In fact, in the pages of *Český Zápas*, (Czech Fight)[10] one learns that in the district of Znojmo in Moravia, both languages were used in liturgical services although, in view of the long-standing antagonism between Czechs and Germans, it was not anticipated that the Germans would join the Czechoslovak Church in significant numbers.

As can be seen, these Statutes left much room for forceful action by "advanced" zealots of the new church, and whenever they had an opportunity, they would seize a Catholic Church, rectory, a printing-shop, or whatever might serve the organization. From the very beginning of the new church, "incidents" concerning Catholic Church buildings became regular occurrences. The situation was further aggravated by conflicting legal claims. The Catholic Church insisted upon ownership of churches as its unalienable right, even when for some reason divine services were no longer conducted there; in this it claimed the guarantees of earlier laws. The Czechoslovak Church, on the contrary, insisted that since the churches were built with the people's money, they should belong to the people, regardless of denomination. In support of this, they claimed that the Catholic Church supposedly had taken some older churches by force after the battle on the White Mountain (1620) and appropriated them and other buildings against the will of the people, the majority of whom were Protestant. Now, three hundred years later, it was argued, the people were requesting "the return" of churches. Where there was only one church in the city, the Czechoslovak Church's members insisted that such a building should be used alternately by both. The Catholic Church's authorities opposed both claims vehemently; first on the legal ground of prior claim and the second on religious grounds because, liturgically, a church building used for heretical services would become desecrated and this should not be permitted.

To spread the claim of "double use" among the people, some zealots of the Czechoslovak Church published a pamphlet titled *O Církvi Československé* (Brno, 1920) under the slogan: "The churches belong to everyone who wishes to serve and praise God!"[11] No wonder, then, that some churches were taken by force, in disregard of the fact that the majority of the local people had remained Catholic. Such specific cases[12] were: in the archdiocese of Prague: Kolín (Filial Church), Tman, Jiloví, Lišany, Přerov; in the diocese of České Budějovice: Lnáře (Filial Church) Kremže (chapel), Tabor, Šaratice (chapel); in the diocese of Hradec Králové: Machov, Jaroměř, Kostelní Lhota, Německý Brod, Chotusice, Čáslav Holohlavy, Radhosť, Červený Kostelec, Kralove Dvor, Skuteč, Vysoké Mýto; in the diocese of Litoměřice: Louny, Velká, Kozov, Prepeře, Turnov, Všejany, Solany, Jenišovice; in the archdiocese of Olomouc: Chudobin, Grygov, Vacanovice, Cholina. Often there were violent fights between Catholics and those whom they considered apostates; even guerilla-like battles involved whole organizations, and buildings might change hands several times.

It should be mentioned that a gymnastic organization, Sokol, was very prominent in the vandalistic seizure of Catholic churches and, resultingly, the Catholic counterpart, Orel, felt constrained to defend them. Further, a great majority of "progressive" teachers in the public schools not only participated in these barbaric adventures, but also engaged themselves in iconoclastic destruction of anything sacred: statues, crosses, images, and other devotional objects. Thus, in 1919, teachers in the Prague schools began to remove the cross from classrooms and about five hundred school crosses were deposited with the city court at Valdstejn Palace. Thereupon, the Order of Christian Brothers and the Association of Catholic Teachers bought them back for ten thousand crowns and deposited them in the Institut Johanneum. Soon this iconoclastic wave began to spread to the countryside, so that the crucifix was removed from

---

[9] This is author's translation of German text, given by Urban, *op. cit.*, p. 61.

[10] *Český Zápas* (Prague), No. 7: p. 3.

[11] This pamphlet: *O Církvi Československé* (Concerning the Czechoslovak Church) (Brno, 1920) was a cleverly structured propaganda piece. Among others, it had very appropriate slogans. For illustration, one reads: "The churches belong to everyone who wishes to serve and praise God. Why should we build the Czechoslovak churches next to empty Catholic churches? The churches are the property of a nation, of peoples and these serve for the purpose of divine services to all who can use them. The churches are built as public buildings in order that they serve the public. These were built by the money of the nation, through the work and sweat of the nation. When our public was Hussite or of Czech Brethren, then the churches were also Hussite or brotherly. When paganism disappeared, the Catholic Church took over the pagan temples and changed these into churches. The Hussites took over the Catholic Church, then the Catholics, after the Battle on the White Mountain, took them back. The churches cannot be owned by one church in a manner as a certain house belongs to somebody." This is taken from Urban, *op. cit.*, p. 63 and it explains its propagandistic effectiveness. One has to realize that by 1920 there was not enough legal protection to insist on it.

[12] J. Doležal, *Český Knéz* (Prague, 1931) pp. 71–72. Antonín Šorm, *Ve jménu Demokracie* (Prague, 1922), p. 26 and *passim*: details on what vandalism has been attempted.

sixteen hundred schools. The statues of the Blessed Virgin, Saint John Nepomucene, Saint Wenceslaus, as well as hundreds of cemetery monuments were destroyed or desecrated; not even historical monuments were spared. In 1920, about three hundred churches, and their sacred furnishings, were expropriated, and about five hundred shrines robbed and dishonored. In Slovakia, although the Slovaks refrained from such insane destruction, the attacks were carried out by Czechs. The memory of such actions would later interfere with mutual understanding.

Priests were often attacked; in meetings with the progressives, they were openly calumniated. Indeed, to be Catholic in those times involved a real risk, especially in Bohemia, where the churches remained empty because people were frightened, and fearful of reproaches from their neighbors. In the schools, matters became intolerable for priests because the majority of the teachers were hostile. There were many cases where the teacher would attack the priest, and go out of his way to teach the very opposite of what the priest maintained; in the minds of children, it produced confusion and disrespect. To avoid all this unpleasantness, many priests avoided going into the schools, others remained in the solitude of their residences. Even on necessary journeys it was difficult for them to escape slander and abuse. It would appear that some sort of conspiracy, either planned or spontaneous, must have existed between the schoolteachers and the ministers of the Czechoslovak Church. At least this would explain why so many teachers were found among the ranks of its leaders and elders. Even though we ascribe such conduct to postwar anti-Catholic psychosis, it does credit to no one.

Another difficult issue was the varying liturgical experimentation conducted by individual priests. According to the Provisory Statutes, the new liturgy was to be mostly in imitation of the Catholic liturgy, but conducted in the Czech language. While the Czech Missal[13] prepared by Dr. Farsky and used for the first time on Christmas, 1919, did continue to be the formula in which the structure of the Mass remained essentially unchanged, in the summer of 1920, Dr. Farsky published the fifth booklet of the Missal, in which there were two formulas of the memorial Mass in honor of Master John Hus: the first one was according to the Roman Catholic manner, and was based on the Biblical readings. The second formula, composed by Professor Tucháček, was entirely different in that the Epistle from the New Testament was replaced by Hus's letter to the Czech nation, and other parts of the Mass were also taken from Hus's writings. Moreover, the Lord's Prayer was done in a Hussite translation and melody. The Mass text was rendered in rather free translation, so that its original authenticity suffered. A still greater surprise marked the arrival of the seventh booklet of the Missal, in which the Mass formula for the Holiday of Czech Independence (October 28), composed also by Professor Tucháček had no Biblical texts at all, but only excerpts from Czech poets and authors. The Epistle was replaced by Komensky's "Ksaft," and the Gospel, by the national oath of those who fought for the nation's freedom. Such innovations not only secularized sacred liturgy, but also alienated the faithful.

The real spirit of the liturgy of the Czechoslovak Church is well reflected in the liturgical guidelines, contained in two handbooks prepared by Dr. Farsky, namely, *Obřadní Příručka Pro Církev Čsl* (Ceremonial Handbook for the Czechoslovak Church) (Prague, 1920). The difference was not so much in the change of liturgical forms, but rather in the insinuated change of meaning. Their religious connotations were transformed into simplified, rationalistic, modernistic and secular thought. Consequently, pragmatic experimentation soon deprived liturgy of its religious content. All ceremonials concerning exorcism or expulsion of evil spirits were omitted; miracles and the supernatural were interpreted in a rationalistic way, because as traditionally accepted, they were out of harmony with modern times. In addition, the meaning of baptism was reinterpreted in a more secular sense. Ceremonials seemed to have been emptied of their traditional, spiritual content and of sacramental connotation, while a vacuum of faith resulted in an absence of prayerful spirit. Thus, the liturgy of the new church seemed to represent a kind of "worship in a secular age,"[14] with little concern for "lex orandi" and "lex credendi," but with great emphasis on national sentiment. The use of the Czech language in the liturgy did meet with great sympathy, but had little impact. The liturgy of the new church had elements which, in the structure of the Mass, were similar to those of the Catholic Church. Nevertheless, with the emphasis on the pulpit rather than on the sacrifice, it was similar to the Protestant Church; while with the score of symbolic elements, it approaches the Orthodox Churches, with the spirit of liturgy, it is in accord with the Free Churches. The minister does not perform the divine liturgy as an objective act by which Christ's sacrifice on Golgotha is miraculously repeated; instead, through the memory of Christ's life, work, doctrine, and sacrifice the faithful are inspired to imitate Christ in his life. The new liturgy placed no emphasis on the minister's role of mediator who

---

[13] As it was described before. Ant. Šorm, *op. cit., passim.* Jaroslav Hradil, "K Otázce Bohoslužeb," *Naše Dílo* (Prague, 1927), pp. 165–174.

[14] Alexander Schmemann, "Worship in a Secular Age," *St. Vladimir's Theological Quart.* 16 (May, 1972): pp. 3–16.

represents the people before God. The Catholic sacramental efficacy, expressed dogmatically as *ex opere operato* is replaced by the Protestant memorial application *ex opere operantis* (through the disposition of the minister). There is no transubstantiation, but only a symbolic presentation of Christ's sacrifice inspiring the faithful to participation. Christ's real presence is replaced by his spiritual presence only, in the manner of a memorial service. Although there is a strict emphasis on ritual prayer performed by the congregation, in its fuller sense, the whole life of the faithful is understood to be included in the act of religious piety, as a prerequisite for man's union with God.[15] This was in imitation of the early Church's agape, which stressed neighborly love as the highest fulfillment of religious satisfaction. In all, the cultus contains the ceremonial presentation of Jesus's life and sacrifice, as the center of the service. The liturgy does not contain the mystical motif of transubstantiation of the offerings. Its main interest is concentrated on the idea of the ethical perfection of the people as actively participating in all parts of the collective worship. These were the aspects of liturgy for which the Czechoslovak Church met with sharp criticism from some renowned authorities, like the Czech historians, Josef Pekař, Ernest Denis, Professor F. Mareš, and others, all of whom objected to a lack of doctrinal substance for the liturgy.

Another problem confronting the new church's leaders was the matter of its exact ecclesiastical status. The urgency of the situation was underscored by the fact that, in the absence of official governmental recognition, it could receive no financial subsidy from the state. It was not at all certain, in the beginning, how or when such a subsidy might be achieved. A bad impression, resulting from several initial turbulent activities of the new church, slowed down interest for speedy action among the members of the government. In fact, recognition came only on September 14, 1920, in the closing minutes of the very last meeting of the Council of Ministers during the rule of Prime Minister Tusar. The anti-Catholic minister of instruction, Mr. Habrman, brought up the petition and gained approval although some members of the Council said later that they had not been fully aware of the real problem. Mr. Habrman's successor, Professor Joseph Šusta, did not favor a new church at all, which suggests that under different circumstances there might have been considerable delay in getting state recognition.

Directly related to this was the question of clerical salaries for keeping baptismal and marriage records, already contracted for in the new church. Further financial problems concerned with maintaining administrative offices of the Church, created an atmosphere of tension, pressure and anxiety.

In its organizational structure, the Czechoslovak Church manifested internal contradictions. On the one hand, the trend toward democratization was deliberately encouraged, while on the other hand, a hierarchical administration was preserved with an episcopacy whose members would be elected for life. There is no doubt that the long delay in completing the constitution of the Czechoslovak Church, (not completed until 1937), was prompted by the difficulty of harmonizing an extreme Presbyterian form with a constitutive Episcopalism. Legally, democratization of the Church was assured by means of election for all ecclesiastical offices, from the administration of religious communities up to the supreme administration of the Church. Equality of clergy and faithful in the administration of the Church was also guaranteed by the irrevocable submission of all church members (clergy included) to the higher supervisory organs of the Church. This was to balance the role of laymen with that of clergy, without giving any precedence to either, and yet preserving the greater functional importance of the clergy to the faithful.[16] This was attempted by Dr. Farsky and was solved gradually, in the course of church synods of 1924 and 1931.

In the face of these many difficult problems, Dr. Farsky and his closest collaborators sought aid and encouragement from established churches which had similar creeds, but were by tradition at variance with Roman Catholicism. None of these attempts really succeeded, but the effort made is worth the telling.

The first church which had contributed so much anti-Catholic propaganda[17] on behalf of the Czechoslovak Church was, of course, the Union of Czech Brethren, since both were, in some way, an outgrowth of Hussitism and Protestantism, and insisted on their claims of close national ties with the people. Prior to the establishment of the Czechoslovak Republic, Protestants in Czech lands, without distinction of nationality or creed, were organized into a single Austrian Protestant Church, and its status was defined in the Decrees of the Ministry of Cults and Education on December 18, 1891.[18] After World War I (1918), this Austrian Church was reorganized into separate denominations along national lines. The Czech Protestants, at their Congress on December 18, 1918, established the independent Evangelical

---

[15] F. M. Hník, *Duchovní Ideály Československé Církve* (Prague, 1934), pp. 164–169; *cf.* F. Pokorný's article in *Český Zápas* of Nov. 17, 1926, where liturgy of the Czechoslovak Church is described as the liturgy of *agapé* of the Early Church.

[16] F. M. Hník, *op. cit.*, pp. 169–184, where the author deals in details of "the Democratization of the ecclesiastical administration and of the position of ministers in the Czechoslovak Church."

[17] Ludvik Nemec, *Church and State in Czechoslovakia* (New York, 1955), pp. 111–145; *cf.* L. Nemec, "The Czech Jednota, the *Avant-garde* of Modern Clerical Progressivism and Unionism," *Proc. Amer. Philos. Soc.* 112, 1 (1968): pp. 74–100.

[18] By the law No. 4 of 1892, amended by the decree of July 24, 1913, No. 155. Vratislav Bušek, *Czechoslovakia* (New York, F. A. Praeger, 1957), p. 139.

Church of Czech Brethren in Bohemia, Moravia, and Silesia.[19]

This Evangelical Church of Czech Brethren is to be distinguished from the Union of Czech Brethren, a Czech Baptist association, which did not apply for recognition.[20] In October, 1919, the government provided the Evangelical Church with the Czechoslovak Evangelical Theological Hus Faculty,[21] an independent faculty with all rights and privileges of a university. This official precedent had an obvious appeal for the Czechoslovak Church, owing partly to its religious affinity with the Evangelical Church, and partly to the necessity for providing an education of future clergy. Cooperation, not fusion, was uppermost in the minds of the leaders of both groups. In fact, the student body and faculty were eventually shared.

Those citizens who rebelled against the leadership of former Roman Catholic priests, stigmatized the result as a sect, a term much resented by adherents of the new church. To gain immediate respect for the new church, Dr. Farsky then began negotiations with the "Old Catholic Church," whose membership was largely confined to the German-speaking Sudeten region, but which had acquired some limited sense of tradition, especially under the leadership of Bishop Pašek. The discussion led nowhere; nor did Dr. Farsky succeed in getting support from the "Old Catholics" in Switzerland and Holland.

Undaunted by these rebuffs, Dr. Farsky and Bohumil Zahradnik-Brodsky turned next to the Orthodox Church.[22] Dr. Farsky's attitude toward the Orthodox[23] was well expressed in a statement he contributed to a Czech newspaper: "The Czechoslovak Church should build a natural bridge between the western and eastern Christian world. The Orthodox faithful are closer to us because of blood relationship and, although both churches have a hierarchy, they also have a democratic organization ...,"[24] The fact that some Orthodox sympathizers were already teaching on the Hus's faculty at Prague may have encouraged Dr. Farsky.[25] Similarities between the Czech Jednota's reform program, with respect to the relaxation of clerical celibacy, and the Serbian Orthodox clergy's struggle to permit the remarriage[26] of widowed priests were, no doubt, contributory factors.

Above all, their mutual appeal to the legacy of the ancient Slavonic vernacular, used in the liturgy since the early days of the Cyrillomethodian Heritage, seemed to point to closer ties. The fact that a great majority of all Orthodox Churches, including the Russian Orthodox Church, were composed of Slavic peoples, helped to produce a consciousness of Panslavism on both political and ecclesiastical levels; and by this, the Czechs were greatly affected. The idea that Orthodoxy was an outgrowth of Panslavism, was promoted by leading influential politicians like Sladkovský, Rieger, Brauner and others. It became the stronger motivating force for all Slavic political aspirations at the end of the nineteenth, and the beginning of the twentieth century. Later, in spite of the great illusion of the Bolshevik Revolution of 1917, it continued to have a surprisingly beneficial, as well as mystical, influence on Czech nationals, so that they had great rapport with anything Slavic, including the Church.[27] It was perhaps in furtherance of this sympathy that, in 1920, the new church took over St. Nicholas Church in Prague, which had preserved the old Slavonic liturgy.

This was not without historical precedent. We know that the chief negotiator for the Utraquist Church, Constantine Anglicus, as early as 1450, had already made two trips to Constantinople. The following year, his activities there had resulted in a message being sent to the Czech Estates by the Greek

---

[19] By unification of Czech Evangelicals of Helvetish and Ausburger branches in Bohemia, Moravia, and Silesia. This became legal by the Decree of the Ministerium of Schools and Public Culture of November 25, 1919, No. 625 of *The Collection of Laws* (No. CXXXV). F. Bednář, "Die Tschechisch-Brüderische Evangelische Kirche" *Die Kirchen der Tschechoslowakei* (Leipzig, 1937).

[20] Frant. Bednář, *Sbírka Zákonů a Nařízení ve Věcech Náboženských a Církevních v Republice Československé* (Collection of Laws and Ordinances in Religious and Ecclesiastical Matters in the Czechoslovak Republic) (Prague, 1929); see those laws concerning Czech Brethren, *passim*. Vratislav Bušek and others, *Československé Církevní Zákony* (Prague, 1931); *idem*, *Czechoslovakia* (New York, 1957), pp. 139–140.

[21] By the law of April 8, 1919, No. 197, of *The Collection of Laws and Ordinances* 40 (April 15, 1919) (Sbírka). This Hus Faculty was not part of Charles IV University, but an independent School of Theology.

[22] Edward Winter, *Die Geistige Entwicklung Anton Gunthers und Seine Schule* (Paderborn, Verlag Ferd. Schöningh, 1931), *passim*. Father Anton Gunther is recognized as the father of the idea of "Old Catholic Church," which spread into Sudeten and later into other Czech regions. The first bishop in Warnsdorf became Pašek, who had great interest of spreading into Czech regions.

[23] John Meyendorff, the *Orthodox Church* (New York, Pantheon Books, 1960), pp. 180–181. D. Attwater, the *Christian Churches of the East* (Milwaukee, Bruce, 1962), p. 130 ff.

[24] *Český Zápas* 3, 33 (March 9, 1920).

[25] Although Protestant himself, it was mainly Dr. Paul Kopal-Stěhovský (Stěhule) who was a lecturer on *Orthodox Thought* and who wrote several studies about this subject, for instance, *Co Vede Československou Církev ku Křestanskému Východu?* (Prague, 1921) and who stood up for Bishop Gorazd's Orthodox Orientation.

[26] In August of 1919, the priests of the Serbian Orthodox Church sent their bishops a memorandum with the ultimate alternative that either the bishops would decide favorably on the widowed priests or these priests would marry without permission. Many priests indeed married, and were suspended. Cf. Alois Hudal, *Die Serbish-Orthodoxe National Kirche* (Graz-Leipzig, 1922), pp. 98–100 and *passim*.

[27] Pawel Kopal, *Das Slawentum und der Deutsche Geist. Problem Einer Weltkultur auf Grundlage der Religiosen Idealismus* (Jena, 1914). Vladislav Šťastný, "Velká Říjnova Socialistická Revoluce a České Rusofilstvi" (The Great October Socialist Revolution and Czech Russophils), *Sborník Matice Moravské* 86 (1967): pp. 5–16.

Church, which welcomed the Czech wish to come to the source of the true faith.[28] The man responsible for this friendly attitude was the Patriarch Gennadius who was, however, the leading opponent of Eastern and Western unification. Indeed, it may be said that the 1451 acceptance of the Czech Schismatics by Constantinople was dependent upon the hoped-for survival of the great schism between the East and West. The advocates of firmness against Rome were inclined to accept the Czech accession primarily as a symbol of thier equal anti-Rome status and only secondarily as a possible accretion of strength against the impending Turkish danger. To the extent that Emperor Constantine XI tried to gain a more general western support through religious unity, the chances for the Czechs were correspondingly lessened. This was the situation which the Utraquist ambassador[29] encountered upon arriving again in Constantinople in 1452. When the negotiations were halted, they were never resumed because the fall of the city and empire in 1453 put an end to all such hopes.

Without speculating further on all the possible motivations for contacts between Prague and Constantinople in the 1450's,[30] the fact remains that the Greeks, as they had promised, did send one of their bishops (who had, of course, true apostolic succession), thus opening up the possibility of a permanent and reliable source for future priests of the Utraquist persuasion. In the context of the mid-fifteenth century, Rome need not have construed these contacts as hostile. By the twentieth century, however, Rome's attitude would scarcely have been one of enthusiasm toward the possible linkage of the Czechoslovak and Orthodox churches which, in effect, would insure ecclesiastical legitimacy and apostolic succession to the recalcitrant Czech priesthood.

At the beginning of May, 1920, negotiations with the Orthodox Church were begun by the attaché of the delegation of Yugoslavia, Mr. Crvčanin. He personally visited Dr. K. Farsky in Prague, and held preparatory talks concerning the matter, after which further negotiations were to be conducted by Bishop Dositej of Nish[31] whose visit was announced for the forthcoming Whitsuntide. The Czechoslovak Church made every effort to be ready for negotiations, and a special group, the "Orthodox Committee," was selected with the following delegates: Dr. Farsky, Fr. Bohumil Zahradník-Brodský, Dr. F. Kovář, E. Dlouhý-Pokorný, Kučera, Sen. Hetes, and Slapák.

At this point, the officials of the Vatican moved to discontinue the talks. By the end of May, the Yugoslav minister of instruction, Dr. Marinkovic, who was traveling through Prague, informed the leaders of the Czechoslovak Church that he would be open to discussion with them at Karlovy Vary (Carlsbad), where he was vacationing. Dr. Farsky hastened to interview him but was disappointed at being bluntly informed that the newly constituted Yugoslavian nation dared not jeopardize its relations with the Vatican by supporting the efforts of the Czechoslovak Church. Supposedly, Dr. Marinkovic told Dr. Farsky: "Yugoslavia cannot afford, for the time being, a Kulturkampf with the Vatican."[32] Soon after, Dr. Farsky was again disappointed in conversations with another Yugoslav official, Mr. Hřibar who, by indirection, hinted that further encouragement was not considered to be in the best interests of Yugoslavia. This negative political attitude became, of course, an omen for further ecclesiastical negotiations between church representatives of both sides.

As mentioned before, the bishop of Nish, Dositej, was sent by the Serbian Orthodox Church to discuss a possible union with the new Czechoslovak Church. He seemed to be well prepared for this role. Born in 1878 of a good Christian family of Vasič, in Belgrade, he received his theological training in the well-known Theological Academy in Kiev, and his advanced learning in philosophy and Protestant theology at the universities in Berlin and Leipzig. During these years he was under the influence of the Russian theologian, Alexios Maltzew,[33] the champion for Cyrillomethodian Unionism; for this very reason, he was a zealous participant in, and promoter of, the Unionistic Congresses in Velehrad. Later he studied in Paris, Geneva, and Bern, where he became well acquainted with the Calvinistic and "Old Catholic" theology. In 1913 he was consecrated and became bishop of the diocese of Nish. During World War I, he was held in captivity and, in 1918, became active in the reorganization of the Serbian Orthodox Church. He was spokesman for church reform, and the promoter of the organizational restructuring of the Orthodox Church in the face of the new Yugoslavian state-church relationship. Until his death, he was bishop of Agram. He was successful in reorganizing all the previously autocephalous Serbian churches, such as the Church of Montenegro, the Patriarchate of

---

[28] Frederick G. Heyman, *George of Bohemia King of Heretics* (Princeton Univ, Press, 1965), pp. 76–78.

[29] M. Paulova, "L'Empire Byzantin et les Tcheques Âvant la Chute de Constantinople," *Byzantinoslavica* 14 (Prague, 1953): pp. 153–225; F. M. Bartoš, *M. Petr Payne, Diplomat Husitské Revoluce* (Prague, 1956), pp. 41–44; idem, "A Delegate of the Hussite Church to Constantinople in 1451–1452," *Byzantinoslavica* 24 (Prague, 1963): pp. 287–292; Otakar Odložilík, *The Hussite King: Bohemia in European Affairs, 1440–1471* (New Brunswick, N. J. Rutgers Univ. Press, 1965), *passim*.

[30] Rudolf Urbánek, *Věk Poděbradský* 4 v. (Prague, 1915–1962) 2: p. 612 ff. Some historians have different views on the matter.

[31] Orazio M. Premoli, *Contemporary Church History 1900–1925* (London, 1932), p. 242 ff.

[32] F. Prášek, *Vznik Československé Církve a Patriarcha G. A. Procházka* (Prague, 1924), p. 81 ff.

[33] He participated in the Second Congress in Velehrad in 1909 and had a lecture: "De Vestigilis Epicleseos in Missa Romana," *Acta II Conventus Velehradensis* (Prague, 1910), pp. 135–143; on page 5 of the *Acta* he is identified as the Spiritual Delegate of the Imperial Russian Delegation in Berlin.

Karlowitz, the Metropolitanate of Czernowitz, the Serbian Church of the Kingdom of Serbia, and the Church of Bosnia-Herzegovina, so that they became united to the Serbian Church in 1920 under the primate of the Serbian Church residing in Belgrade, and who was also over all the Orthodox in the new state of Yugoslavia. The ecumenical patriarch of Constantinople approved this arrangement on March 9, 1922, and recognized the head of the Church as patriarch.[34]

Before the war (1914–1918), the Serbian patriarch had jurisdiction over the diocese of Mukacevo in Ruthenia; and there was always a tendency for the Serbian Orthodox Church to patronize the Orthodox Church in Czechoslovakia. With this historical background, it is clear that the Serbian Orthodox Church was in a legitimate position to fulfill the expectations of the Czechoslovak Church.

In spite of the political rebuff from Yugoslavia in May and June, Bishop Dositej was welcomed in Prague on August 22, 1920, and negotiations were held there from August 23 to 29. On August 23, Mr. Bohumil Zahradník-Brodský presided at the conference, while on August 24, Dr. Farsky took a leading role in the conferences. Based on these negotiations, a document by the Serbian Church was composed to announce its conditions, which Bishop Dositej stated as follows: (1) unconditional acceptance of the Nicene-Constantinopolitan Creed of the Serbian Church, (2) acceptance of the regulations and laws of the Serbian Orthodox Church, (3) the language of the liturgy should be Czech, but on important feast days should be Old Slavonic, (4) priests of the Czechoslovak Church should be permitted to marry, but bishops were not allowed to do so, (5) the church should be called the Czechoslovak Orthodox Church (*Pravoslavná Církev Československá*).[35]

These conditions were difficult for the Council of the Czechoslovak Church to accept. In fact, one of its members, Dr. Dvořák, proclaimed them as completely unacceptable, because the Czechoslovak Church, which tried so hard to throw off the slavery of the Roman Church, would fall again under the domination of another church. Nevertheless, after turbulent discussions, a group led by Bohumil Zahradník and A. Ševčík won enough favorable votes for acceptance of the conditions. Some members hoped that reforms might be achieved later. At the very last minute, the *avant-garde* of those not in favor of these conditions succeeded in adding the following reservation, "All rights of freedom of conscience and principles of free religious development must be preserved."[36] It is interesting to note that Fr. Matthias Pavlík was a great promoter of this reservation, although he was also a zealous proponent of Orthodox orientation for the Czechoslovak Church. This shows that the Czechoslovak Church was rather pressured into rapport with the Serbian Church by difficulties, including financial ones, and she did not act with totally free deliberation.

Negotiations were concluded with solemn celebration of the divine liturgy in St. Nicholas' Church in Prague on Sunday, August 29, by Bishop Dositej together with the Orthodox priest, Dr. Crvčanin, a member of the Yugoslavian delegation, and a Russian priest, a resident in Prague. The liturgy was attended by a great number of people and was an impressive experience to all present. Dr. Farsky utilized this event in his homily by showing a historical connection with this liturgy and the aspirations of the Czechoslovak Church. After him, the Rev. Keating Smith, a minister from Westfield, Massachusetts, who had come to Czechoslovakia as a delegate of the American Episcopal Church, spoke in English and stressed the need of this rapport among the churches. The external agreement was, of course, much stronger than the internal consensus of the churches on both sides. In general, the result of these negotiations was felt as not very promising.

On September 3, 1920, by way of compromise, a Czechoslovak memorandum was prepared in reply to the Serbian Orthodox Church. It read as follows:

To the Most Reverend, Most Holy Sabor (Council) of the United Serbian Orthodox Church in Belgrade:
In the name of the Czechoslovak Church, the undersigned Central Committee requests the union of the Czechoslovak Church with the Serbian Orthodox Church under the following conditions:

I. The Czech nation cherishes the memory of the great work of the holy apostles Cyril and Methodius who brought the light of Christian truth to the Czechs, and who established the foundations of Czech as well as Yugoslav and all Slavic culture. Unfortunately, the German hierarchy tore apart the bonds which united us with all eastern Slavs and, as a result, our nation came under the domination of Rome, which always has been the enemy of our nation and of all Slavic aspirations. It was our great priest and martyr of blessed memory, Master John Hus, who through his teaching concerning the freedom of conscience, fought for the moral renewal of the nation, and for its separation from Rome as well as for Christian understanding.

But, in spite of all political and other difficulties which this man and the Czech nation had to experience because of conflicting outlooks on life, a fresh understanding and Christian renewal of Slavic solidarity became reality. Only after having achieved political independence did our people return to this great thought, related to both Sts. Cyril and Methodius and to Holy John Hus, all of whom were responsible for bringing us the light of Christ's

---

[34] Victor Pospischil, *Der Patriarch in der Serbish-Orthodox Kirche* (Vienna, Verlag Heider, 1966), *passim*. John Meyendorff, *The Orthodox Church* (New York, Pantheon Book 1960), pp. 161–162.

[35] This is reported by Urban, *op. cit.*, pp. 71–72.

[36] This is open door for double standard of liberal orientations of the Czechoslovak Church, for which this new church became known.

teaching, so that we became members of the great Slavic family under the guidance of Christian faith. The Czechoslovak Church, as guardian of this idea, expresses its willingness to accept the teaching of the Serbian Orthodox Church, following that of the seven Ecumenical Councils, and to follow the ordinances and laws of the United Serbian Church with the reservation of freedom and conscience and free religious development.

II. With regard to certain great difficulties, and in view of the character of the Czech nation, the Central Committee of the Czechoslovak Church proposes the following points:

(1) The Czechoslovak language will be the language of the Liturgy, and will be used in the whole Mass and public functions. The Czechoslovak Church will try to see that the young clergy learn old Slavonic, so that they will be able, one day, to celebrate Mass in the old Slavonic vernacular.

(2) We ask, further, that the ceremonies, i.e., Holy Mass, as well as other functions, be carried out in the present contemporary manner. In the course of time, the necessary books, prayers, and ceremonies will be adapted so as to become different from those of the Catholic Church, and more fitting for the new church. All this will be updated as long as these traditions are not contrary to the customs of the people.

(3) We ask that the members of the Czechoslovak Church be democratic, so that the priests will be sent out for spiritual administration only, and with the consent of the parish church councils. In regard to those higher clerical offices, including bishoprics, we ask that these offices be filled with the consent of the faithful, and that no one should become a bishop if the majority of the people are against him.

(4) We ask that, after union is accomplished, our priests will not have to undergo a new ordination; analogically, as the Roman Catholic Church would not ordain Orthodox priests when they change from the Orthodox Church to the Roman Catholic Church.

(5) We ask that our priests be permitted to marry, not only before, but after priestly ordination, and not only once, but even twice or thrice.

(6) We ask that, unless the prohibition against marriage by candidates for episcopal office is not abolished by the Ecumenical Council, then, as long as we do not have enough single candidates for this dignity, married men be given permission to be consecrated as bishops.

(7) We ask that the United Serbian Orthodox Church send its bishop to the Czechoslovak Republic, to help organize, and be the ordinary of our Church, until such time as we have our own Czechoslovak bishops. Expressly and urgently we request that the Most Reverend Bishop Dositej be sent to us because we have full confidence in him.

(8) We ask that after organization of our Church is completed, and our bishops consecrated, they should take over the leadership of the Czechoslovak Church as an independent and autocephalous one. In this regard, especially since there is a justifiable fear that the Roman Catholic Church may attempt to paralyze all connections of our nation with the Serbian Orthodox Church, by establishing a Roman Catholic patriarchate in our Republic, we request that the consecration of our bishops be as soon as possible so they may participate in our Ecumenical Council, to be held in the year 1921.

(9) We ask that the economic position of our priests be justly and adequately provided for. The priests should then be salaried in category A, as applied to state employees, and as officials (with academic education).

(10) We ask that, for the time being, since we cannot open our own faculty and institute for our seminarians, fifteen of our students be accepted in the Theological Seminary in Belgrade for an education.

(11) We ask that there should be no restrictions for women, if they have the ability and intelligence, to become members of the parish Church councils.

(12) Since under the name of "Orthodox" many Czechoslovaks might wrongly suppose the same ecclesiastical circumstances as existed in Russia before the war; and the impression might be created that the autonomy of the Czechoslovak Church would be hindered, we ask that our Church be called either the Orthodox Czechoslovak Church (*Československá Církev Pravověrná*) or Czechoslovak Cyrillomethodian Church (*Československá Cyrilometodějska Církev*), or simply the Czechoslovak Church.

Indeed, we ask that these religious conditions be fulfilled with consideration and concern for the union of the Slavs. In view of the fact that many already irrelevant, Catholic Church-imposed customs, and centuries-old traditions must be disposed of, we ask for time to build up our Church in harmony with western times. We want to follow the Serbian Orthodox Church in the footsteps of Sts. Cyril and Methodius and Master John Hus, and if moral and material help from the brotherly Orthodox Church is given to us, the ideals of all progressive Czechs will be fulfilled. We will be united not only through the bonds of blood, but also by the ties of Christian faith.

We ask you to answer our memorandum as soon as possible, and we assure you of our respect and deep love. Central Committee of the Czechoslovak Church.[37]

After this memorandum had been finished in its official version, Mr. Bohumil Zahradník-Brodský proposed the dissolution of the Central Committee and its replacement by another one with a different purpose. This really took place, and a new Central Committee was elected consisting of thirty members, the chairman of which was again Dr. Farsky. On September 6, 1920, a special delegation of the new Czechoslovak Central Committee solemnly gave this memorandum to the delegate of the Serbian Church in the presence of Minister Djorice at the Yugoslav Embassy. The next day, Bishop Dositej also received a copy, and left immediately for Belgrade to present it for consideration to the conference of Bishops called the Archjerejski Sabor.

This memorandum, full of ambivalence and contradictions, characterized the policies of the new Czechoslovak Church. On one hand, its representatives were willing to conform to conditions set by the Orthodox Church (concerning occasional old Slavonic liturgy and acceptance of the Nicene Creed); on the other hand they wanted to follow their own policies and demands (such as freedom of conscience and free religious development) while also striving for some

---

[37] This is author's translation of German text, given by Urban, *op. cit.*, pp. 72–76.

kind of independence (as we can see in their objecting to the name "Orthodox"). Their emphasis on "moral and material help" reveals, to a great extent, the pragmatic attitudes which occupied their minds, and which were dictated mainly by their determination for survival. In all justice, however, it must be said that these apparent differences resulted from the radically different minds represented. While the progressive Czechs were striving toward the orientation of their new church, based mainly on principles which are elsewhere characterized as *Religionswissenschaft*,[38] or as political ecclesiology,[39] the Serbian Orthodox tried to modify this Czech liberal thought by emphasis on traditional tenets concerning theological faith and Christian ecclesiology. This was not the usual confrontation between degrees of progressivism and conservatism, but rather one between real opposites.

No wonder there were mixed feelings on both sides although, for the time being, they were not displayed as fully as they would be later; but certain dormant difficulties would shortly demand pragmatic compromises.

Both sides, however, knew the score. The ambivalence of the Czechs was evident. They were anxious to get the "status of church" by association with the Orthodox, but they also were determined to follow the themes of modern secular thought by advocating twentieth-century secularism. It was precisely because of these characteristics that, from the very outset, the Czechoslovak Church was ostracized by the majority of serious church leaders. As a result, she also had a difficult time gaining government recognition which eventually was achieved on September 19, 1920, and then, only by coincidence rather than by deliberation. Since she did not enjoy this recognition at the time of the memorandum, one can understand why so much pragmatism had been employed to gain a unity with the Serbian Orthodox Church. However, once there was state recognition, the leaders assumed a more confident attitude. It is no wonder that the memorandum, as presented to the Serbian Orthodox Church, did not get the favorable response the Czechs had hoped for, but was regarded with increased caution by the Orthodox.

Meanwhile, some of the representatives of the Czechoslovak Church thought that it was time for clarification of their stand concerning the status and creed of the new church. They were motivated, not only by their own ideas, but also by the pressures of public opinion. If the new church was to survive the crisis of identification, some plan of development would have to emerge.

This prompted members of the Central Committee to convene on November 4, 1920, in Prague, where all the concerned matters were discussed, and planned procedural steps were set up. There were two phases: (a) preparatory work of committees, and (b) publication of the committees' work at the first church congress[40] (called *Sjezd* in Czech), to be held on its first anniversary (January 8, 1921). The urgency of theological clarification concerning creed (according to the first seven Ecumenical Councils), Mariology, Eucharist, the cult of saints, relics and pictures, creation and scientific view, doctrine of the human soul and eschatology, the trinitarian doctrine and interaction between education and science, and other aspects, was so pressing that they dared not delay, or try to escape by postponement. The problems of this so-called theological vacuum already had waited too long to be filled. This was the goal of the preparatory work which was organized into categories to be carried out by pertinent committees. Accordingly, six committees were set up:

(1) The Dogmatic and Liturgical Committee, one of the most important, was composed of members: Dr. Farsky, Dr. F. Kovář, Professor J. Tuháček, and Father Matěj Pavlík. They had a most difficult task trying to clarify theological tenets of the Serbian Orthodox Church, and comparing them with those of the Roman Catholic Church, and then formulating the stand for a new Czechoslovak Church.

(2) The Educational Committee, composed of Professor F. Spisar, Mr. Oxar Maly, teacher J. Vaněk, with Rev. Rudolf Pařík in charge, was concerned with instruction and education in religion.

(3) The Committee for the Organization and Administration of the Church, composed of Dr. Gustav Procházka, Mr. Ružička, Mr. Hoffer, and Mr. Šlapák, was to elaborate guidelines for organizational and administrative policies.

(4) The Committee for Public Relations, composed of Mr. J. Kolinský and Rev. E. Dlouhý-Pokorný, was to create, coordinate, and organize editorials for journals, newspapers, and other communication media.

(5) The Committee for Legislation, composed of Fr. Ferdinand Stibor, Dr. Svojtka, and Dr. Němeček, was charged with providing the legal basis of all church activities and institutions.

---

[38] Alexander Schmemann "Worship in a Secular Age," *St. Vladimir's Theological Quarterly* **16**, 1 (1972): pp. 3–16.

[39] Bernard F. Donahue, "Political Ecclesiology," *Theological Studies* **33**, 2 (June, 1972): pp. 294–306.

[40] Dr. Josef Hanuš, *The First Council of the Czechoslovak Church* (Washington, D.C.), NCWC Release of April 5, 1921: pp. 1–4; Mila Liscova, *The Religious Situation in Czechoslovakia* (Prague, 1925); F. M. Hník, *Za Lepší Církvi* (For a Better Church) (Prague, 1930) passim. Valný Sjezd Církve Československé Konaný v Sobotu a v Neděli, dne 8.a9. Ledna 1921 v Praze (General Congress of the Czechoslovak Church, held on Saturday and Sunday, of January 8 and 9, 1921 in Prague) (Prague, Vol IX of Liturgy of the Church, 1921).

(6) The Committee for Finances, composed of Rev. R. Stejskal, Brzkovský, Závorka, and Bautz, was commissioned to search for financial resources, and to provide the funds for all expenses of the Church.

These committees were confronted with various kinds of difficulties as would be usual with the beginning of a new institution, especially a church; their efforts were those of pioneers in many directions. Often, their work was hindered by an unfavorable public, which was more curious than interested in this somehow "peculiar church" and its even more "peculiar doctrinal tenets." A common aim of all the committees was eventually directed to one purpose; to reach a consensus which would become a platform from which would be elaborated the new church's program. This had to be done with considerable speed, yet with a practical approach, a perspective outlook, and in conformity with the times. The work of the committees was to be shared with all members of the religious church communities from which delegates for the forthcoming church council were to be elected. This would implement the democratic process and not only distribute responsibility among all the church membership, but represent the membership proportionally at the Congress. It was decided that one delegate would represent a collective of one thousand members, and that all participants must be delegated by church communities. This applied to all members of the Central Committee, without exception.

Following this preparatory work, the first Church Congress was held in the Hotel Albergo dell'Oca in Prague on January 8-9, 1921, with an attendance of 300 delegates, of whom about 109 represented unofficially recognized church communities of 193,665 members. The prepared program was much too involved for the delegates, who were simply lost in their attempts to go about their business, and were completely unable to find the way for solutions. Theological and other problems were simply beyond their reach. In spite of their attempts to get a consensus on some topics, the delegates eventually had to agree to content themselves with setting up guidelines for further procedures. After many discussions and deliberations, there was general agreement as to the guidelines;[41] these were written up and well articulated by Father Matthias Pavlík, and became the official framework and basis on which all coherent problems and ideological orientation and build-up of the Czechoslovak Church were to be solved. They read as follows:

---

[41] F. Prašek, *Vznik Československé Církve a Patriarcha G. A. Procházka* (Prague, 1932), pp. 92–95. F. Cinek, *K Náboženské Otázce v Prvních Letech Naší Sanostatnosti: 1918–1925* (Olomouc 1926), pp. 60–65.

Today's Congress of the Czechoslovak Church is not competent to resolve all the specific dogmatic questions as stated in the program. This would be possible only if and when these questions were theologically described to us, and if they were analyzed in all their aspects. This did not happen nor would it be possible. Even the ancient church councils did not make resolutions, as long as some questions were not completely clarified. So, neither can we decide upon questions which need a thorough professional yet popular presentation.

If we should now decide on dogmatic tenets as they are introduced in the program, it would be an unscientific and undemocratic way of doing things. Our church communities would have to be properly informed, on the basis of valid ideological and historical facts, yet in a way they would understand; so that in the entire Church there would be a consensus after these problems had been solved.

Some problems are related to our communities—these are all basically practical and organizational ones—while others, and these fall into the framework of dogmatics, would have to be reconsidered and resolved in and by our communities. Hence, for the present, there is no way that we can deal exclusively with those pressing problems which should be treated alone. It is precisely the dogmatic questions which should be solved so as to fit into the framework of the general guidelines.

These guidelines have to be consonant with our own times, yet must be in accord with an ideologically exact science. We must emphasize that we recognize the unrestricted freedom of science; and that science for us is self-understood, indisputable, and indispensable, so that all the religious fields will have to be treated by scientific methods as far as science and scholarly research are able.

We are convinced of the universal validity and relevance of the law of evolution, to which religious throughts are subject, and by which Christianity is regulated. In view of this fact, we recognize that Christian dogmas and decrees of the Church Councils are "gradual necessary steps in the general development of Christian thought."

Under the strong influence of this evolutionary thought, we want to attempt a critical revision, and introduce a new terminology for all those concepts of Christian thought which we have accepted from previous generations, with a view of their contemporary meaning; and we will not be disturbed by the past which cannot be of help to us. Our desire is rebirth and the growth of religious and moral life.

In view of this evolutionary thought, we hope to come to conclusive knowledge as to what was or was not essential in Christianity, or whether it is only a reflex of Christian society isolated to certain times. We hope that we will be able to rid ourselves of foreign customs which originated from the mentality of certain nations (mainly Greek, Roman, and Oriental) and from ancient times, so that we may become children of God on the basis of the pure and joyful message of Christ.

Through these efforts, we hope to eradicate today's grave religious crisis, and bring it a positive conclusion. Jesus Christ is the cornerstone of all our religious efforts. His doctrine and His life are our goal and basis. The sonship of God, as it was lived and announced by Christ, is our salvation and hope. With Him we stand with full consciousness, from Him we can gain strength so as to grow into the image of God and bring all our people, as our brothers and sisters, to the heavenly Father. Without Jesus Christ, all our undertakings would be meaningless. We are and want to be Christians in an ideological, fully committed, and honest manner. Moral rebirth is the only aim of our Church.

Our great goal is the new, pure type of Christendom where unimportant differences would disappear; because of past differences, there arose various church denominations; but, for the present, we must share in God's Word until that time when we will be but one flock and one Shepherd.

Pure Christianity must be lived by individual people, and since man is a member of mankind and the child of a certain nation, he should live, think, work, and die in an ideological and acceptable atmosphere of which he should not be deprived, and in accordance with whose historical development he is a part. He should have an opportunity to live his Christianity according to the customs of his nation and its important traditions. He should have a choice to live his Christian ideals according to the ideology and atmosphere which suits him directly and individually, and it is because of this that, of necessity, greater communities of Christians organize themselves nationally, and later incorporate themselves into national churches. Together, these constitute the universal Church of Christ as has happened in Oriental Churches, and as a principle for the Evangelical Church. This, some day, the Czechoslovak Church will also be. She is the Church of Christ because her foundations are the teaching of Christ and, at the same time, she is a national church because she wants to live among and with the people. She identifies herself with the historical development of the Czech people as an organic part of their life.

This determines the relationship of our Church with other churches. Our Church rejects every interference with its own life—and it does not interfere with the lives of other churches. The relationship among churches should be one of brotherly love, led by independence and equality. It is, however, necessary that national churches perfect and influence each other in the building of the Kingdom of God on earth. We desire a close connection with the Serbian Church, and ideological and practical intercourse with the Church of Czech Brethren.

Our ideological goals urge us to be interested in those theological and popular works by which all individuals and church communities would be prepared for their salvation. It is our duty to work diligently and precisely for the solution of religious questions, and to find the historical basis for all these points: religious knowledge, revelation, faith, religious forms and organizations, Christianity, the Person of Christ, the scriptures, creed, the Church of Christ and Christian churches, tradition, dogmas, spiritual, moral, and social problems of contemporary and future forms of Christianity. This necessary work must rest on principles which will be the key to all those questions of faith, which we have inherited from past Christian generations.

It may be necessary to found a modern religious periodical with high standards, and perhaps with no definite religious orientation, in order to have an outlet for religious discussions with all the people, especially members of several churches (I have in mind the Czechoslovak Church, the Church of Czech Brethren, and the Serbian Church), and including those people without any denomination. Moreover, it will be necessary to publish a collection of modern religious books to broaden the horizon of the Czech atmosphere. Therefore, it is mandatory for all churches to unite in working on this, and to invite also those persons who stand outside the church to participate.

People should not be afraid to work together on these common goals. The Serbian Church brought up that nation from paganism. Her theology has modern orientation, and she does not avoid relationships with the secular world, and does not exclude herself from its influences. The Serbian Church is selfconscious; she has to have concern for the needs of today, and for this reason she will hold a council this year to acquaint herself with the new political atmosphere, and prepare herself for future problems which she did not experience in the past thousand years. This is why it is worth studying the type of Christianity which the Orthodox represents. We have to be mindful of the great influence which, after the World War, orthodoxy had on the internal life of the people, especially those in Russia. The Church of Czech Brethren, which is a direct product of the Czech reformation, and which kept her purity of inheritance unspoiled by political influences, is able to communicate, to use the learning of her great theological masters, as well as those of the religious West. As a result, this work will bring to all of us much moral and scholarly enrichment.

From the factual points of historical and ideological continuity, we want to have the last and the best formulation of Christian thought as it is accepted by all Christian churches, and which is contained in the creed of the Constantinople Council. We want to be identified with the first seven Ecumenical Councils from which the Roman Catholic Church went astray in her unnatural development, and arrived at her doctrine concerning the primacy of the Roman bishop, including his claim to infallibility. Therefore, we co-identify ourselves with the first seven Ecumenical Councils as the Czech Reformation did in the past, and proclaim ourselves as true sons of our fathers as we insist on the evolutionary principles of Christian thought; and we stand firm on the principle of the freedom of conscience, as we have it in the program of our Church, as also expressed in the memorandum sent to the Serbian Church. It is against this background that we all share the freedom of religious conviction.

In the meantime, we ask all our brothers and sisters to think about religious questions in love and tolerance, to avoid all fights over special religious dogmas, as well as violence against the freedom of religious conviction, but rather to strive for a moral life on the principles of Christ.

By the conclusion of my *Referat*, I propose that the Central Council should elect a commission for the purpose of organizing the theological work according to the guidelines or directives given above. This commission would have to found a religious journal, a theological library, and revise theological studies.[42]

These guidelines, surprisingly, reveal the fact that the idea of union with the Serbian Church was not favored by the Czechoslovak Church. They even contradicted the Serbian memorandum and left it unanswered, although it had urgently sought this interchange between both churches. The caution about speaking openly would further indicate that all delegates did not agree with such union of the whole Church with the Orthodox Church, but preferred to restrict their relationship to mutual cooperation.

The most interesting observation revealed in these guidelines is the pragmatic inclusion of all religious traditions in relation to the Czechoslovak people, in spite of their inherent conflicting relationships in the past; this inclusion was intended simply to gain a sympathetic following. Thus, recourse to the seven Ecumenical Councils would appeal to the Orthodox;

---

[42] This is the author's translation of German text, given by Urban, *op. cit.*, pp. 80–85.

an emphasis on Cyrillomethodian heritage[43] would play on the national sentiments of all Czechs; an appeal to Hussitism would appease all liberals; the reference to Protestantism would capture understanding; a stress on the scientific basis of religious understanding should elicit the sympathy of modern agnostics and of all those with secular tendencies. This all inclusive pragmatism in the program for a new church is a peculiar mixture of everything, with something for everyone. The most daring of all these items would seem to be the unanimous acceptance of the principle of the freedom of science without reservation, and with all its consequences, even if and when employed in religious fields, to appease all modernistic minds, and all those advocates of the much too arrogant Religionswissenschaft who have so little appreciation of theology.

In addition to these guidelines, the assembly of delegates accepted the statutes[44] which, in forty-five paragraphs, represent the constitutional basis of the Czechoslovak Church. If these are compared to anything, they certainly resemble, at least in certain points, the Jednota's reformist attempts expressed in *Návrh Československého Duchovenstva na Obnovu Církve Katolické v Československé Republice* (Proposal of the Czechoslovak Clergy on the Renewal of the Catholic Church in the Czechoslovak Republic) of 1918.[45] The statutes spell out the regulations and responsibilities of elders, of general religious communities, the Council of Bishops, and the Central Committee of the Church. To give some idea of what the nature the new church would be, the first paragraph of the statutes offers this definition of the Church:

> Those Christians form the Czechoslovak Church who believe in the teachings of Jesus Christ, following the interpretation of the first seven Ecumenical Councils, who confess the Nicene Creed, and who accept traditions of the Slavic Apostles Sts. Cyril and Methodius, and of Master John Hus.

The second paragraph is not humble either, for it says:

> The Czechoslovak Church is a universal or Catholic Church in purest meaning of the word. Its liturgical language is a native one!

This shows how the authors of these statutes were inconsistent: on the one hand they attacked the Catholic Church whenever and wherever the opportunity presented itself; on the other hand they borrowed anything they could from the Catholic Church, especially what they found good for the new church. They liked to stress its national character, and yet wanted to have it Catholic as well.

The Czech theologian, F. M. Hník, sees it differently:

> The Czechoslovak Church does not consider Catholicity in the exclusive sense of superiority, as does the Roman Catholic Church; the latter is willing to write off from the Christian world a major part of those somewhat varying Christians who do not correspond to her arrogant, spiritual, and political rule. As opposed to intolerant, canonical Roman Catholicity, the Czechoslovak Church offers the inclusive Catholicity of Jesus, where the measure of the universal Church of Christ in the intensity of His Spirit, prevails on the borders of dogmatic vocabulary and national and interracial prejudices.
>
> For the Czechoslovak Church, the apostolic church does not rest on apostolic succession and on the numerous privileges derived from this succession, but is the source of those motives for loving God and for intensiveness of faith, which were the fruit of the Spirit of Jesus in early Christian religious communities.
>
> The Czechoslovak Church springs from the conviction that the Church is not the supreme institution in this world, but is the Kingdom of God; that it never was the intention of Jesus to establish the Church with uniform dogma and a complex hierarchical apparatus, but rather to insure the spreading of the Gospel. The Roman Catholic Church uses the words of Jesus to Peter for strengthening of her universal claims: "I say to you, that thou art Peter, and on this rock I will build my Church, and the gates of hell will not prevail against her. And whatever you shall bind on the earth, it will be bound also in heaven, and whatever you shall loose on the earth, it will be loosed also in heaven" (Matt. 16: 18 19). However, is it not obvious that numerous parables of Jesus' concerning the Kingdom of God do not have this single testimony about the establishment of the Church, or one analogy in other Gospels, or that other places in the New Testament contradict it? (as I Cor. 3: 11; Eph. 2: 20)
>
> Following the example of the historical Christian churches, the Czechoslovak Church does not want to compel obedience to the Church, or to any system of dogmatic doctrines; and does not believe that the authenticity of the Church should depend on external notes. By her return to the historical Jesus, she puts the emphasis on the internal spiritual correlation with the Kingdom of God, for the spread of which, the Church is instrumental; and which, by logical necessity she developed from the work begun in the realm of Christ's love through His life and His sacrifice.
>
> The Czechoslovak Church in her very beginning appealed to Christ, and was aware of the fact that her existence and her Christian character did not depend on the judgment of historical Christian Churches, but on

---

[43] Vaclav Chalupecký, "Slovanska Bohoslužba v Čechach," *Věstník České Akademie Věd* (Prague, 1950), pp. 68–80; Josef Vašica, *Slovanská Liturgie v Českých Zemích* (Prague, 1932). L. Nemec, "Recent Reinvestigation of Cyrillomethodian Sources and their Basic Problems," *Czechoslovakia: Past and Present*, ed. by M. Rechoigl (2 v., The Hague. Mouton, 1964), pp. 1151–1174, *passim*.

[44] A more detailed content of these statutes was mentioned before. These were elaborated with relation to the memorandum which was sent to the Serbian Church and became the framework for the guidelines and served as the foundations of a new Czechoslovak Church.

[45] Published in the *Supplement* to issue No. 1 and 1 of *Právo Lidu* (Jan. 1, 1919). *Cf.* Josef Doležal, *Česku Knéz* (Prague, 1931), pp. 59–60. This was a sixty-six page memorandum sent to Rome and which later became an official program of the Jednota. *Cf.* J. S. Baar-Fr. Teplý, *Na Obranu Reformního Programu Jednoty Katolického Duchovenstva Československého* (Prague, 1920); L. Nemec, "The Czech Jednota . . . ." *op. cit.*, pp. 85–99 and *passim*; Dr. Karel Farský, *Přelom. Vzpomínkové Fevclletony k Dějinám Církve Československé* (Prague, 1920), *passim*.

her own loyalty to spiritual ideals which she was determined to make a reality.[46]

This expression of theological thought concerning the ecclesiology of the Czechoslovak Church is too vague and evasive for anyone to see the Church's nature in a proper dogmatic perspective and biblical context. One might say that confusion in Christology is reflected in the confusion of ecclesiology, and in the framework of thought just mentioned. A more appropriate title would be the Czechoslovak Religious Association rather than the Czechoslovak Church.

All in all, it may be said that this first Congress of the Czechoslovak Church did not bring about any clarification of its dogmatic tenets, and, as a result, it did not gain the momentum of a truly national movement; rather it was a kind of face-saving through guidelines and statutes, presented to the eyes of some radicals and progressives. Many schismatic churches sent their representatives. The Episcopal (Anglican) Church of the United States was represented by the Reverend Mr. Gollier; the Russian Orthodox Church, by Professor Jastrebov; the Evangelical Protestant by Dr. Stěhule; the Serbian Orthodox by Rev. Mr. Grovanin; and others, all prepared to make addresses. This illustrates the extent of anti-Catholic agitation as a vehicle of propaganda against the vast majority of the Catholic population of Czechoslovakia, against whom the new Czechoslovak Church represents eloquent protest.

As February 15, 1921, approached, the date set for the official census to be conducted under the supervision of Professor Dr. Ant. Boháč, a Protestant and well-known enemy of the Catholic Church, anti-Catholic propaganda increased in hostility and violence. Sad to say, this propaganda was not only tolerated by some Czechoslovak government officials, but was helped positively by them in many ways. Thus, one million, two hundred thousand crowns from the government were gratefully accepted by the First Congress of the new church, and it was only one of many examples of such largesse. The anti-Catholic press, especially that of other churches, added to the magnitude of poisonous attacks and created a fearfully tense atmosphere for the weaker Catholics. Intimidation, scandal, sarcasm, and slander were not infrequently used. Hostile controversy and uncompromising polarization between the Czechs and Rome reached its peak when, in a journal of the Evangelical Church of Czech Brethren, there appeared this frontal attack by the free thinkers organization in *Volná Myšlenka* and by the Czechoslovak Church:

The time approaches when it becomes necessary for the Czech nation to judge and condemn Rome according to the words of President T. G. Masaryk. The forthcoming census must prove that our republic is not Roman anymore. Otherwise, our nation would be saying that our State is not worthy of its ancient past, its ancestors and its freedom. We appeal to all Czechs to leave the Roman Catholic Church before the census and join the church of their choice and conviction.[47]

As a result of this anti-Rome propaganda many Czechs left the Roman Catholic Church and joined the national church. On January 8, the 300 delegates of the Council represented 193,665 members; whereas, less than six weeks later, on February 15, there were 525,333 listed as belonging to the Czech Church. On the whole, the census showed the following religious composition of the Czechoslovak state:

Entire population	13,613,172
Roman Catholic	10,384,833
Without any belief	724,504
Greek Catholic	535,543
Augsburg churches	526,206
Czechoslovak Church	525,333
Jews	353,925
Czech Brothers	234,100
Helvetians	209,502
Greek Orthodox	73,097
Old Catholic	20,255
Free Reformed	5,095
Herrnhuter	4,044
Baptists	2,107
Methodists	1,461
Anglicans	459
American Orthodox	149
American Catholic	43
Salvation Army	16
Other religions	5,380

Measured against the norms of geopolitics, it would seem that most members of the Czechoslovak Church resided in Bohemia (437,377 or about 83 per cent). Some 85,855 members (about 16 per cent) were located in Moravia and Silesia. Only slight traces of membership could be found in either Slovakia or Carpatho-Russia. In the entire Czechoslovak Republic, then, with its total population of some 13.6 million people, slightly fewer than 4 per cent indicated allegiance to the Czechoslovak Church. With appropriate distinctions between districts, it might be said that those having a predominantly German-speaking population, and those having a Slovak-speaking population were least affected. Still, the loss of over one-half a million members of the Roman Catholic Church in such a short period indicated serious internal

---

[46] F. M. Hník, *Duchovní Ideály Československé Církve* (Prague, 1934), pp. 152–154. The author deals with the problem in chapter II of this book, "The Nature and Authenticity of the Church in the Teachings of the Czechoslovak Church," pp. 147–160. This is the author's translation of the Czech text hereby given.

[47] Appeared in *Český Zápas* (Prague) **4,** 5 (February 4, 1921). This appeal paraphrases the frequently quoted words of T. G. Masaryk that "Rome has to be judged and condemned!" *Cf.* T. G. Masaryk, *Los von Rom* (Boston, Unit. Hist. Society, 1902); *idem, Moderní Člověk a Náboženství* (Prague, J. Leichter, 1934) *passim*; Josef Vrchovecký, *T. G. Masaryk a Náboženství* (Prague, 1937) *passim*: cf. Romanus, "Von der Modernen Husitenkische" *Katholiken Korrespondenz* (Prague, 1921), pp. 195–200, 205–210.

bleeding, if not exactly a hemorrhage. On the whole, the loss to the Catholic Church was tremendous[48]

All endeavors to influence the result of the census failed because the adherents of the Czechoslovak Church still numbered only about 1,000,000 and the majority of these were in Bohemia. In Moravia, there were only 150,000 apostasies.[49] Although propaganda made use of terror, asserting that the new Church was really the Czech Catholic Church, many apostates, after having learned that they were victims of deceit, returned to the Catholic Church.[50] After their apostasy, many workers, inspired by the Social Democratic leaders, either entered the Czechoslovak Church or remained without any confession whatsoever. Nine years later, there were 853,000 of no religious affiliation, whereas adherents to the Czechoslovak Church numbered only 793,000. Dr. Ant. Boháč wrote about the obvious success of the Czechoslovak Church:

> Those who left the Catholic Church, but did not want to be outside any Christian Church, favored the new Czechoslovak Church with much greater sympathy than they did the Protestant churches. At the last census (1930) the number of memberships of the Czechoslovak Church increased 47.01 per cent, and could have had an increase of more than 50 per cent if some religious communities on the occasion of schism in their church, had not transferred to Orthodoxy.[51]

Catholics decreased in percentage from 95 to 75 per cent. The nation remained prevailingly Catholic, but progress was delayed.[52]

This statistical exposition is the best indication that many people viewed the Czechoslovak Church as a mode of atheism. Undoubtedly, it had its analogue in the Austrian *Los von Rom* movement.[53] After the census had been taken, the leaders of the Czechoslovak Church called on the archbishop of Prague, Francis Kordač, asking him for the use of Catholic churches. He answered: "As a guardian of the Church, I cannot give any such approval, and I repudiate the suggestion." The leader of the delegation replied: "We will look for another way to reach these smaller churches."[54] They then approached the government requesting their use. The suggestion, although supported by Mr. Francis Krejčí, was strongly opposed in Parliament by Monsignor John Šrámek and Rev. Krojher.

The leaders of the Czechoslovak Church used all available means to justify their excesses legally. Anticlerical teachers assisted the strongly anti-Catholic newspaper, *Prager Tagblatt*, which informed the public that the governmental commission had decided that civil weddings, henceforth, would be obligatory, that Catholic holy days would be suppressed, and all official records were to be removed from the Catholic rectories and handed over to the State chanceries.[55] The purpose for spreading such rumors, was to create an atmosphere of tension and of hysteria, to make it more difficult for Catholics to be steadfast.

The census, coming on the heels of such unchristian tactics, brought sharp criticism to the new church, at home and abroad. As its membership increased, there were also increased complaints against the provisional status of the church, and demands were made for a better creed.

At this juncture, the first serious internal differences of opinion became manifest in the new Czechoslovak Church; one group, satisfied with having simply broken with Rome; and a second group, dissatisfied with the teachings, customs, and liturgy of the new church, and wanting to go much further in the rebellious process.

These unresolved differences, perhaps, stimulated the leaders to look, once again, to the Serbian Orthodox Church for aid and comfort. But protests arose within the Central Committee itself over the failure of Belgrade to respond to the Memorandum of September 3, 1920. Accordingly, it was decided to set a deadline to force some response. The communication directed to the Serbian Orthodox Church read:

> As we have not received the answer to our memorandum of September 3, 1920, we ask for a definite answer by March 31, 1921. If it is not possible to answer all our points, we ask you to tell us whether the Serbian Orthodox Church would have the Christian and fraternal love to consecrate three of our candidates for the office of bishop—they would come to Belgrade for this purpose. We ask you to do this as soon as possible, as we cannot postpone the solution of the question of consecrating priests any longer. In case we should not get any answer

---

[48] Mila Liscova, *The Religious Situation in Czechoslovakia* (Prague, 1925), pp. 36–60; Urban, *op. cit.*, pp. 86–89; P. Kirsch "Religiousbewegung in der Tschechoslowakischen Republik" *Katholiken-Korrespondez* (1924), p. 100 ff; F. Dvornik, "Evolution de L'église Catholique en Tchecoslovaquie Depuis la Guerre," *Le Monde Slave* 7 (1930): *P*. 2; 5–6 (1933): pp. 260–275.

[49] Dr. Josef Hanuš, *Religious Chronicle of Czechoslovakia* (Washington, D. C., 1921). *NCWC Release* of April 5, 12, 1921, M. 2; *cf.* Emanuel Rádl, *La Question Religieuse en Tchecoslovaquie* (Prague, the Gazette de Prague, 1922), *passim*.

[50] Blažej Ráček, *Československé Dějiny* (Czechoslovak History) (2nd ed., Prague, Kucíř, 1933), pp. 694 ff.

[51] Dr. Ant. Boháč, "Přehled Nejdůležitějších Výsledků Posledního Sčítáni Lidu. I. Náboženské Význání v Kombinaci s Národnosti v Zemích Českých," *Statistický Obzor* 14 (June 1933): pp. 175–180. (This is a review of the most important results of the last census of the people concerning religion and nationality.)

[52] *NCWC Release* (Washington, D.C.) (March 12, 1921), pp. 1–2. *Cf.* Josef Doležal, *Politická Cesta Českého Katolicismu 1918–1928* (Prague, 1928), *passim*; details difficulties Catholics had in these years; Aug. Neuman, *Katolíctví a Naše Osvobození* (Olomouc, 1931), *passim*.

[53] Franz Stauracz, *Los von Rom* (2nd ed., Hamm in Westf. Verlag on Breen 1900), *passim*. "De Los-von-Rom Bewegung in Oesterreich," *Hist. Pol. Bl.* 126–127 (1900–1901) in numerous articles. *Lexikon für Theologie und Kirche* VI. p. 653.

[54] *Ibid. NCWC Release* (Washington, D.C.) (February 21, 1921), p. 2 ff.

[55] L. Nemec, *Church and State in Czechoslovakia* (New York, 1955), pp. 128–129.

whatsoever until March 31, 1921, we really would regretfully regard the negotiations as finished.[56]

Without waiting for the arrival of this dead-line, the Central Committee of the Czechoslovak Church decided, at their meeting of March 5, 1921, to renew contacts with the Evangelical Church of Czech Brethren, and to enter into contacts with professors of the Hus Faculty in Prague, with the request that they also assume the task of training students in the study of theology. It would seem that the larger number of members in the national church after the census increased also the need for ministers; but the hoped-for supply from among the apostate Catholic priests was disappointing. From the statistics immediately after the census, some indication of the clerical supply problems might be seen in the following data:[57]

Priests adhering to the new Church, as clergy:		Priests choosing their return to lay status:
Archdiocese of Prague	29	17
Diocese of Budějovice	4	30
Diocese of Hradec Králové	11	31
Diocese of Litoměřice	10	20
Archdiocese of Olomouc	7	7
Diocese of Brno	3	0
Totals	64	105

Obviously, some provisions would have to be made to insure an adequate flow of ministers for the new church. In this regard, the assistance of the Hus faculty proved of great importance.

From the data given above, it would appear that the national church had failed to attract the numbers that the leaders had anticipated. Why was this so? Professor F. M. Hník of the Hus Faculty, writing in *Za Lepší Církvi* (For the Better Church),[58] attempted a rationale best indicated by his subtitle: "Psychological Study Concerning the Reasons for Transfers into the Czechoslovak Church." According to Hník, some new members were seeking reinforcement of their nationalistic feelings as Czechs, sentiments less clearly supported in the more universal Roman Church. Others sought a renewed church, and not finding it adequate to their search, either left or remained in a condition of indifference. To stem the ebb and flow of these spiritual pilgrims, the leadership of the Czechoslovak Church needed (1) its own consecrated episcopacy in apostolic succession, and (2) a continuing education of its own clergy. The Central Committee pursued both objectives vigorously.

The problem of apostolic succession was particularly difficult, as no Roman Catholic bishop had come over to the new church. Yet, the vast majority of the priests and laity had once been Catholics. Their cultural conditioning predisposed them to seek some sense of spiritual legitimacy in the form of an authentic episcopate: natural, desirable, and proper.[59]

In this context, the Central Committee of the Czechoslovak Church was astonished to receive the following letter which had been forwarded from Belgrade:

The Holy Assembly of Bishops
of the Serbian Orthodox Church
A.S. No. 132
Karlowitz on 18 of Nov., 1 December 1920.

The holy assembly of the bishops of the Serbian Orthodox Church welcomes with joy the wish of the clergy and faithful in the Czechoslovak state to change to the Orthodox Church—to the Church to which they had belonged from the very beginning, and which is closely connected with the names of the great apostolic teachers Cyril and Methodius.

Faithful to tradition and the spirit of the Orthodox Church, this holy assembly of bishops welcomes your wish, but is averse to undermining the foundations of any church or any Christian community, or to minimize their missions, especially in these times when, all over the world, Christianity is forced to engage in the hardest fight against the spirit of negation; and when unity and the greatest firmness is needed for all the churches of God to stand together.

Faithful to the tradition and spirit of the Serbian Orthodox Church, this holy assembly of bishops regards askance any suggestion or desire to make proselytes of any other Christian church.

On the other hand, this holy assembly of bishops considers it its duty to help in a sincere wish to change to the Orthodox, especially if initiative to this movement comes spontaneously from the Czechoslovak clergy and faithful. The Serbian Orthodox Church cannot, or would not, deny its help to the Czechs, since in the fifteenth century such a union had been seriously taken into consideration or attempted, and pertinent negotiations had been interrupted only by the fall of Constantinople.

This holy assembly of bishops is also of the opinion that by fulfilling the Czechoslovak wish, she is discharging her duty by making it possible for the newest church to be included in uninterrupted succession with the oldest one. Therefore, the holy assembly of bishops has decided:

(1) Responding to numerous requests of the Central Committee for this change, the assembly of bishops sends its incumbent, His Eminence Bishop Dositej, Bishop of Nish, as a true interpreter of the teaching of this holy, united, and apostolic eastern church, and as a wise adviser for the inner building up of the organization of a new sister church in Czechoslovakia.

---

[56] This is the author's translation of German text, found at Urban, *op. cit.*, p. 90. Here is the first concrete and urgent request for a bishop, although the only purpose of these negotiations with the Serbian Orthodox Church has been to get some bishops from them.

[57] Josef Doležal, *Český Kněz* (Prague, 1931), p. 71.

[58] F. M. Hník, *Za Lepší Církvi* (For the Better Church) (Prague, 1930) was published on the tenth anniversary of the Church as recollection and reflection of the actual situation of the Czechoslovak Church.

[59] Kuneš Bauer, *Myšlenkové Proudy v Československé Církvi* (The Religious Currents in Czechoslovak Church) (Olomouc, 1924), pp. 36–37.

Concerning certain issues in this matter which were expressed in the requests and wishes by the Central Committee of the Czechoslovak Church, the assembly of bishops, in its attempts to be helpful in the right direction, and especially in the benefit and salvation of this church, decided the following:

(1) With the approval of the supreme Church Council, the liturgical books should be properly translated into the Czech language.
(2) They should be accepted, only if and when everything of essential teaching of the Orthodox Church concerning consecration of the Holy Sacraments is introduced and observed.
(3) We agree that the establishment of the Czechoslovak Church will be uniformly united, so that the spiritual administration can be organized on the pattern of parish communities. Referring to the election of parish clergy, the faithful will elect suitable persons whom the bishop would ordain (through imposition of hands). Clergy and faithful may elect and propose candidates for bishops, from whom the synod of bishops would select those who were most worthy of episcopal consecration and dignity.
(4) It should be accepted with understanding that special instructions will be given to these bishops.
(5) The Czechoslovak clergy is to be allowed to marry, as well as ours. The matter of a second marriage of the clergy will have to be discussed and final resolutions will become binding for the entire Orthodox Church.
(6) Our Serbian Orthodox Church assumes that her sister Czechoslovak Church has sufficient numbers of well educated and qualified candidates who could, according to canonical regulations, become bishops as in other Orthodox churches.
(7) Responding to the petition, it sends the most reverend bishop of Nish, Dositej, as interpreter of the teaching of the Orthodox Church, and as adviser to special problems related to the build-up of the Czechoslovak Church.
(8) Always united with brotherly love toward the Czechoslovak people, the Serbian Orthodox Church has only one goal—to assist, with God's help, her brothers to establish the autonomous (autocephalous) Czechoslovak Orthodox Church, similar to other Orthodox churches.
(9) The Serbian Orthodox Church hopes that the Czechoslovak government will agree to the formation of a new Orthodox church in the Czechoslovak Republic and that the financial status of the clergy will be acceptable to the government as well as to the faithful.
(10) This holy assembly of bishops sends this letter as an answer to all your questions.
(11 & 12) The Serbian Church is as Orthodox as any other church. Since the Committee of the Czechoslovak Church has turned to the Serbian Church for help until such time as the Czechoslovak Orthodox autocephalous (independent) Church can set up her own church laws, as well as her own internal administration, the Serbian Orthodox Church agrees to accept temporary jurisdiction over the Czechoslovak faithful and will extend to them a motherly care. This church should call itself: *Pravoslavná Československá Církev Svatého Cyrila a Metoděje* (Orthodox Czechoslovak Church of Sts. Cyril and Methodius).

The Chairman of the Episcopal synod of the Serbian Orthodox Church
Archbishop of Belgrade and Serbian Patriarch:
signed Dimitrej
Secretary: signed Ros.[60]

It is interesting to note the skillful diplomacy evident in this latter document. While the Orthodox synod speaks constantly of a "change" (or transfer) of the Czech nation to the Orthodox Church, the Czechoslovak Church memorandum of September 3, 1921, had been talking only about the "union" or "joining to," "unity or perhaps association with." The Serbian Orthodox Church proposed a "corporate union," whereas the Czechoslovak Church meant only ideological, material, and organizational assistance. In view of the fact that some points of the memorandum (like #5 and #6) were rejected, some (like #8) postponed, and some evasively circumvented, this reply was admittedly a great disappointment, especially since even the material help that the Czechoslovak Church was looking for was not only not promised but would have to be supplied by the Czechoslovak government. The Serbian Orthodox Church was willing to confer apostolic succession only on condition that the Czechoslovak Church became an Orthodox sister to her, but not to another Christian church. The mission of Orthodox Bishop Dositej had been carefully restricted to giving an interpretation of the teaching of Orthodoxy, and to giving advice on how to set up an Orthodox Church in Czechoslovakia.

This Orthodox document made no pretense at ambiguity, nor did it leave any room for other possibilities, but unequivocally pressured the Czechs for a corporate union. It was like a dictator's manifesto, to be accepted gracefully but unreservedly by a weak brother, under the big brother's conditions.

This was too much for the independent-minded Czechs who wanted to be treated as equals among equals, and not as taking dictation, even if it were from brother Slavs. Furthermore, the Serbian Orthodox Church could not have thought much of the ideological vacuum in the Czechoslovak Church if they felt it had to be filled by the Orthodox.

Evidently, the Orthodox did not want to become partners in any form of *Religionswissenschaft* of which the Czechoslovak Church boasted. Instead, they insisted on traditional theology and ecclesiology; and their statements met with violent response. When the document was read to members of the Central Committee at the meeting held on March 16, 1921, in Prague, the agitation was so strong that some members could not believe their ears. Some did not want to make any acknowledgment, and some preferred to

---

[60] This is the author's translation of the German text found in Urban, *op. cit.*, pp. 92–94. This text in Czech may be found in *Český Zápas* (Czech Fight) 4, 14 (April 8, 1921), and was also reproduced in F. Cinek, *K Náboženské Otázce v Prvních Letech Naší Samostatnosti* (Concerning Religious Question in the First Years of our Independence) (Olomouc, 1926), pp. 72–74.

ignore it in silence. Only a few were for accepting it. When thirty-six members of the Council were called to vote, eighteen were for and eighteen were against replying to it. This tie was broken when the activist teacher, Vaněk, voted against replying; thus it was decided to ignore its existence. This decision disturbed everybody present, and the bitterness of debate was so upsetting to the visiting representatives of the Orthodox Church, that Mr. Crvcanin and thirteen members of the Committee indignantly left the meeting in protest at having subjected their guests to such embarrassment.

Now, the roots for the second internal schism, i.e., the Czechoslovak-Orthodox Schism, had been planted. Opposed even to answering the Orthodox document, were the following members of Council: Kysilka, Kolinský, Tuháček, Gajdik, Hrdlička, Hains, Pařík, Šillinger, Farský, Pavlík, Polešovský, Zeman, Osvald, Šlapák, Procházka, Kozák, Němeček, and Stržínek.[61] Some, of course, changed their minds, especially Father Matthias Pavlík, who later became a great proponent of Orthodox orientation. For the present, all negotiations were stalled and the deadlock was broken only a week later when the Central Committee held its meeting on March 23, 1921; here it was decided that negotiations should be reopened by answering the Orthodox document. After prolonged deliberation, it was agreed that the following new memorandum be sent to Bishop Dositej:

Mr. Bishop:

We turn to you in brotherly respect and love, to inform you that the Council of the Central Committee of the Czechoslovak Church is of a firm and unanimous opinion that the answer of the assembly of bishops of the Serbian Orthodox Church was in many aspects, not satisfactory to us and our faithful.

We ask, Mr. Bishop, that an assembly of bishops (Sabor) of the Serbian Orthodox Church further take into consideration that our mutual differences do not contradict our Slavic sentiments but that, on the contrary, we emphasize specifically that we were brought up on the Slavonic idea of our great founding fathers in the belief that, between two Slavic brother-nations, friendly cultural and religious relationships shoud not only be maintained, but become even deeper. Although our nation will remain faithfully Slavonic, based on the spiritual traditions of the great Slavonic nations, our people do not want to change (transfer) to Orthodoxy, or to form a new Orthodox Czechoslovak Church. With great joy we welcome you, Mr. Bishop, as a wise counsellor, and intermediator between us and the assembly of bishops; and this is why we have come to you: to explain to you our doubts and wishes.

While we are going to refer to the individual aspects of the memorandum, and compare them with those in the answer of the assembly of bishops, let us say: Points #1 and #2 from the letter of the assembly of bishops we take into consideration, but we want the Censorship Commission for liturgical books to be composed of Czechs, the members of the Czechoslovak Church who reside in Prague and live in the spirit of Czech religious traditions; and it is, of course, understood that everything that is beautiful and becoming in the Orthodox liturgy we will carry over into our ceremonies, that the substance of the Mass liturgy, and the seven sacraments will be kept; there cannot be any doubt of this.

We accept point #3 but with the reservation that the Czechoslovak Church will elect the candidates for bishoprics, will determine the number of persons, and that nobody and nothing will influence us in this respect. As soon as our Church is independent (autocephalous), the election and consecration of bishops will be a matter within our Czechoslovak Church.

Point #4 is entirely in agreement with that of the assembly of bishops and is acceptable under the condition that the synod acknowledges the ordinations and marriages of our priests.

Points #5 and #6 are acceptable with a reservation that prohibition of a second or third remarriage of the priests, as well as imposed celibacy of bishops in the Orthodox Church, are not dogma, but a matter of church discipline. We are glad to hear that there are efforts in the Orthodox churches to bring this question to the attention of the Ecumenical Council, so that, hopefully, it will be justly resolved and rectified. We propose that, towards the end of this year, the matter should be resolved by the Ecumenical Council. For the future, however, we think this should be a matter of discipline in the independent Czechoslovak Church.

Points #7 to #10 are accepted without any change. We only want to express our desire that the organization of our Church, as well as the consecration of bishops, should not be postponed any longer, because the development and common good of the Church does not tolerate further delays. In this matter, we cannot afford any further postponement, and all questions should be settled in the course of two months; at the latest, by July 20 of our calendar.

Point #11—the Central Committee of the Czechoslovak Church insists on the demand of its membership that women should be members of the Church Council of Elders, and would like this point recognized by the synod of bishops.

Point #12—for many other, but especially for national and psychological reasons, we ask that the name of our Church in the future be called the Czechoslovak Church. Until this Church has her own bishops and her own assembly of bishops, it will be under the jurisdiction of Bishop Dositej. As soon as this Church becomes independent, she will administer her own matters according to the needs of the time, the principles of freedom of conscience and free religious development.

In case all these conditions are accepted, we ask you for an immediate consecration of our bishops.

Prague, April 3, 1921
For the Central Committee of the
Czechoslovak Church in Prague.[62]

This memorandum reveals impatience and anxiety as well, and it is written with a rather strong sense of self-confidence, addressed to a man who well knew the Czechoslovak situation, the Most Reverend Bishop

---

[61] These are registered by Urban, *op. cit.*, p. 95, who has also those members who were in favor of the Orthodox document. These were the following: Svojtka, Kuklik, Truhlář, Závorka, Heteš, Kondelka, Vacková, Žídek, Zmatlikova, Tichý, Brzkovský, Kučera, Sen. Zahradnik-Brodský, Rejholda, Nevole, Malý, Dlouhý-Pokorný, and Šebek.

[62] This was published in *Český Zápas* 7, 22 (April 6, 1921) (Prague). This is author's translation of the German text, given by Urban, *op. cit.*, pp. 96–97.

Dositej, and whose influence was being used to bring the synod of bishops of the Orthodox Church toward a better understanding of the problems facing a new church. All in all, this memorandum seems to be demanding in only one respect: to secure the consecration of a bishop by which apostolic succession would and could be gained, and then be continued in the Czechoslovak Church. This was decided as a matter of policy at the meeting of the Central Committee, held on April 2, 1921, that the episcopal office should be independently superior although connected with the priesthood. The crux of the problem was about the source from which this episcopal office should be obtained. No church was overly willing to share the benefits of the episcopal office with another church, especially with one which did not conform with all creedal and disciplinary requirements, and which was too progressive in comparison.

Dr. Farsky, a spokesman of the new church, lacked the necessary diplomatic skills to keep this in balance. As time went on, his statements, especially in journals, became more daring and embarrassing. Neither did his ready sarcasm spare the Orthodox Church:

> The Orthodox Church, which has not had any reforms since the year 787, when she had the last Council (and that without the participation of Slavs who are truly the principal holders of Orthodoxy), is in urgent need of reform. The question is, whether the Church is able to carry them out. Many doubt it. Therefore, the Czechoslovak Church, having to face reaction, reformation and revolution, does not want to bind the young state to Orthodoxy. She wants to accept the episcopal consecration out of friendly, brotherly and Christian willingness, without any obligation, while on the other hand she is willing to live in friendly relationship with the Serbian Church, and with the entire Orthodox world.[63]

It was this attitude of progressivism and modernism which was so characteristic of the Czechoslovak Church, and which suggested that she might look for opportunities elsewhere as well. For this reason the Evangelical Church of Czech Brethren became a very inviting prospect. She had the same Hussite program, and her membership came mostly from the Roman Catholic Church, as did the Czechoslovak Church. Furthermore, this Church of Czech Brethren had its own history of hardship in searching for apostolic succession. Back in 1467, Brother Michael, who had apostatized from the Catholic Church, succeeded in receiving his consecration from the Waldensians.[64] Later, he consecrated Brother Matthias as bishop of the Czech Brethren. Perhaps it was this historical past and the memory of mutual heritage that was the bond between both churches. Moreover, the determination of the Czechoslovak Church to obtain episcopal office, was so intense, that the manner of its conferment was of lesser importance. It was even suggested that the episcopal dignity might be conferred simply through an imposition of hands by the elders, according to the pattern of the primitive church.

Thus, especially the union of the Czechoslovak Church with the Evangelical Church of Czech Brethren is only a question of time, since nowhere does it appear that the Czechoslovak Church would have to change any of her fundamental tenets and decrees, nor would she be pressured to accept any from the other side.[65]

Evidently, it was the principle of religious freedom which was so strongly in the mind of the Czechoslovak Church and made her so reluctant to accept restrictive conditions from any other church.

Why, then, did the Serbian Orthodox Church continue to keep in touch with the Czechoslovak Church? This can be explained only by her political aspirations to play the role of "Mother Slavic Church" and replace the Russian Orthodox Church, isolated after the Bolshevik Revolution of 1917. Thus she would also be the protector of the new Church.[66] This is why the Yugoslav government had such interest in promoting the union and why the Czechoslovak Ministry of Foreign Affairs would inform the Yugoslav delegation in Prague on March 19, 1921, that the arrival of the delegate of the Serbian Orthodox Church, Bishop Dositej, was welcome to help organize the Czechoslovak Church.

It must, of course, be kept in mind that, as everywhere else, in the Czechoslovak Church there was great fragmentation and division, difference in views, in orientation, in aspirations and motivations. Basically, the Czechs were more radical than the traditional Moravians and, as a result, a movement of moderation would soon evolve in Moravia.[67]

We must keep in mind that Moravia was mainly the land where the Cyrillomethodian Heritage was taken seriously as a historical legacy for both Slavic solidarity and church unity. In fact, the whole history of Moravia was under the shadow of Sts. Cyril and Method; under their influence national patriotism and Catholicism went hand in hand, in the harmony of undivided service and dedication to God, nation, country, and church simultaneously. It was

---

[63] *Český Zápas* 4, 14 (Prague, April 8, 1921).

[64] In 1467 the Brethren, breaking definitely with *Ultraquists*, founded their own organization, directed by three elected priests who were consecrated by a Waldensian bishop. *Cf.* Francis Dvornik, *The Slav in European History and Civilization* (Rutgers Univ. Press, 1962), pp. 207–208; J. Bidlo, *Akty Jednoty Bratrské* (Prague, 1915); F. M. Bartoš, *Dějiny Jednoty Bratrské* (Prague, 1923); R. Říčan, *Jednota Bratrská* (Prague, 1956).

[65] Urban, *op. cit.*, p. 98.

[66] The Serbian Orthodox Church came from the influence of the Patriarchate of Moscow into the sphere of the Patriarchate of Constantinople after World War I (1918), and subsequently received the status of autonomous-authocephalous-Patriarchate with residence in Belgrade (1919). *Cf.* Donald Attwater, *The Christian Churches* of the East II (Milwaukee, Bruce, 1926), pp. 81–86.

[67] M. Pavlik-Gorazd, *O Krisi v Církvi Československé. Otázka Pravoslavné Církve v Československu* (Prague, 1924), pp. 15–20 and *passim*.

understood in this way by such Slavic giants as Joseph Dobrovský,[68] Francis Sušil,[69] and especially Antonin C. Stojan,[70] who brought it to public expression in the Unionistic Congresses at Velehrad.[71] There, in Slavic solidarity, the Orthodox and the Catholics were longing for church reunion and an exchange of national sentiments.

III. CZECHOSLOVAK-ORTHODOX SCHISM

Moravian members of the Czechoslovak Church, influenced especially by their Cyrillomethodian past, had always retained a sense of traditional moderation, even in their expression of religious reform and revolt. They saw a union with the Orthodox only in the light of an extension of their traditions.

Thus, one of the zealous promoters of union with the Serbian Orthodox Church, Rev. Josef Zídek, minister of the Czechoslovak Church in Chudobin near Litovel in North Moravia, invited Bishop Dositej for friendly unofficial conversations. Subsequently, on April 21, 1921, the Czechoslovak Church Assembly of Delegates from all church communities in Moravia held a meeting in Olomouc with an attendance of 130 delegates under the chairmanship of the Reverend F. Polešovsky. Bishop Dositej explained the stand of the Serbian Orthodox Church, that acceptance of the first seven Ecumenical Councils and of the Nicene-Constantinopolitan Creed would be sufficient basis for the consecration of candidates who had been elected from within the Czechoslovak Church on April 3, 1921. These candidates were: Rev. Ferdinand Stibor for Silesia, Rev. Matthias Pavlík for Moravia, Rev. Emil Dlouhý-Pokorný for the Diocese East of Bohemia, and Dr. Karel Farský for the Diocese West of Bohemia. In regard to this Assembly of Moravian delegates in Olomouc, a subsequent public communication was published through the Czech press[1] to clarify the the situation. It read as follows:

We look upon the Czechoslovak Church, as a fully independent, autocephalous church, with the spirit of her own national tradition and history, but within the framework of the great Christian family of Churches of Christ, with the development of their own independent forms of the Christian Religion, all of which are in harmony with the principles of the one, holy Catholic and apostolic Church. Our only effort is to help the Czechoslovak Church attain this independence within the shortest possible time, and we want to help her with our own advice, as once upon a time we were helped by Sts. Cyril and Methodius.

We hope that it will be to the benefit of the Czechoslovak nation when we, a great religious unit, become one with the Slavonic East, where Czechs, one of the Brother Slavic nations, a most cultural and progressive nation, can exert a great mission for the political welfare, but more especially for the cultural, ideological brotherhood of all Slavs. We hope that we can be of some religious help to the Czechoslovak nation since we, as all other Slavic Orthodox nations, still have a living religion, the true religion of Christ, rooted in moral life, a religion which has not yet been corrupted by the influence of rationalism. Our aims are the sincerest; coming, as they do, from a Christian and brotherly Slavic heart. We have not wanted to achieve anything else, and we entrust our sincere efforts to the hands of God.[2]

This strongly worded declaration was deliberately framed to reflect the real situation. On May 7, 1921, a meeting of the Central Committee of the Czechoslovak Church was held in Prague, with full attendance, and it promulgated the following resolution:

The Czechoslovak Church is based ideologically according to Statutes and decisions of the Church Congress of January 8–9, 1921, on the first seven Ecumenical Councils and on the Nicene-Constantinopolitan Creed; and while keeping the title "Czechoslovak Church" she will, in official business contacts with the Eastern Orthodox Churches, use the name "Orthodox Czechoslovak Church" (*Československá Církev Pravoslavná*). In view of the fact, that this common ideological basis of eastern apostolic churches is being accepted, we ask that, for the benefit of religious life, the candidates already elected from religious communities of the Czechoslovak Church, be consecrated bishops as soon as possible.[3]

This official proclamation created an atmosphere of credibility, which motivated the Serbian Orthodox Church to respond. By affirming that the Czechoslovak Church was "ideologically based on the seven Ecumenical Councils and on the Nicene Creed," her formal claim of being of "Orthodox status" was established. In response to this proclamation, and as a result of the decision of the Episcopal Conference of June 16, 1921, the Serbian Orthodox Church forwarded to the Central Committee of the Czechoslovak Church the following document. It reads as follows:

To the Central Committee of the Czechoslovak Church in Prague

The Holy Synod of the Serbian Orthodox Church appreciates the resolutions of the Congress of Delegates of the Czechoslovak Church, held on April 21, 1921, in Olomouc in Moravia, as well as the resolution of the

---

[68] Josef Vajs, "Dobrovský a Biblická Kritika. Joseph Dobrovský 1753–1829" *Věstník Statí* (Prague, 1929), pp. 358–370.

[69] Alois Kolísek, *Cyrillo-Methodějstvi u Čechů a u Slováků* (Brno, 1935), pp. 47–48; Jan Vychodil, *Frant. Sušil* (Brno, 1898); Vlad. Šťastný, *Památce Fr. Sušila* (Brno, 1904).

[70] Josef Olšr *Služebník Boží, Antonin Cyril Stojan, Olomoucký Arcibiskup* (Rome, 1966); F. Cinek, *Arcibiskup Dr. A. C. Stojan* (Olomouc, 1933); idem, *Velehrad Víry* (Olomouc, 1936).

[71] Peter Esterka "Toward Union: The Congresses at Velehrad," *Jour. Ecumenical Studies* 8, 1 (Spring, 1971): pp. 10–51; Maurice Gordillo, "Velehrad e i Suoi Congressi Unionistici," *Civilta Cattolica* 2 (Rome, 1957): pp. 577–590.

[1] *Český Zápas* (Prague, of May 6, 1921) where entire text is, and partly given in Urban, *op. cit.*, p. 100.

[2] This was essentially part of a speech which Bishop Dositej gave at the conference of Moravian delegates in Olomouc. This part was published for its influence, with its patriotic emphasis, and its display of national sentiments. It was, in a way, a good piece of public relations between two Slavic nations, affirming themselves in their mutual solidarity.

[3] This is given by Urban, *op. cit.*, p. 101, in author's translation from German text. It could not be checked in Czech journals.

Central Committee held in Prague on May 7, 1921, and from their meeting on June 16, 1921, sends this communication.

The Holy Synod of the Serbian Orthodox Church is of the opinion that these two resolutions mean that the new National Czechoslovak Church, on the basis of her sisterly religious tie with the Serbian Orthodox Church, as well as with other eastern Orthodox churches, accepts the Nicene-Constantinople Creed and the first seven Ecumenical Councils, i.e., as the bond by which the Czechoslovak nation has been connected with us and the other Slavs and the Orthodox East for many centuries past. These resolutions were given to the Supreme Sabor (Council) of the Serbian Orthodox Church, i.e., to all bishops, in a volume for their inspection and final decision. It is our most sincere wish, that there will be persons at the head of the sister Czechoslovak Church who are worthy of their vocation, and who are fully aware of their duties and responsibilities, and who are conscious of the importance of the traditions of the Slavic apostles, Sts. Cyril and Methodius. The Serbian Orthodox Church is ready to allow the member of this committee, Bishop Dositej, at his own request, to stay for some time in Brotherly Czech land to finish the work for which this Holy Synod of the Serbian Orthodox Church is to be responsible, i.e., to establish a spiritually united church, bound by blood and language with other sister churches. It is the single and earnest wish of the Serbian Orthodox Church, to experience soon such development and organization of the Czechoslovak Church that it will be not only independent, but also autocephalous, able to take on responsibility for the religious and moral life of her faithful; and that she, as a full-fledged member, can be accepted into the great Union of All Eastern Orthodox Churches. With this desire and the most sincere brotherly sentiments, the Serbian Orthodox Church is ready to do everything in her power to help a nation, for whose culture and great Slavic soul she has such great admiration and respect; so that the Czechoslovak Church may be recognized within the framework of the Eastern churches, ready to work in the name of the Holy Brothers, Cyril and Methodius, through whose heritage the sons of the glorious Czech land, into which the Slavic Brothers came from Moravia, will prosper in the moral and religious progress, and help to build up the national ideals also with the Serbian nation.

May God, to whose hands we entrust the progress and completion of the Czechoslovak Church, constantly lead this Church from one good thing to another, and may His love penetrate the hearts of all your brothers.[4]

Encouraged by this positive stand of the Serbian Orthodox Church and inspired by the possibility of reaching the episcopal office by way of this Church, the Central Committee of the Czechoslovak Church convoked the Second Congress of the Church to be held on August 29, 1921, in Prague; and at this Congress, the earlier May 7, 1921, decision of the Central Committee concerning reorganization of the Church was confirmed. A unanimous vote was recorded for a change in name from Central Church Committee to the Central Council. Furthermore, it was decided that the first original paragraph of the statutes concerning requirements for the church membership should also be changed to indicate change of structure as well, and to read as follows:

Christians who believe in the teaching of Jesus Christ according to tradition of the first seven Councils and the Nicene-Constantinopolitan Creed and follow the traditions of the Hussite movement, all in the spirit of the contemporary state of human culture, constitute the Czechoslovak Church.[5]

The purpose of this change was to mitigate the modernisitic phrase: "following freedom of conscience and religious development"; the moderate statement "in the spirit of the contemporary state of human culture," was substituted. This was evidently done to appease the traditional Serbian Orthodox Church. The Congress further confirmed all candidates who had been elected by religious congregations; one exception was that of the already married Rev. E. Dlouhý-Porkorný, who was replaced by Rev. Rudolf Pařík, a candidate for the diocese of East Bohemia with residence in the city of Kutná Hora. The reason behind this was the ancient tradition of the Orthodox Church which was in principle against the consecration of married men for bishops. Father Pařík was single and acceptable. Father Dlouhý-Pokorný had been married and by that fact disbarred from the episcopal office. He was, instead, made temporary superintendent in an administrative function of the diocese. This was another concession made to the Orthodox Church by the Czechoslovak Church. In general, it can be said that the Czechoslovak Church, at this time, tried to accommodate herself whenever this was possible, by exhibiting good will and understanding.

The man who was to a great extent responsible for this transition from a radical to a moderate stand of the Czechoslovak Church was a Moravian, of course, and none other than Father Matthias Pavlík[6] (1879–1942), who himself would later undergo a spiritual transformation. In view of the fact that Pavlík was the first man to beome an Orthodox bishop from the Czechoslovak Church, a need for more detailed biographical data would seem to be in order.

Born on May 20, 1879, in Velká Vrbka in Moravia, the son of a farmer, Matthias attended the gymnasium in Kroměříž, where he graduated with exam of maturity in 1898. Thereafter, he entered a seminary, studied at the theological faculty at Olomouc, and was ordained a Roman Catholic priest in 1902. During his studies at the gymnasium and later at the university, he showed great interest in the Russian Orthodox Church. Because of this interest, he undertook a trip to Kiev in 1900. Later, he became interested in Cyrillomethodian unionism and partici-

---

[4] This is author's translation of German text in Urban, *op. cit.*, pp. 101–102.

[5] See F. M. Hník, *Duchovní ideály Československé Cirkve* (Prague, 1934), pp. 147–168.

[6] There seem to be discrepancies in a translation of his first name: In Czech his name is *Matěj* Pavlík, which should be translated as *Matthias* Pavlík, but in the majority of textbooks and studies, he is called *Matthew* Pavlík. In Czech this means *Matouš* Pavlík and not *Matěj*.

pated in some unionist congresses in Velebrad. After his ordination, he became assistant pastor in Karlovice, and then in Brumovice in Moravia. He was zealous in pastoral activities and active in politics of the Christian Democratic party, and later in the Catholic People's party.[7] Being of a rather scholarly type, he was a zealous student of nineteenth-century Czech history and, to pursue his studies in this direction, requested his transfer to Vienna or Prague to be able to use the libraries there. Archbishop Theodor Kohn of Olomouc refused his request and instead appointed him editor of the Czech Catholic journal *Pozorovatel* (Observer) in Kroměříž, in Moravia. Owing to subsequent controversies he had with other members of the editorial staff, he resigned this position and became a spiritual director of the Institution for the Mentally Ill in Kroměříž, where he remained for fifteen years. With the arrival of Czechoslovak independence, in 1918, Father Pavlík founded a newspaper, *Právo Národa* (The Right of Nation), serving as editor until he was affected by a grave eye illness. During the turbulent years of religious unrest in the newly established Czechoslovak Republic, he was a very active member first, in the Jednota, then in the Club of Reformist Priests, and finally among the zealous promoters of the new national Czechoslovak Church, becoming a member of its Central Committee in 1920 and, after 1921, its principal spokesman. Through his skilled journalistic abilities he contributed greatly to the public promotion of a new national Czechoslovak Church and participated in both church schisms: the Czechoslovak Schism in 1920, and the Orthodox Schism in 1921. As an Orthodox bishop bearing the name of Gorazd-Pavlík, he excelled as an organizer and administrator and, as a writer, he contributed popular as well as serious literary products.

Among his other works, worthy of note are the historical studies: *Myšlenkové Směrnice Církve Československé* (Kroměříž, 1920); *O Úkolech a Orientaci Církve Československé* (Olomouc, 1922); *O Krisi v Církvi Československé, Otázka Pravoslavné Církve v Československu* (Prague, 1924) and others, all with special attention to Czechoslovak and Orthodox churches. Always a Czech patriot, he suffered greatly during the Austrian era, and the occupation of the Protectorate of Bohemia and Moravia. He acted heroically during the dark era of Nazism; especially in the difficult days following the assassination of the Reich's Protector, Reinhard Heydrich, by protecting Czech patriots involved in the conspiracy against the Nazi regime. He was executed by the Germans in September, 1942.[8]

Professor Alois Spisar, with whom he lived for a long time during his stay in Kroměříž and from whom F. Pavlík took advice about practically everything, had a powerful influence on him. Professor Alois Spisar had been instrumental in helping in different projects in the newly founded church. He inspired Pavlík toward certain goals some of which eventually materialized in the framework of a new church. This sincere interest in the national Church led Spisar to become involved in the numerous meetings,[9] seriously appraising or criticizing doctrinal tenets of the Czechoslovak Church, so that his views became generally well respected in and outside the Church. Professor Spisar's contributions are a valuable deposit for the study of the Czechoslovak Church as he was one of the sources of its doctrinal content. Unfortunately, when Fr. Pavlík became Bishop Gorazd and, as such, was pressing toward union with the Orthodox, Professor Spisar disassociated himself from his protégé and became his staunch critic, although remaining in the Czechoslovak Church and following the progressive current of the Church. Father Pavlík went his traditional way, greatly influenced by Cyrillomethodian unionism and his special interest for Slavic orientation.

Upon reflection, one can easily see that it was not at all accidental that Pavlík should be chosen to become the first Orthodox bishop (Gorazd) and representative of the Czechoslovak Church. His detailed studies of the Orthodox Church, his special predilection for, and interest in, Slavic history, as well as his interest in clerical unionism and reformism, and finally his acquaintance with the Serbian Bishop Dositej, had helped him towards his change of outlook. He

---

[7] Jan Drábek, *Z časů nedlouho zašlých: vzpomínsky na Dr. Mořice Hurbana* (From times not too long past) (Rome, Christian Academy, 1967), pp. 92–93, and *passim*.

[8] Theodoric J. Zubek, the *Church of Silence in Slovakia* (Whiting, Ind.; Lach, 1956), pp. 217–218; Bishop Gorazd of Prague, who together with Orthodox priest Wenceslaus Cikl, the curate Vladimir Petřek and orthodox lay functionary J. Sonnewend, was executed by Germans in September, 1942.

[9] In addition to his numerous articles in newspapers and journals he was author of these books:

Ideové směrnice církve čsl. a bratr biskup Gorazd (Prague, 1924).
Ideový úkol církvi v náboženské krisi dneška (Prague, 1926).
Evangelium Ježíše Krista a naše doba (Prague, 1929).
Křesťanská věrouka v duchu církve čsl. pro školy měšťanské a střední (Prague, 1932).
Křesťanská mravouka v duchu církve čsl. pro školy měšťanské a střední (Prague, 1932).
Církev československái Slovok stejnojmennému článku Prof. Dr. Hromádky v Křesťanské revui, ročník V., čís. 7–10 (Prague, 1932).
Moderní subjektivismus a úkoly theologie. Inaugurační přednáška (Prague, 1933).
Náboženství Ježíse Nazaretského (Prague, 1934).
President T. G. Masaryk, náboženský člověk a myslitel (Prague, 1935).
O milosti v duchu čsl. církve (Prague, 1935).
Dějiny náboženství před Kristem (Prague, 1936)
"The Doctrinal Basis of the Czechoslovak Church." In: *The Czechoslovak Church* (Prague, 1937), pp. 53–76.

It is an impressive spectrum of studies with concern of doctrinal tenets of the Czechoslovak Church and contemporary philosophical and theological thought. He is also author of several textbooks and handbooks used in the secondary schools.

wanted to compensate for an inner shallowness of the Czechoslovak Church and, therefore, was in search of the inward depth to be found in a new church.

Having acknowledged the fundamental doctrines[10] of the Orthodox Church, the Czechoslovak Church had fulfilled all conditions set for the consecration of the bishops. Under the pressures of Bishop Dositej, final conferences were held concerning the consecration of bishops in special Sabor of the Serbian Church, with only the final decision to be made. About the second half of September, 1921, Father Pavlík, then administrator of the Moravian-Silesian diocese of the Czechoslovak Church, received a telegram concerning his scheduled consecration to take place at Belgrade, Yugoslavia. He was to be the first one consecrated, because his election had been confirmed and approved by Sabor, but there was some protest and resentment expressed against the election of Dr. Karel Farsky and Rev. Rudolf Pařík, both candidates for Bohemia. To emphasize the importance of the event, a delegation consisting of twenty-five delegates went, on September 19, from Bratislava to Serbia. The delegates were: from Bohemia, Professor Alois Tuháček; from Silesia, Rev. Ferdinand Stibor; from Moravia, Director F. Polešovský, Professor Hrdlička; clergymen Kostka, Žídek, Koudelka; and lay delegates Slavinger, Mazáč, and others. The delegation was accompanied by Protodean Niketic and a representative from Carpatho-Ruthenia, Dr. Bogatyrec.[11]

Bishop Dositej met this delegation in Nove Sadi; the occasion was memorable because Bishop Dositej was also a metropolitan of the Serbian Church. A magnificent reception was held at the patriarch's residence, *Sremski Karlovtsi*. On September 20, the Synod of Bishops approved all the documents and ratified Father Pavlík's choice for bishop of Moravia and Silesia. On September 21, the delegation went to Truska Gora, where the bishop-elect entered the monastery and chose as his monk's name Gorazd, which had been the name of St. Methodius's pupil. Immediately he was ordained superior-abbot of this monastery. The delegation then proceeded to Belgrade where, again, his selection as bishop was solemnly announced. On September 25, 1921, Pavlík-Gorazd, in solemn ceremonies, which lasted about four hours, was consecrated by Patriarch Dimitrij according to the rites of the Serbian Orthodox Church. Gorazd preached a spirited sermon about the goals of the Czechoslovak Church, and Bishop Dositej responded with an enthusiastic exhortation for Gorazd to bring back the belief to his Czechoslovak faithful as Methodius's pupils, Gorazd, Sava, Clement, Angelar, and Naum had brought the light of faith from Moravia to the Southern Slavs. On the same day, the city of Belgrade gave Gorazd a splendid reception attended by many public officials including Lord Mayor Mitrovic of Belgrade. The next day, (September 26), Gorazd was received by Prime Minister Pasic, minister of culture, and the lord mayor of Belgrade, and was awarded the Order of St. Sava, one of the highest Serbian orders.[12] The attendance of the multitude of people was described in the press as larger than any ever witnessed before. The membership of the Czechoslovak Church was incredibly exaggerated in the news account, probably to praise the missionary efforts of the newly united Serbian Church. Participation of all government authorities in this event indicates the magnitude of political prestige which the Yugoslav government hoped to gain.

However, the fact that Gorazd was consecrated, while the other two Czech candidates, Farský and Pařík, were deemed by the Synod of Bishops as too modernistic in their theological views,[13] and that both subsequently refused consecration, proved ominous.

When the delegation returned home the next day (September 27, 1921), preceding Bishop Gorazd who arrived five weeks later (on October 30), they found the Czechoslovak Church in great turmoil. At the root of the trouble was the question of candidates for the bishoprics. When it became known that Dr. K. Farsky had been elected to be bishop of the diocese of West Bohemia and, *ex officio*, the patriarch of the entire Czechoslovak Church, there was an avalanche of protests. These protests were organized in Prague, especially Smíchov, and spread over several districts, such as the city of Benešov and others. These protests were forwarded formally to the Synod of the Serbian Church, to the Czechoslovak government, and to the Ministerium of Education. In general, Dr. Farsky was accused of unbelief and wickedness; and for this reason, it was said, he could never be the leader (patriarch) of the entire Church. The protests were organized by clergymen like Jake Rab, Bautz, Brzkovský, and especially Heteš, who was influenced by Bohumil Zahradník-Brodský. Evidently frustrated ambition motivated the opposition. Heteš was envious that he himself had not been elected as bishop and the rivalry was greatly blown up before being circulated by the press.[14] Heteš had been the business manager of the Printery and Press Company of the Church, a great friend and agent for the ministerial councilman and writer Bohumil Zahradník-Brodský, but he had been reprimanded by Dr. Farsky

---

[10] Frank Gavin, *Some Aspects of Contemporary Greek Orthodox Thought* (New York, Amer. Rev. of Eastern Orthodoxy, 1962), *passim*; Sergius Bulgakov, *The Orthodox Church* (New York, 1935), *passim*.

[11] These names are mentioned by Urban, *op. cit.*, pp. 105–106.

[12] F. Cinek, *K náboženské otázce v prvních letech naší samostatnosti* (Olomouc, 1926), pp. 89–95 ff.

[13] Matthew Spinka, "The Religious Situation in Czechoslovakia," *Czechoslovakia*, ed. Robert J. Kerner (Berkeley, Univ. of California Press, 1949), pp. 296–297 and *passim*.

[14] *Český Zápas* 4, 39 (Prague, of Sept. 30 1921) described inside story concerning their rivalry.

because of mismanagement and, as a result of this bad relationship, the attack on Farsky was interpreted by many as a personal vendetta. Actually, the Heteš affair was only a cover-up for the Farsky-Zahradnik-Brodský contest, and the public protest obviously was aimed at forestalling Dr. Farsky's consecration. The disputes were settled at the first Synod of Clergy, held on November 15, 1921, in Prague, but the scandal is rather interesting because it involved two former friends and collaborators who had favored the cause of the Czechoslovak Church. The fact of the matter is that both Farsky and Zahradník were very ambitious, antagonistic, and inclined to be dictatorial in nature.

The return of Bishop Gorazd to Prague, together with Bishop Dositej of the Serbian Church, provided an opportunity to soften the unseemly rivalry. The event was celebrated by solemn pontifical liturgy at St. Nicholas Church on October 31 with a great attendance of faithful and public authorities; and Dr. Farsky, as principal spokesman, emphasized the relationship between the two churches as one of equality, saying:

> The Reverend Serbian Orthodox Church preferred to regard our Church as a free, entirely equal companion rather than have us transformed into a dependent church. Despite all difficulties, our Serbian brothers did not let themselves be deterred from their intention to establish our episcopate when the circumstances permitted, but they gave a foundation such that, through their support, our Church would be fully and from all sides, independent, totally structured and self-administered. Credit must be given to the Serbian Orthodox Church for giving existence, organization, and activity to her sister church.[15]

This praise, full of self-confidence and self-consciousness, expressed clearly enough how Dr. Farsky, as the Patriarch of the Czechoslovak Church, understood the mutual relationship between the two churches. He made sure that the independence of the Czechoslovak Church was well defined, and was to be taken seriously. Further, he let it be known that he expressed the consensus of all members of the Church.

There were some who did not approve of the Orthodox orientation at all, saying that the situation was not much different from that in the Catholic Church. They began to criticize Bishop Gorazd, who appeared always with miter and crozier, and other pontificalia; whereas they preferred simplicity, as more congenial to the Czechoslovak Church. Others resented Gorazd for being more Orthodox than the bishop of the Czechoslovak Church should be. In their opinion, Bishop Gorazd was too much concerned about the faith and was constantly stressing its connection to the seven Ecumenical Councils and the Nicene Creed. Journalistic propaganda attacked some Orthodox dogmatic tenets as being contradictory to modern science and irrelevant for modern times. While Moravia was more traditional and conservative, the adverse propaganda was loudly proclaimed in Bohemia and in the Czech papers. The different attitudes were also reflected in the different journals; while in Bohemia the leading organ *Český Zápas* (Czech Fight) was sarcastic and highly critical of everything, the Moravian journal *Za Pravdu* (For the Truth) was moderate and objective. This difference followed the lines of the differing Moravian and Czech characteristics.

It was on the basis of a decision by representatives of all the religious communities in Moravia, held on May 27, 1921, that the newly established diocese of Moravia and Silesia began publishing a new journal *Za Pravdu*, on July 7, 1921. It was here that Bishop Gorazd, in the face of intemperate attacks in the Czech journal *Český Zápas* against the Orthodox Church, published his decisive defense titles, "*Aby Bylo Jasno*" (For the Sake of Clarity).[16] He pointed out that it was illogical to call themselves "Czechoslovak Orthodox Church" and simultaneously to carry out hostile propaganda against the fundamental tenets of the Orthodox Church. It was his view that the majority of the faithful stood for traditional views, that is, mass, sacraments, priests, structures, etc. Therefore, it was imperative to accommodate the policies of the Czechoslovak Church in this direction and not to promote the radicalism of the progressives at the cost of traditional Christian creed.

This propaganda, hostile to the bishop, was politically supported by the Socialists and Communists (who had come into legal existence[17] in May, 1921), and by the National Socialists, who broadcast radical progressivism in all directions. Many teachers, too, were extreme nationalists and aided the critics; Protestants were also instrumental in bringing to public attention what could be embarrassing to traditional circles. Thus, the Protestant journals reproached the Czechoslovak Church for sticking to traditional Catholic forms, especially for celebrating mass, which Communists called "damned idolatry." The Czechoslovak Church defended herself saying that she had to consider the psychology of the masses, the majority of whose members had been accustomed to the ceremonies and who wanted to retain them. Protestants, of course, called this consideration of "psychology" undemocratic and insisted that there should be more emphasis on the modern approach and a modern philosophical outlook.

---

[15] *Český Zápas* 4, 45 (of Nov. 11, 1921) here is author's translation of partial text, given by Urban, *op. cit.*, p. 100.

[16] *Za Pravdou* nos. 8–10 (of Feb. 23 and of March 9, 1922), it was a series of articles, which later were used in a pamphlet form. *Cf.* F. Cinek, "Pozoruhodný projev biskupa církve československé, "Posléze jasno" *Našinec* no. 54. (Olomouc, March 3, 1922); *ibid.* (no. 54 March 7, 1922); (March 10, 1922).

[17] Zdeňka Holotíkova "Historické kořene vzniku Komunistickej strany Československé" (The Historical base from which Czechoslovak Communist party was born) *Historický Časopis* 19 (1) (1970): pp. 9–30.

With the increased tempo of criticism, the need for balancing the extremes became increasingly obvious. On July 25, 1922, a meeting of church counsellors was held in the city of Pardubice for the purpose of discussing the burning questions relating to the Orthodox orientation of the Czechoslovak Church. The principal speakers were Professor Nermuť from Olomouc and Pastor Hota of Nymburg. After spirited discussion of conflicting views, the following resolution, authored by Rev. E. Dlouhý-Pokorný, was finally accepted.

The counsellors of all three dioceses of the Czechoslovak Church gathered at this meeting on July 25, 1922, at Pardubice, insist on the directions of the Congress of the Czechoslovak Church of January 8 and 9, and of August 29, 1921 in, the following formulation: 1. The Relationship between the Czechoslovak Church and the Orthodox Churches is expressed in the first Article of our Constitution; Christians, believing in the teaching of Jesus Christ according to tradition of the first Ecumenical Councils and Nicene-Constantinople Creed and following the traditions of Hussite Movement—everything according to contemporary state of human culture, form the Czechoslovak Church, with a clear understanding that the Church has the freedom to remain faithful to its basic idea: (a) To form among the Czechoslovak people a Christian, national and modern church, with Christian and moral teachings, with service of divine worship and discipline. (b) In the manner of the Orthodox and other Christian churches, to take the decisions of the seven Ecumenical Councils and Nicene-Constantinople Creed as the basis and starting point for a development toward religious reformation within the Czechoslovak nation, in the spirit of the Gospels, of general Christian traditions, of the national Hussite and the Czech brethren traditions, as well as the contemporary standard of human culture. The Assembly of all three diocesan councils of the Czechoslovak Church authorizes the Central Council to end the negotiations with the Serbian Orthodox Church concerning these matters as soon as possible.[18]

This Resolution, because of its contents, was not given to Bishop Dositej by the Central Council until October 18, 1922 (over a year later). It represented a compromise between traditional and progressive wings of the Church, but the compromise could not conceal some unresolved questions. It was actually an opening in both directions and could be interpreted and rationalized in several ways. However, to understand properly this rivalry between traditional and progressive members of the Czechoslovak Church and their view and policies, one has to keep in mind that the real target was always the Catholic Church. The Catholic Church was, in fact, a barometer of the atmosphere in which both traditionalists and progressives had to breathe. The heyday of radicalism, progressivism, and all kinds of eccentricism, rampant since 1918, was slowed down by the Constitution of February 29, 1920, which permitted some breathing space to the moderates. The Census of February, 1921, was the outward expression of that change in the atmosphere.

Czech and Moravian Catholics expected to have some legal defense against numerous excesses of the progressive movements. Constitutional life and the unceasing attacks against the Catholic Church evoked in the government certain efforts to regulate church-state relationships. The government of T. G. Masaryk and Eduard Beneš tried to solve the situation.[19] Since the census had proved that the nation would remain predominantly Catholic despite the antithesis between Reformation and Counter-Reformation, the minister of foreign affairs, Dr. Beneš,[20] went to Rome to learn more about the situation from a Catholic point of view and to prepare a concordat. After discussing all possibilities with the secretary of state, Monsignor Cerreti, Dr. Beneš found that his trip was only of an informational character, although the Vatican wanted to make an honest agreement. The problems of ecclesiastical properties, of bishops and their appointment, were basic to the position of the Church. By special authorization of Pope Benedict XV, some affairs had already been settled in Prague between the government and the apostolic auditor, Monsignor Clemens Micara, in October 1919. On May 3, 1922, Vaclav Pallier was sent by the Czechoslovak government as minister extraordinary to the Holy See, and in the fall of 1923 the new nuncio, Monsignor Francis Marmaggi came to Prague and presented his credentials to President Masaryk. During the talk, the president explained that the life of nations, as of individuals, must be based on moral religious principles.

Dr. Beneš tried to regulate the relations between church and state with especial reference to international considerations. For that reason he went to Rome on three separate occasions. These negotiations resulted in their instituting full diplomatic representation. During the negotiations, Beneš was advised by Monsignor Borgongini-Duca[21] that the Holy See would be insulted if a national holiday to honor John Hus were proclaimed. It is apparent that all these efforts of Dr. Beneš were based only on motives of political prestige and expedience. Meanwhile, in internal policy, the Czechoslovak government allowed all forms of attacks and disturbances at home.[22]

Great excitement in educational circles was caused by the so-called "small bill of education," enacted on June 15, 1922, whereby religious education was made relatively obligatory; that is to say, it was made dependent on the decision of parents. The law of 1922,

---

[18] Originally given in Czech, *Český Zápas* 5, 31 (of July 26, 1922); this is author's translation of German text, given by Urban, *op. cit.*, p. 112.

[19] Joseph Schmidlin, *Päpstgeschichte der Neuesten Zeit* (4 v., Muenchen, Verlag Josef Koesel and Friedrich Pusset, 1933–1939) **4**; p. 132.
[20] *Schmidlin, op. cit* **4**: p. 288.
[21] *Osservatore Romano*, August 28, 1925.
[22] Orazio M. Premoli, *Contemporary Church History* (London, Burns, 1932), p. 242 ff.

No. 226, and later, by Cabinet Decree of 1925 No. 64, authorized the exemption of children from seven to fourteen from compulsory religious instruction if their parents requested it. The same provision also exempted children "without religious denomination" from compulsory attendance in religious classes.[23] This, of course, favored the non-Catholic minority, and the Czechoslovak Church took maximum advantage of this relaxed legislation in the name of religious freedom, aided by the concentrated propaganda of all liberals. This overview will give some indication of the prevailing atmosphere in which the proponents of all different segments of views had to adapt, eliminate, struggle, polarize, or change to comply with the rapidly changing times. Opportunism took preference over principles, with purpose and motivation dictating the choice of means. The status of the Catholic Church became the negative norm whereby various groups sought to establish their *raison d'être*. The Czechoslovak Church was determined to use all forces, as she did, to play the role of a "contemporary, modern and progressive church." This is how the internal struggles within the Czechoslovak Church became a reverberating discord of many voices. This is why the confrontation of the Orthodox orientation, with the progressive determination of the national church, had to take its course.

Another example of the Czechoslovak Church's determination to enlarge her membership, was by Bishop Gorazd's journey in August, to the United States of America, where he hoped to recapture those Slovaks and Czechs, whom he had missed earlier, especially in Slovakia. Many Slovaks in America, after earning some money, would return to their mother country.[24]

Gorazd's success in America was practically nil. Although he could not influence the American Czechs at all, he was able to establish six communities for the "National Catholic Czechoslovak Church" in Palmerton, Perth Amboy, Masontown, Monessen, New York, and McKeesport.[25] Two of them were established by Tokar, a former Catholic priest. Even less effective was Gorazd's mission among the Slovak American clergy, although he did win over to his side two Slovak priests, Fathers Balley and Šebesta. One of the reasons for Bishop Gorazd's failure was that, in general, all the American Slovak clergy were separatist, i.e., they wanted to see an independent Slovakia, while Gorazd represented a unified Czechoslovakia. This difference of political outlook created much division among the Slovaks at home as well as abroad.

Besides this unsuccessful apostolate among his countrymen, Bishop Gorazd also participated in the General Convention of the American Episcopal Church, held in Portland, Oregon, from September 6 to September 14, 1922. Here he delivered a talk in Czech (which was translated into English) in the name of the Czechoslovak Church, but he expressed only his own Orthodox concepts which, as previously noted, were opposed by the majority of the members of the Czechoslovak Church at home. As he explained it, the Orthodox orientation of the Czechoslovak Church, would insure their mutual support. This union, he explained, was brought about on the basis of decisions reached at the last Congress of the Czechoslovak Church, held on August 29, 1921, when both churches agreed that their dogmatic tenets were similar and mutually compatible. This union was never really consummated because the actual corporate union envisioned did not materialize, but resulted only in cooperation. Contact with the Episcopal Church Convention was provided by the Reverend Keating Smith, who had been a guest at the liturgical celebration held in St. Nicholas' Church in Prague back on August 29, 1920; but this effort came a little late since the Serbian Orthodox Church had already mediated the episcopal office to the Czechoslovak Church through the consecration of Bishop Gorazd. Thus, the American journey of Bishop Gorazd scored positively in some points,[26] but did not influence the thinking of the majority of the members of the Church at home. It was rather an interesting phenomenon. Bishop Gorazd's explanations did not accurately detail the reality of the Czechoslovak situation.

This last-mentioned fact was brought to light by the publication of a new catechism, in which the new church's teaching was formulated for the first time, and in which two basic orientations, Orthodox and modern progressivism, were set apart. Disputes about doctrinal tenets reached a decisive stage with the appearance of a new Czechoslovak catechism (*Československý Katechism učebnice Pro Mládež a věřící Čsl. Církve* (Příbram, 1922) (A Handbook for Youth and the Faithful of the Czechoslovak Church) authored by Dr. Karel Farsky and Professor Francis Kalous from Příbram. Obviously, to publish a question-and-answer catechism was a sheer imitation of the Catholic Catechism which had been used in Catholic schools during the Austrian era, and had been

---

[23] Vratislav Bušek, *Czechoslovakia* (N.Y. Frederick A. Praeger, 1957), pp. 134–135.

[24] Joseph J. Rouček, "The American Czechs, Slovaks, and Slavs in the Development of America's "Climate of Opinion," *Czechoslovakia: Past and Present*, ed. M. Rechcigl, Jr. (The Hague, Mouton, 1968) **2**: pp. 815–843.

[25] See geographical distribution of Slovak parishes in the United States of America in *Jednota Katolický Kalendár na rok 1972* (Middletown, Pa., Jednota Printery, 1972), pp. 165–186; there are some vital statistics on parishes and priests as well, pp. 186–204; Slovaks were always religiously minded and well organized ethnical groups with numerous parishes and schools.

[26] F. Cinek, "Spojení církve československé's protestantskou církví episkopální" *Našinec* no. 56 (Olomouc, March 9, 1923); Alois Spisar, *Ideové směrnice církve československé a bratr biskup Gorazd* (Prague, 1924), *passim*.

taken up by Catholic bishops in the Czechoslovak Republic with minimal adaptation.[27]

This new Czechoslovak catechism was divided into four principal parts and having 13 independent subdivisions split up into 136 questions and answers. Its contents and index can be comprehensively outlined as follows:

I. Religion: A. The Life of the World. B. The Knowledge of God. C. Teachings of Jesus Christ or Christianity. D. Jesus—The Heroic Sufferer of Mankind.
II. The Commandments and Legacies: A. The Divine Election. B. Commandments. C. Legacies.
III. Divine Worship: A. Religion as a Private Matter. B. Religions as a Public Matter. C. Ceremonies. D. Mysteries (Sacraments).
IV. The Church: A. The Concept of the Church. B. Constitution and Organization of the Czechoslovak Church.

This catechism held to common religious terms like God, Creator, Jesus, Redeemer, Holy Spirit, heaven, hell, sin, repentance, but in most cases they are given a new meaning. Thus, God is the living law of the world (question 3). God Himself is spirit and the absolute truth (question 4). Man can recognize Him only partly in single events and laws of nature, especially in his (own) inner self (question 9). He is also called creator dominating the world, because He created the world (question 8) and creation is the life of the world, because in the world new creations come into being or are being created constantly (question 7). Man, himself, can become co-creator, a god, as father and mother are (question 16). The divine enthusiasm in man is the Holy Spirit (question 20) with whose help man can unite himself with God (question 19). God is man's father (question 32) and those persons who have understood (penetrated into) the divine truth, are God's sons and children (question 31). Only in this sense Jesus is to be understood as the Son of God. He predominates only because He, Himself, has understood the divine code of law best and has explained it best to man (question 12). He, Himself, is not God, He is only one of the prophets who reveal the divine law to men (question 11). He is the greatest of them (II,4); besides Him there are other famous prophets like Moses, Socrates, Mohammed, Zarathustra, Buddha, Confucius (II,6) and those who have to be considered especially as Czech prophets, such as Cyril and Methodius, Hus, Komenský, and the national liberators of the Czech people (II,7). Among these famous prophets Jesus takes, so to speak, the position of "primus inter pares." Through His death on the cross He overpowered man's wickedness and weakness (1,43); therefore, He is called victor over death, and redeemer (Christ) of mankind (question 1,45).

Sin is departure from the divine law (1,49) and hell is human life without the divine law (1,51). Repentance is the decision of sinful man to return to the divine truth (question 53) to achieve thereby a new unification with God (or forgiveness) (question 54). He who rids himself from sin is in a condition similar to being re-born or risen from the dead (question 57). He who is united with divine truth participates in divine life and lives eternal life. The term grace does not occur in the catechism; nor does the thought that Christ has saved mankind in a vicarious way. Instead, Jesus is said to have saved mankind from sin and hell only through His truth (question 48). The divine judgment is constantly taking place in the lives of individual people as well as of nations (question 35).

The section called "Legacies" introduces the opinions of famous Czech personalities; among them we find the four Prague articles which were added to the commandments and considered as equal to them.

The term "service of mass" is said to be the service offered to God, consisting in the carrying out of God's will by serving one's neighbor (III, 1 and 2). Prayer is a spiritual dialogue with God (III, 5). About the Church we read:

(1) The community of all Christians is the one Church.
(2) The Head of this church is Jesus Christ.
(3) Jesus wants His church to be based on a strong belief in the gospel.
(4) The individual beliefs and deeds are parts of the one Church.
(5) The individual confessions (denominations) also call themselves churches.
(6) There are about 300 churches of that kind; therefore, no church is right in calling herself Catholic at the cost of other churches.
(7) Besides the Czechoslovak Church, the best-known churches are the Protestant Church, the Orthodox Church, and the Roman Papal Church.
(8) It is the task of every church to lead its members to religion in the spirit of Christ and to arouse their love for their neighbors.[28]

This Czechoslovak catechism became highly controversial and was under attack from representatives of traditional Christianity. The definition of God as the living law of the world was labeled as the "worst pantheism" and the denial of Jesus Christ's divinity

---

[27] Much catechetical and pedagogical material was published for teaching religion for grade, high school, and colleges in Czechoslovakia. Theological faculties had pedagogical chairs and professors were promoters of new methods. The most recent were *Podlahův Katechism*, then cathechetical handbooks by Dr. V. Kubíček, Dr. J. Kašpar and Professor Josef Hronek from University of Prague. *Cf.* J. Hronek, *Přehled Katolické theologic české* (Prague, 1935), pp. 61–67.

[28] This division, structure, and doctrinal content of the *Czechoslovak Catechism* was taken from the outlines of Urban, *op. cit.*, pp. 114–116. These outlines are taken from the oldest edition, published in Příbram in 1922, as it has been announced for the first time in *Český Zápas* 5, 35. In following editions, material content and structure was little altered, but basically preserved. *Cf.* F. Cinek, "Církev zbudovaná na frázích" (Church built on the phrases) *Našinec* no. 33 (Feb. 2, 1923).

put the Czechoslovak Church in a position of being ostracized as a church without foundation, and as a product of modernism. In all other points, her doctrinal tenets were styled as vague reproductions of religious views mixed with *Religionswissenschaft* and *Weltanschauung*, as the Germans generally called liberal theological trends, to be interpreted according to the times.

It was most obvious that this catechism was in complete disagreement with the seven Ecumenical Councils and the Nicene-Constantinopolitan Creed on which the entire union with the Serbian Orthodox Church was supposedly based. As a result, the catechism met with strong criticism by Bishop Dositej, and he lost no time in rejecting it:

> I consider it my duty for the sake of my peace of conscience, before God and in the name of the entire Church, as well as in the interest of the young national and friendly Czechoslovak Church, for which I have worked with full Christian love, and continue to do work as a responsible protector, to state: The catechism authored by Dr. K. Farsky and Professor F. Kalous, published at their own cost, but approved by the Prague Diocesan Council, contradicts in its contents the decision of the Church Council of August 28, 1921, according to which the Czechoslovak Church in her teaching on faith and morals is founded on the basis of the seven Ecumenical Councils and the Nicene-Constantinopolitan Creed. Furthermore, the contents of the catechism contradict the basic Christian principles of the Cyrillomethodian tradition and the dying legacy of the great martyr and holy master, John Hus; and this means it is opposed to the return of the Czechoslovak nation to the original apostolic belief
>
> The catechism probably contains only the private ideas of Dr. K. Farsky and Professor Kalous, but it is certainly and completely outside of the body of any Christian creed. I ask the entire Czechoslovak Church, all brothers and sisters, to remain faithful to the faith and the principles of the apostolic Church and not to leave the body, on which the Czechoslovak Church placed her first organization and her first council.
>
> Delegate of the Serbian Orthodox Patriarch
> Signed: Dositej, Bishop of Nisch[29]

On another occasion Bishop Dositej went so far as to call this catechism a "theological absurdity."[30] It was characterized in a more kindly, but none-the-less ambiguous way by the well-known Catholic theologian, Msgr. Francis Cinek, professor of the Cyrillomethodian Faculty at Olomouc as a "unique feature in Czech literature."[31] Professor J. Konečný called it a "symbol of disintegration of Christianity."[32] These and many other statements were certainly not complimentary; and the majority of Catholic, Protestant, Orthodox, and other scholars were in agreement that the Czechoslovak catechism represented, to say the least, "an unusual theological rarity" in a bad sense.

Bishop Dositej's attack drew a violent response from Dr. Farsky, who accused the bishop and the whole Orthodox Church of insolence. Immediately Bishop Dositej left for Prague for a long conference with Farsky and after it was over, declared promptly that his mission in the Czechoslovak Church was finished. He returned depressed to his native Serbia; and, on November 30, 1922, the Synod approved his action without reservation. With this, all rapport of the Czechoslovak Church with the Serbian Church was about finished.

To make the break more emphatic, the Diocesan Council for East Bohemia, on October 3, 1922, did approve the catechism as official; whereupon it was recognized as the official doctrine of the Czechoslovak Church. As a result, the Synod of the Serbian Orthodox Church would consecrate neither Dr. K. Farský nor the Rev. Rudolf Pařík, both of whom had been selected as candidates for episcopal consecration for Bohemia, one for East and the other for West Bohemia; and, on February 26, 1923, the Serbian Church officially and publicly declared her stand in a communication to the Central Council of the Czechoslovak Church in the following words:

> As it has turned out, the May 7, 1921 resolution of the Central Council of the Czechoslovak Church in Prague which was accepted by the Congress of Delegates of the entire Czechoslovak Church held in Prague on August 29, 1921, and which served as the basis of today's friendly relationship between the Czechoslovak Church and the Serbian Orthodox Church, has been absolutely negated and voided by the contents of the Czechoslovak catechism; therefore we consider it necessary to say that any further explanations and negotiations would be meaningless. If one partner does not observe an arrangement which was previously agreed upon in a friendly manner, then results of such an action must become clear. . . .[33]

By this action not only all negotiations with the Serbian Orthodox Church came to an end, but the alienation of Moravia from Bohemia was also effected. The Diocesan Council of Moravia, at its meeting on October 16, 1922, condemned the Czechoslovak catechism as follows:

> The Diocesan Council of the Czechoslovak Church, in its meeting held in Olomouc the sixteenth of October, has decided to abide by Bishop Dositej's statement in its entirety; and declares that it does not consider the contents of the approved Czechoslovak catechism pub-

---

[29] This was published in *Český Zápas* **5**, 42 on October 16, 1922; this, however, is the author's translation of German text, given by Urban, *op. cit.*, p. 117; the first time it appeared in diocesan Moravian paper *Za Pravdou* on October 12, 1922. *Cf.* F. Cinek, "Biskup Gorazd slavnostně odsoudil československý katechismus," *Našinec*, no. 24 (30 of Jan. 1923); K. Statečný, "Centrálne otázky věrouky církve československé," *Nasě Dílo* (Prague, 1927), pp. 7–50.

[30] Premoli, *op. cit.*, p. 242 ff. and *passim*.

[31] *Ibid*.

[32] Jan Konečný "Československý katechismus a rozklad křestanství," *Časove Úvahy* **283** (Hradec Kralové, 1922): *passim*.

[33] M. Pavlik-Gorazd, *O Krisi v církvi československé. Otázka pravoslavné církve v Československu* (Prague, 1924), pp. 25–26.

lished in Prague, by the Councils of the East and West Bohemian dioceses, as the teachings of the entire Czechoslovak Church, but as only the private theological opinion of the brother authors. In taking this stand, this Diocesan Council calls attention to the fact (1) that this catechism does not correspond with the first paragraph of the Constitution acknowledged by the State, by which the Czechoslovak Church in her entire teaching of faith tends toward the acceptance of the first seven Ecumenical Church Councils and of the Nicene-Constantinopolitan Creed, and (2) it contradicts the decision of the entire Church Council of the Czechoslovak Church held in Prague on January 8, 1921, where it had been announced that the Czechoslovak Church would join the members of the Eastern Orthodox Church as an autonomous and equal member.[34]

This inspired some followers of the Orthodox orientation in Bohemia also to take a stand of protest against the Czechoslovak catechism, since it was also unacceptable to them. Thus, on November 5, 1922, the Czech journal, *Národní Listy*, published the proclamation of some religious communities, such as the city of Benešov, Prague VII, Tabor, Sviňov near Budějovice, Solan, and others, that they also stood for the Orthodox orientation, and it accused the leaders of the National Czechoslovak Church in Prague of deceiving the people in this matter. To the surprise of all, the leaders of Prague's Czechoslovak Church answered by excommunicating all their opposing members. This note concerning "excommunication" pronounced by the national Czechoslovak Church, which had boasted of its great tolerance and freedom of all kinds of opinions, was rather interesting, since practically all members of the Czechoslovak Church were themselves in some way or another excommunicated from the Roman Catholic Church, and they all had ridiculed that "antiquated practice" of the Catholic Church which now suddenly became modern enough to be used by them against their dissidents.

The same thing happened in Moravia, but in reverse. Some members of the Czechoslovak Church in Moravia did not agree with a majority of Orthodox orientation and made a *coup d'état* in leadership and in a new orientation of the Czechoslovaks in Moravia. Dissatisfied with Bishop Gorazd's leadership, they took over the editorship of the Church with clergymen Hrdlička, Polešovský, Rezek, and Urban. Their tactics were to attack Orthodox ideas rather than their principal representatives, and thus they created chaos and confusion.

The Diocesan Assembly of Delegates, held in Olomouc on November 23, 1922, followed a similar approach. On the program there was to be a formal re-election of the bishop's Diocesan Council by delegates of twelve religious communities recognized by the state. The presence of Dr. Farsky and Professor Kalous clearly indicated that a change in direction might be discussed as well. There were eighty-three delegates (sixty-three laymen and twenty clergymen) present, and yet only delegates of the twelve religious communities were allowed to vote; including the clergymen and religious teachers, they totaled forty-two. As a result, the Diocesan Council was elected again. Furthermore, the proposal of Director Polešovský against that of Fr. Žídek was accepted. It read as follows:

The Assembly of the Delegates of the Moravian Diocese of the Czechoslovak Church, held in Olomouc November 23, 1922, declares, with the agreement of the delegates of the Prague Diocese and of the Central Council, that it insists on the unity of the Czechoslovak Church and the decisions of the Church Councils, and it rejects all efforts to destroy this unit. Bishop Gorazd-Pavlik was elected the bishop of the Moravian Diocese.[35]

This was intended to create an impression that there was unity and agreement between Dr. Farsky and Bishop Gorazd, but it took unfair advantage of Bishop Gorazd who was, at that time, in the United States of America; and who reacted vehemently when he was informed of what had happened. He sent two messages in which he expressed his views concerning the situation. The first letter reads:

Brothers and Sisters! I am sending you friendly greetings from distant America. I am writing amidst an influx of work. From the diocesan paper I learned that the Diocesan Assembly carried out the election of a bishop and of the Diocesan Council. Regarding the inner development in our Church, in which I am personally involved, and which I deeply regret, I take the liberty to admonish you that I fully agree with the statements which I had expressed earlier in the study on the work and the orientation of the Czechoslovak Church. These statements are in agreement with decisions of the entire Assembly of our Church and are, in my strong opinion, the only way toward the unity and successful work of our Church.

I do hope that the Diocesan Assembly will not let itself be misled by agitation, and will not be deterred from the direction which is positively a religious one. As our Church is democratic and there is no one person justified in deciding what the Church should and should not be doing, the possibility cannot be excluded that the majority of brothers and sisters in our diocese might refuse to identify themselves with my views concerning the orientation of the Church. If this were the case, it would be unwise to elect me as bishop and, under such circumstances, I would not accept the election at any price. I would ask the Diocesan Assembly to take this explanation of my point of view into consideration.[36]

The second letter was addressed to the former Diocesan Council and it contained a very strong criticism

---

[34] *Za Pravdou* no. 42 of October 16, 1922; this is, however, the author's translation of German text, given by Urban, *op. cit.*, p. 119.

[35] *Za Pravdou*, no. 47 of November 23, 1922; *cf.* also *Český Zápas* 5, 48 of December 1, 1922; this is the author's translation of German text, by Urban, *op. cit.*, p. 120 ff.

[36] M. Pavlik-Gorazd, *O úkolech a orientaci církve československé* (Olomouc, 1922), *passim*. *Cf.* Vladimír Grigorič, *Pravoslavná Církev v Republice Československé* (2nd ed., Prague, 1928), p. 127 ff.

about the Czechoslovak Catechism and of the leadership in Prague. It read as follows:

Dear Brothers! Although far away from you, I am thinking of you. The news which has reached me fills me with sorrow. Since I did not want to leave America and neglect the work which seemed to hold out such great hope, I could not personally get involved in the development of events.

I deny the accusation that I have not shown enough responsibility for my actions. I have always stuck by my actions, and I will always do whatever in my ecclesiastical life I shall have to do. My stay in America convinces me of the righteousness of my previous activity within the Church.

I do not deny that I experienced a serious religious crisis myself, for it was during this crisis that my Christian basic concepts were born, and during my psychological upheaval they became even stronger, although normally they would have faded out. Especially, from the time when I was called to work at the head of the Moravian and Silesian Church, I have felt an immense responsibility. I have thought intensively about the future of the Church. The result was my study on the orientation of the Church. I still fully agree with this study. It corresponds with the guidelines given at the Assembly of the Church Delegates on January 8 and 9, 1921. The Orthodox orientation is not and could not be an illusion, since it corresponds best with the actual needs of the majority of our brothers and sisters; and if then, there had not been widespread confusion, which is our weakness, our Church would have been already constituted and interiorly consolidated. The Orthodox orientation enables us to develop in a democratic spirit, and with a corresponding growth.

With the Orthodox orientation any dictatorial regime is entirely excluded; and this is a problem which our Church has tried to avoid from the very beginning. I still will have an opportunity to show how our Church, through a dictatorial regime, would be damaged ideologically, morally, and materially.

In this category of Church matters, one has the right to take into consideration the publication which appeared under the title, *Czechoslovak Catechism*. It was edited and published as the religious book for the youth and faithful of the Czechoslovak Church, but no explicit statement has shown that the Moravian and Silesian Diocesan Council had been informed as should have been done, since it is unlawful to edit books without previous permission and approval of the Professional Commission, which was authorized by the General Assembly of January 8 and 9, 1921, and which authorization was never revoked.

The *Czechoslovak Catechism* was published by the Diocesan Council of Prague as the textbook which everyone, not well acquainted with the matter, might take as an official statement of the Church; but this is, however, not true in regard to the formal and real matter. Nowhere do we find it explicitly stated that the Moravian and Silesian diocesan authorities were even consulted. Yet, since the Professional Commission was set up on January 8 and 9, 1921 (and there has been no revocation of that authorization), all publications must be submitted for study to this Commission; and no Diocesan Council is qualified to publish in any other way. With regard to material content, especially on certain points, the tenor of the book, seen from an all-round perspective, disagrees with the Gospel as well as with the concepts held by the first Christians, the decisions of the Councils, and the belief of the present Christian churches. Christ (and His work) is portrayed without reference to divine grace;

on the grace of Christ as the Son of God, is based the eternal unity with God. Grace is, however, the necessary and indispensable force, the meaningful sign of Christianity. Without grace, there is no Christian religion; it is then only Christian ethics. Materially, also, in the *Czechoslovak Catechism*, Christ is portrayed as only one of the greatest prophets, in whom no divine grace, in any aspect, is shown to be working. This is rather a handbook for ethics, but not of religion. Whether mere ethics is sufficient for our nation, and especially for the members of our Church, or whether we should be content with a free ethic, is a question that has still to be resolved. The Czechoslovak Catechism damages and destroys our Church inside and outside. It creates and continues to spread the bad impression at home as well as abroad, that there is no need for any church, especially not for the Czechoslovak Church; after the publication of such a Catechism, no Church would have any appeal. Yet this catechism is being imposed on the hundreds of thousands and millions of those who already have entered this Church, or who might later enter it. Even in America, it is simply impossible to build up a Czechoslovak Church on such a basis.

On the basis of this catechism, any church would be reluctant to consecrate our bishops. If, in the very beginning, it had been thought that the teaching of the Czechoslovak Church would be formulated as it now appears in this catechism, then it must also have been regarded as nonsensical to introduce the episcopal system, and foolish to negotiate for episcopal consecration. If, after making the Roman Catholic Church alien to our nation, the Czechoslovak Church wants to be truly Czechoslovak, i.e., a totally national church which could fulfill a great mission as happened with other Slavic Churches, and wants to be so acknowledged by the Protestant Churches, there is only one thing to do, and that is to reject this Czech catechism. I mention the similarity with other Slavic churches because I was a co-consecrator of the new Russian-Orthodox Bishop Adam Filipovský on October 25, 1922. I am, therefore, in agreement with Bishop Dositej and with the brotherly Diocesan Council of Olomouc. After having been confronted with such a dictatorial decision, it is now high time to proclaim that we are against everything which is harmful to our Church's existence, everything which would be against her acceptance and recognition by others.

I ask the Diocesan Council to acknowledge my explanations, and read them in the Assembly to be held on November 26, as was announced in the Diocesan Journal.[37]

Of course, these letters of Bishop Gorazd were not published in either of the church journals because of the danger of disturbing the unity and creating unrest among the faithful of the Czechoslovak Church. Bishop Gorazd, therefore, made a great appeal to the Slovak-American people, informing them about the real situation which existed in the Czechoslovak Church at home, and defending its program as conformable to the Orthodox tradition and rejecting entirely the *Czechoslovak Catechism* with this proclamation, a portion of which reads as follows:

And I, the only rightly and validly elected Bishop of the Czechoslovak Church, declare that I reject this book-

---

[37] Vlad. Grigorič, *op. cit.*, pp. 125–127; this is author's transl. from Grigoric's text.

let entirely. This is not a real Czechoslovak catechism because it could have been such only if and when it were proclaimed as such by the Church Council. This booklet published in Prague contains the private views of the authors, Dr. Farsky and Professor Kalous, as they themselves already have admitted, and by this admission, it cannot be the catechism of the Czechoslovak Church.[38]

With this proclamation, of course, any further apostolate of the Czechoslovak Church abroad lost effectiveness and the reputation of the new Church lost appeal even among free-thinking Czechs, of whom many lived in America. It created a decisive polarization among the faithful at home, and the momentum of a national church, as such, was lost in the national state. This all happened because the Czechoslovak catechism failed to offer any definite formula of faith, which would be satisfying enough to inspire or even appeal to the faithful who anxiously sought eternal salvation.

When Bishop Gorazd returned home at the end of January, 1923, the confusion in his Moravian diocese had almost reached its peak. Since the former official journal, *Za Pravdou*, had been seized by progressive wings of the Czechoslovak Church, the traditional followers of Bishop Gorazd founded a new organ titled *Náš Směr* (Our Direction), for the defense of the Orthodox orientation; later, for increased emphasis, the name was changed to *Pravoslavný Směr* (Orthodox Direction), with its first issue on January 19, 1923. Dr. L. K. Kopal-Stěhovský was selected as editor-in-chief. He was then instructor of Protestant theology at the Hus Faculty at Prague, a long-time proponent of union of the Czechoslovak Church with the Orthodox Church, and author of the several books, one of which was titled, *Co Vede Československou Církev ku Křestanskému Východu* (What Leads the Czechoslovak Church toward the Christian Orient?) (Olomouc, 1921). He was also a leading opponent of the modernistic theses of progressives of the Czechoslovak Church. It was he who attacked Dr. Farsky, accusing him of deceiving the Czechoslovak public,[39] and it was he who in his devastating, critical article against the progressive leaders of the Czechoslovak Church in Prague, titled "Christianity Over Freemasonry?"[40] showed that their Church had been degraded to the level of Freemasonry.

However, there were a great number of faithful who still identified themselves with the progressive ideas expressed in the Czechoslovak catechism, not only in Czech dioceses but also in the Moravian Diocese. Thus, for Bishop Gorazd, consecrated by the patriarch of the Serbian Orthodox Church, and irrevocably committed to the union with the Orthodox Church, only two possibilities remained: (1) either to separate from the Czechoslovak Church completely, with the small number of his followers; or (2) to give up the fight against the majority of the progressives, and renounce his bishopric in the Czechoslovak Church.

After serious consideration and conferences with many influential churchmen and laymen, he decided to make one last effort. On March 5, 1923, he informed the Moravian Diocesan Council that the present circumstances made it impossible for him to remain a bishop and to have responsibility for the further development of the Czechoslovak Church. The Diocesan Council decided to call a Diocesan Assembly for March 28, in Přerov in Moravia, where Bishop Gorazd could explain his decision to all delegates of the church communities. It caused great anxiety in the entire Czechoslovak Church, since Bishop Gorazd was their only consecrated bishop and was the only source from whom they could obtain apostolic succession for other candidates already selected, such as Dr. K. Farsky, Rev. Rudolf Pařík, and Rev. Ferdinand Stibor. Looking for such an opportunity, they had waited too long. After the break-up of negotiations with the Serbian Orthodox Church, it was painful to think that Bishop Gorazd might separate or resign because, especially after the recent *Czechoslovak Catechism* situation, there would be no other church willing to mediate apostolic succession by consecrating candidates who, because of their modernist views, had already been refused consecration by the Serbian Orthodox Church.

Furthermore, there were psychological reasons why this question was so important: the common people were genuinely concerned about apostolic succession, owing to their faith in and desire to be part of a true church which could find itself with the historical continuity from apostolic times. Surprisingly enough, even among the progressive members, this concern was more widespread than was thought desirable by some of the church leaders.

At the beginning of 1922, when negotiations with the Serbian Orthodox Church were being held, Dr. Farsky had to suppress rumors being spread about the Czechoslovak Church's ongoing negotiations with the American Methodist Church because at that time, the faithful did not see any reason for it. After all, the Methodist Church could not consecrate bishops with apostolic succession. Dr. Farsky's denial of the rumors reads as follows:

> I need not prove that the entire story about negotiations for union with the Methodist Protestant Church is a mere lie. Brother Emil Dlouhý-Pokorný would have been discredited with me in the Czechoslovak Church, and would have been so infected with the poison of "Protestantism" that all negotiations of the Czechoslovak Church with the West would have been broken; and, in spite of all the energy expended by Bishop Gorazd,

---

[38] *New Yorský Denník* no. 2789 of December 24, 1922; this is the author's translation from Slovak text, published above.

[39] *Národní demokracie* (Hague), no. 265 of Nov. 12, 1922, where a strong attack against the Central Council of Czechoslovak Church in Prague may be found.

[40] *Pravoslavný směr* (Orthodox Direction (Prague)) no. of Jan. 19, 1923, where this article may be found

we would have been condemned, because we, supposedly, would have striven to mislead the Czechoslovak Church.[41]

This self-defense of Dr. Farsky's reveals the resentment which many of the faithful in the Czechoslovak Church felt against any protestantizing tendencies squeezing their way into the national church.

Another indignant denial of the same story but with the supposed help to come from the Presbyterian System, appeared in *Národní Politika* of April 25, 1922.[42] This was called a mystifying fabrication, because the Presbyterians could not be helpful in securing the episcopal office, since they themselves do not share in any continuity of apostolic succession; and *quod non habes, non potes dare* could have been applied here. Even the common faithful knew this principle well enough, and this was why the greater part of the Czechoslovak Church looked to the churches with episcopal structures, and avoided those of the evangelical type.

Before proceeding any further, it seems necessary to clarify "apostolic succession" the focal point of the controversy going on between the factions of the Czechoslovak Church. First of all, the discussion of apostolic succession regards what may be called a traditional teaching[43] but as developed from the beginning of the twentieth century. There was not a single Christian confession which was not involved in it, because apostolic succession of some sort has been recognized as a basic condition for the very existence of Christian communities, to the extent that it serves as an ideal criterion for their comparative classification. As Javierre notes,

looking at gradations within the spectrum from left to right, so to speak, we find some confessions radically opposed to the idea of succession; others accept it as applying only to the transmission of doctrine; still others would extend it to include the ministry; then, the so-called "catholic" confessions would also require the strict collegial succession of their bishops; and, finally, Rome, which adds the pope as the head of the College of Bishops.[44]

Owing to the intensified cooperation of theology and history, the thesis of apostolic successions became in time suitably moderated, and ceased to cause the scandal it used to.[45] By 1950 the divine origin of the ministry was commonly recognized;[46] some non-Catholic writers do not hide their nostalgia, as ministers, for unity in descent from the apostles.[47] Some even study sacramental ordination with a frank sympathy.[48] Others try out formulas of equivalence, in the hope of narrowing the function of bishop to dogmatic teaching, in places where sociological conditions would seem not to admit its broader application.[49]

Later the problem of apostolic succession was interpreted in terms of its essence. Hans Küng insists that

Apostolic succession is, therefore, primarily a succession in apostolic faith, apostolic service, and apostolic life. This means, in the negative sense, that there is a juridical narrowing of the concept to see apostolic succession primarily in a continuous chain of impositions of hands—as if such a chain of ordinations by itself could supply the apostolic Spirit! In the positive sense, it means that the point of the succession lies in the constantly renewed daily loyalty to the apostles.[50]

Anyone can readily ascertain that in Catholic circles the term "apostolic succession" is usually used in a narrow sense. It is restricted to hierarchical succession in the Church, even though "apostolicity" is regarded as a note and a hallmark of the whole Church insofar as her origins and her doctrine are concerned. This terminological restriction is tied up, in the general tendency of Catholic ecclesiology, so as to place primary stress on the role and authority of the hierarchy. Limiting the notion of apostolic succession in the Church to the succession within the hierarchy might be taken to mean that the hierarchy is set up as against the People of God. Since, however, apostolic succession within the hierarchy is meant to serve the People of God, it can only be understood in relation to the apostolic succession of the whole Church. It is only because apostolic succession resides in the whole Church that it can be applied to the hierarchy as serving the faithful.[51]

After noting that the apostolic succession of the hierarchy "cannot be isolated from the total reality transmitted, the Church herself," Congar goes on to make this point, "Buried in the reality of apostolic succession is the principle of sobornost."[52] It suggests that there is some type of control exercised by the whole Church, some scheme of reception. There is abundant testimony of this in history, but it was

---

[41] *Český Zápas* 5, 2, this is the author's translation of German text, given by Urban, *op. cit.*, p. 127.

[42] *Český Zápas* 5, 20, reported this news which appeared in *Národní Politika* of April 25, 1922.

[43] Antonio Javierre, S. B. B., "Notes on the Traditional Teaching of Apostolic Succession," *Concilium* 34 (1968): pp. 16–27.

[44] Antonio Javierre, *op. cit.*, p. 17.

[45] E. Schlink, "La succession apostolique," *Verbum Caro* 69 (1964): pp. 52–86.

[46] *Cf.* recent symposia *Das Amt der Einheit* (Stuttgart, 1964), *passim*; "Ministère et Laicat," *Verbum Caro* 69 (1964): pp. 71–72.

[47] E. Fincke, "Das Amt der Einheit," *Verbum Caro* 69 (1964): (1964): pp. 77–190.

[48] M. Thurian, "L'ordination des pasteurs," *Verbum Caro* 57 (1961): pp. 199–213.

[49] J. J. von Allmen, "Le ministère des anciens. Essai sur le problème du presbytérat en ecclesiologie reformée," *Ministère et Laicat* in *Verbum Caro* 69 (1964): pp. 214–256.

[50] Hans Küng, "What is the Essence of Apostolic Succession," *Concilium* 34 (1968): pp. 28–35, especially p. 29.

[51] Johannes Remmers, "Apostolic Succession: An Attribute of the Whole Church," *Concilium* 34 (1968): pp. 36–51, especially p. 38.

[52] Yves Congar, "Apostolicité de ministère et apostolicité de doctrine," *Catholocisme* 1 (Paris, 1948): pp. 107–108.

lost sight of in professional theology through an emphasis on the juridical aspect of things.[53]

Renewed consideration of the hierarchy as a service to the community seems to offer a great change to play down their "juridicism," which is so often objected to.[54] Within this perspective, it would seem, treatment of the apostolic succession of the whole Church should be given precedence over that of hierarchical succession. This is well suited to the Orthodox theology and would greatly facilitate the road to ecumenical dialogue, by being more inclusive than exclusive. The apostolic succession was and is a point of importance, indeed, but its interpretation indicates rather an "attribute to the whole Church."

To return to our account, under the circumstances, the Assembly of Delegates of all religious communities of the Moravian dioceses held in Přerov on March 28, 1923, was a turbulent one. The fact that a representative chargé d'affaires of the Yugoslav Embassy in Prague, Mr. Crvcanin, was again present, indicated that the Serbian Orthodox Church in Yugoslavia had a great interest in the development of Orthodox orientation in a National Czechoslovak Church. On the other hand, the presence of Dr. Farsky, Professor Kalous, Rev. Stržínek, and the elected episcopal candidate, Rev. Rudolf Pařík, as delegates of the East Bohemian Diocesan Council was an omen which revealed the determination of the progressives to press their influence toward the final victory. On the whole, ninety delegates and about one hundred other members of the Moravian diocese took part in the Assembly, most of them followers of Bishop Gorazd. He made a two-hour speech, attacking the rationalism of the radical wing, and singling out, for emphasis, Dr. Farsky. The bishop then explained why he could not feel responsible for the future development of the Church, because of this rationalistic modernism, the liberal theological progressivism, and religious secularism. Dr. Farsky defended all these advanced trends but his defense was attacked fiercely by a layman, Mr. Brosman, teacher from Knoice, who reproached Dr. Farsky with inaccuracy and falsity. The debate became rather wild. Dr. Farsky left the Assembly and took the train that afternoon to Prague. The remaining delegates of Prague fought for Dr. Farsky's modern ideas and warned the delegates not to tear the Church apart.[55]

Bishop Gorazd had prepared a long resolution and had it read to the Assembly urging them to accept it. It contained, among other points, the Nicene-Constantinopolitan Creed. The twelfth paragraph of his speech was the most important one, for it pledged that all the church communities which accepted this resolution would be considered independent in matters of belief and morals. The bishop would be entitled to accept into his jurisdiction any petitioning church communities of other dioceses and, in return, he would also guarantee freedom to those communities in his own diocese which did not agree with his proposals. It was a rather important document of understanding and of tolerance and reads as follows:

(1). Since the resignation of Bishop Gorzad, the only rightly elected and validly consecrated bishop of the Czechoslovak Church is pending, and the whole movement depending on it is, therefore, made to suffer, we beg him to recall his resignation and to take his place again, to continue the work of building up the national church and its religious and moral renewal for a better future of the Czechoslovak nation. We thank him for everything he has done so far for the Czechoslovak Church here and in America. We agree with his outlook and are in complete accord with his plan because it corresponds to all the decisions of the General Assembly of the Czechoslovak Church and, with God's blessing, gives the greatest assurance of permanent success.

(2). We acknowledge our Lord Jesus Christ as the highest Head of the Universal Church.

(3). We reject the teaching that the apostle Peter was called to be the Prince of the other apostles, and that the Roman bishop, as the direct successor of the apostle Peter, is the head of the Church and stands above the Ecumenical Councils.

(4). We reject all teachings which the Roman Catholic Church, after her separation from the primitive church, has introduced, such as the teaching concerning hell and indulgences, as well as any specifically Roman, i.e., legally instituted form of religion. Further, we reject foreign liturgical language, compulsory celibacy of priests and the absolute Roman system.

(5). We recognize the authority of the Bible and of ecumenical church councils in matters of faith and morals; we adhere firmly and whole-heartedly to the Nicene-Constantinopolitan Creed, which reads: We believe in one God, the Father all-ruling, maker of heaven and earth, of all things visible and invisible. And in one Lord Jesus Christ, the only-begotten Son of God, begotten from the Father before all ages, light from light, true God from true God, begotten not made, of one substance (homo-ousion) with the Father, through whom all things came to be, who because of us men and our salvation came down from the heavens, and became flesh from the Holy Spirit and Mary the Virgin, and became man; was crucified on our behalf under Pontius Pilate, and suffered and was buried, and rose on the third day according to the Scriptures, and went up into the heavens, and is seated on the right hand of the Father, and will come again with glory to judge the living and dead; and of whose kingdom there will be no end. And in the Holy Spirit, the Lord and Life-giver, who proceeds from the Father, who is both worshiped and glorified in company with the Father and the Son, who spoke through the prophets: in one holy, catholic and apostolic church. We confess one baptism unto the remission of sins: We await the resurrection of the dead and the life of the age to come. Amen.

(6). We stand firmly on the Episcopalian system because it is based on apostolic institution and it corresponds

---

[53] K. H. Schelkle, *Jüngerschaft und Apostelamt* (Freiburg, 1961); D. Semmelroth, *Das Geistliche Amt* (Frankfurt, 1958).

[54] Yves Congar, "La hierarchie comme service selon le Nouveau Testament et les documents de la Tradition," *L'Episcopat et l'Eglise universelle* (Paris, 1962), pp. 67–99; David M. Stanley, *The Apostolic Church in the New Testament* (Paramus, N.J., Paulist Press, 1970).

[55] This description of the events is to be found in Urban, *op. cit.*, pp. 127–129 and *passim*.

to the needs of our religious movement, and we do not want the Presbyterian system which the oldest Protestant churches, after centuries long experience, abandoned to return to the Episcopalian. We recognize the seven sacraments as those obtaining in all apostolic churches.

(7). We want to live in our Church, the nationally organized Church of Christ, which has the continuity of the universal Christian Church as is indicated in the accepted declaration of faith. However, she would be so adapted to her own historical background that our Church would find her proper place and be able to blend into the mainstream of the Czech and Slovak people, one Czechoslovak nation. On the basis of an accepted confession, we want to live in the community of all Orthodox Churches, especially the Slavic ones, but with insistence on autonomy, i.e., autocephaly or independence, as generally understood. We want to live in friendship with other churches, such as Anglican, old Catholic, Czech Brethren, Slovak Evangelicals, and others, and we want to work with them on all generally Christian matters in brotherly love and with regard to our own ecclesiastical characteristics and our own system.

(8). We want further to strive so that, during the time of the Czechoslovak Republic, today's Czechoslovak Orthodox Church would be so built up to become a truly spiritual mother of the Czechoslovak nation, and the mighty foundation of our whole nation and state.

(9). We accept the development in our religious Christian life according to ideological, moral, and organizational principles with the understanding that such development must be real and not destructive of Christianity.

(10). We accept the freedom of science, to decline and accept certain flexible aspects of the Church, or others which may be accidentally necessary.

(11). We recognize freedom of conscience in the sense that no man should be persecuted because of his religious conviction, but we reject attempts to force a falsely understood freedom of conscience; also the Church should tolerate confessional choice.

(12). As to the developing internal relationship in the Czechoslovak Church, we emphasize that, although we intend to stay in that Church, we do not agree with the present central leadership in Prague. We insist that every religious community should accept the decision of today's Diocesan Assembly, to be autonomous in the area of teaching faith and morals, as long as the present crisis (as to free development for the good of the faithful), remains unsettled. Such an autonomous entity is to be fully independent in all matters of faith and morals, and independent from the Central Church of Prague; yet we would cooperate with her in all organizational matters, until the crisis subsides. Further, until such crisis is resolved, all now-existing decisions of the central leadership are to be held as null and void. Hence, we regard as temporarily void article 4,41 and artt. 42c and d, which refer to the pastoral jurisdiction which the patriarch, bishop of Prague claims over the whole Church; and art. 40, according to which the Central Council is empowered to demand unity of faith and divine worship.

In case individual communities within the Moravian diocese should disagree with this decision, we would absolve them from the decisions of the Constitution, which might hinder their freedom of choice. This freedom would continue until they determine whose jurisdiction (bishop's or diocesan Council's) they prefer. For our part, we request on behalf of Bishop Goradz and his Diocesan Council that, until the crisis is resolved, he be empowered for the sake of faith, to receive into his jurisdiction, all those religious communities who might request it.

—————Given at Přerov on March 28, 1923.[56]

To be consistent, those who had fought for unity within the Church, had to reject this resolution. Professor Paul of Holešov in Moravia angrily shouted that the acceptance of this resolution would mean the destruction of the entire Czechoslovak Church. Bishop Gorazd, however, insisted on the acceptance of the resolution; otherwise he would renounce his position as bishop. Professor Haňavka from the city of Brno tried to arrange a compromise, but without success. As it was getting late, most of the delegates had to leave the Assembly to catch their trains. Later, although most of the members had left, Alois Ševčík, chairman of the Assembly, asked for a vote on Bishop Gorazd's resolution. Twenty-five voted for, eleven voted against the resolution. The result was that Gorazd remained a bishop in the Czechoslovak Church. This resolution was the declaration of independence for the Orthodox orientation. It was a great victory for the traditional minority of the Czechoslovak Church but the internal crisis continued, spread more widely, and grew in intensity.

However, the majority of the progressives were not willing to yield one inch and, as a result, fragmentation, division, and separation were to enter their final phases. The following month, the Central Council in Prague had a meeting (on April 12) during which they declared themselves as not opposed to a free, independent development of the Orthodox orientation, but it should not be inside the Czechoslovak Church. This was, in other words, an "invitation" to those of the Orthodox orientation to leave the Czechoslovak Church and found a church of their own.

The Central Council's declaration at this Prague meeting spoke in a clear and decisive manner: the integrity of the progressive, modernistic and liberal Czechoslovak Church should and would be observed by every means. We read:

The Central Council of the Czechoslovak Church held a meeting on April 12 in Prague with an attendance representative of all four dioceses. The topic of discussion was the crisis arising out of the negotiations with the Serbian Orthodox Church. The result of the negotiations was that the proposal of Bishop Gorazd of Olomouc, to the effect that the communities of the so-called Orthodox orientation should form an independent unity with separate legislation and guidance, was rejected by a majority of votes. Thus, the Orthodox orientation would be free to organize itself separately according to wishes expressed in the Assembly of Delegates of the Moravian diocese, held in Přerov on March 28, 1923, and as indicated by acceptance of the resolution, but it must be outside the Czechoslovak Church. The Central Council could not accept their resolution because it would have gone far

[56] This is the author's translation of Czech test, given by Kuneš Bauer, *Myšlenkové proudy v československé církvi* (The ideological currents in the Czechoslovak Church) (Olomouc, 1924), pp. 88–92 and *passim*.

beyond the Church's limits for unity. It decided, therefore, to grant complete freedom to the Orthodox orientation in regard to organization, but it must be completely independent from the Czechoslovak Church.[57]

Although, or in spite of, the fact that the situation had been clarified and decided by and for both sides and, in major part with the open ends to each side, Bishop Gorazd did not intend to form his own church at this time. He tried to speak for the Orthodox ideas, union and orientation within the Czechoslovak Church as much as he could. He did this so that no one could reproach him for not having made every effort to save the unity of the Czechoslovak Church. He tried to get the Moravian diocese under his command and to win it for the Orthodox idea. For this reason he dissolved the official organ *Za Pravdou* (For the Truth) and claimed it as his own property. Some members, like Professor J. Urban and Rev. Kořínek, protested, but their efforts were in vain. The bishop also dismissed the uncooperative members from the Diocesan Council and replaced them with his favored people. By this activity, he alienated many people, and even created some enemies among his former friends. Others attacked him as being "undemocratic." Professor Růžička, from the city of Uherský Brod in Moravia, vehemently accused him of completely neglecting the opinions of the lay people who, at least, should be listened to.

We cannot blame Bishop Gorazd that he turned from the left to the right during his three months' stay in Serbia (as he wrote to one of the brothers in Prague), so that not only did he accept the Orthodox teaching of faith and morals, but also became a monk. This is a matter of his conscience, but he should not try to force us to accept his views. We stick to the decisions made at the Council on January 8, 1921, initiated and propagated at that time by Brother Pavlík, to preserve unity in the Church. He has destroyed this unity by his changed views.[58]

This diatribe, largely justified because of Gorazd's frequent changes and spiritual crises, nevertheless shows why his ambivalent approach and lack of resoluteness had no beneficial effects on anyone, but rather demoralized those who would have been willing to follow him unreservedly. What a contrast to Dr. Farsky who, although often wrong, was always decisive; and for this reason was able to keep the majority of his followers against the odds of time and circumstance. Bishop Gorazd had attempted to proceed with caution; but now, when everything was said and done, he was found to lack that decisiveness which would have guaranteed his position as the real spokesman for the needed majority.

In this dilemma, Bishop Gorazd sent questionnaries to his clergy to ascertain their opinions. Later his newspaper stated proudly that the entire clergy supported him in his opinions. However, the truth was that not all of the clergy were supporting him. Thus, on December 8, 1922, the religious communities of the political districts Moravská Ostrava and Nový Těšín separated from the Moravian diocese and united with the Silesian diocese (founded on November 8, 1922), whose elected bishop, Rev. Ferdinand Stibor, was an outspoken opponent of the Orthodox orientation. In *Palcát*,[59] a Silesian diocesan newspaper, he fought a bitter and effective fight against Bishop Gorazd.

Meanwhile, several members of the Orthodox orientation went their own way, leaving the Czechoslovak Church, and joining the Prague Czechoslovak Orthodox religious community. *Pravoslavný Směr*[60] announced that some hundred families in the city of Tabor had joined the Czechoslovak Orthodox religious community because they found no satisfaction within either the Czechoslovak or the Protestant Church.

Confusion increased with the suprising news that the elected episcopal candidate for the diocese of East Bohemia, Rev. Rudolf Pařík, had renounced his election on May 27, 1923, although remaining in residence for some time as a clergyman at the city of Kutná Hora. Still more shocking news came when, on November 2, 1923, he withdrew his signature from the second edition of the *Czechoslovak Catechism* (*Československý Katechism*), which he had approved a year earlier (on October 3, 1922). It was said that he had not known at that time that Bishop Dositej was against the catechism; and that, moreover, he had felt a responsibility to carry out the decisions of the Diocesan Council, made according to Fr. Huta's proposal. Now, after serious consideration, he had come to the conclusion that the Czechoslovak Church could not do without the old Christian belief, expressed in the Nicene-Constantinopolitan Creed.[61]

---

[57] *Český Zápas* 6, no. 16 of April 20, 1923; hereby is fragmentary author's translation of German text given by Urban, *op. cit.*, p. 131.

[58] *Český Zápas* 6, no. 18 of May 4, 1923; F. Cinek, "Doznaný vzvrat církve československé" (The Disintegration of the Czechoslovak Church) *Našinec* no. 60 (Olomouc, March 14, 1923); *idem*, "Biskup Gorazd organisuje rozkol v církvi československé," *Našinec* no. 106 (May 9, 1923).

[59] *Palcát* was a very controversial journal seeing to the needs of the Silesian Czechoslovak Church. It was published for four years only. This name *Palcát* is taken from the Hussite terminology with the meaning of Žižka's readiness for the fight. It reflected the very controversial and belligerent nature of Bishop Stibor, who was among the first revolutionaries against the Catholic Church, and who was among the first to marry while still a Catholic priest in Radvanice.

[60] *Pravoslavný směr* nos. 18 and 19. This was the organ of the Orthodox Church in the territory of Czechoslovakia. It was a replacement for the former organ *Za Pravdou* (For the Truth), which ceased to be published. See my note before, concerning the circumstances about changes.

[61] *Za Pravdou* 6 48 of November 8, 1923, which contains the whole story about Rev. Rudolf Pařík's change of stand. It does not disclose his real motivation. Pařík later became pastor of the Czechoslovak Church in Silesia. He was basically a good natured clergyman, who spiritually remained a Catholic priest.

After all this, there was once again an attempt to unite both parties who were fighting each other so vehemently. Without Bishop Gorazd's knowledge, the Assembly of the Moravian Council of Elders was called into session in Přerov, Moravia, on November 15, 1923. They decided to put a request before the entire Diocesan Council, to form a special commission whose assignment it would be to study and examine the respective views of Bishop Gorazd and Dr. Farsky, compare them, and prepare a directive for the Czechoslovak Church. Finally, Bishop Gorazd was asked to prepare for the consecration of the elected bishops of the Czechoslovak Church, to be carried out as soon as possible.

This attempt to bring the two parties together was in vain. Bishop Gorazd published his answer: "My Point of View as to the Decisions Made by the Assembly at Přerov," [62] wherein he stated that it was impossible for them to unite again. The differences with regard to the idea of God, the Church, eternal life (eschatology), and other religious and theological problems, were so great that it was impossible to find some *via media* (middle way) between them. He further insisted that the crisis could only be solved by renouncing the *Czechoslovak Catechism* which was the crux of all the trouble. Finally, in reference to the petition that he should take care of the consecration of bishops, he answered that he could not consecrate new bishops because the rules of the Orthodox Church would not allow it. Therefore, there was nothing left for the Czechoslovak Church except for her to ask some other autocephalous Church to do it for her.

With Gorazd's clear statement concerning doctrinal matters, and his categorical refusal to consecrate bishops, the last hopes for unity were forever crushed. There was no hope for reconciliation, as the situation was beyond the point of no return.

During this time, on May 27, 1923, and to replace the resigned Rev. R. Pařík, the Diocesan Assembly for East Bohemia chose as bishop, Dr. Gustav A. Procházka, who was pastor of the Czechoslovak Church in Jenišovice near Turnov in Bohemia. To the surprise of all, this Assembly sent a petition to the episcopal conference of the Serbian Orthodox Church requesting the consecration of the newly chosen episcopal candidate Dr. Procházka. This almost unbelievable event can only be explained as a result of the general confusion of the times. The Serbian Orthodox Church could not possibly cooperate because past negotiations had been discontinued on the basis of the Czechoslovak Church's doctrinal inadequacy. It was a daring attempt but it proves the respect and faith the people had toward the episcopal office. In 1922 Dr. Farsky himself had made an unsuccessful bid for episcopal consecration from the Anglican Church,[63] with the help of the evangelical theologian, Dr. F. Žilka, professor of the Hus Faculty in Prague. It was said that the Anglican Church rejected him because of the unchristian character of the *Czechoslovak Catechism*. After such an experience, the action of the Diocesan Assembly must have been desperate to get consecration from anywhere possible. Evidently, it was not possible.

In the meantime, the fights, controversies and exchanges between the two antagonistic blocs continued. Eventually, the leaders, especially in the Czechoslovak Church, came to the conclusion that they could not continue these struggles without losing their members again. Some of the faithful were leaving in disgust and returning to the Roman Catholic Church. This was an effective warning to the church leaders, especially since there were also former priests returning to the Catholic Church.

The leader of the Silesian Diocese, Father Ferdinand Stibor, formerly pastor in Radvanice, now chosen for the episcopacy, addressed the members of the Church in an article titled "Quousque" with the subtitle "How Long Shall We Remain Witnesses of This Disgusting Fratricidal Comedy?" [64] He made a great impact with this rhetorical exclamation. It reads as follows:

I am the oldest of those who once participated in the founding of our national church, and therefore, I think I am entitled to defend it. We did not establish our Church for some priests to make their dogmatic stand stricter, neither did we found it for this or that bishop, but we built it in order that the Czechoslovak nation might have a free, truly Christian Church as a substitute for the Roman Church, free from the various superstitious and ritualistic hindrances of Roman or Greek-Orthodox culture. We cannot expect a man of twenty years to believe in St. Nicholas as he did in his childhood. In the same way, we cannot force the Czechoslovak nation, now so culturally developed, to accept religious ideas of the first centuries after Christ, when the Church was in its early stages of development. Anybody who does not understand that, is not mature enough for our Church. If he was only looking to our Church as a substitute, he ought to get rid of his Roman soul. There is nothing left for such a person but to return to the Roman hypnotist. The matter is quite natural. Influences after the *coup d'etat* were stronger than was the Roman attraction. The soul under this influence could go back to her Lord. Yet when, after struggling for five years, all of a man's energy has been used up, hypnosis might cause him to return without resisting, and quietly follow the suggestion of the hypnotists.[65]

He was for a traditional theology, and all modernistic theses were very repugnant to him.

[62] It was published in *Za Pravdou* nos. 37–38, and it was rather unexpectedly resolute and harsh.

[63] *Pravoslavný směr* no 14, 1922, had notice about this attempt. It is interesting to note that there was little publicity concerning these unsuccessful attempts.

[64] It was published in *Palcát*, the organ of the Diocese of Silesia, in the issue of Nov. 23, 1923, and later republished in *Český Zápas* 7, 2 of Jan. 12, 1924.

[65] This eloquent warning, given by one of the most radical members of the Czechoslovak Church, is replete with the fear that "hypnotic influence" is still strong enough to lure people back. This is author's transl. from German text, given by Urban,

This warning, given by one of the most radical revolutionaries in the movement, is replete with the fear that the "hypnotic influence" of Roman Catholicism was still strong enough to lure people back.

This warning was suggested by the impending frustration and disappointment already experienced by some members of the national Czechoslovak Church who were beginning to return to their original mother church. The internal struggles of the Czechoslovak Church were hardly inviting even to the former Catholic priests who, in their frustration, decided to re-affirm their loyalty to the old Church, especially since the *Czechoslovak Catechism* which had little or nothing to offer.

Statistics of clerical membership in the new Czechoslovak Church indicated a total of 288 of these unfortunate ones by 1924, in this proportion: Hradec Králové diocese, 68; Olomouc, 35; Litoměřice, 47; Prague, 63; České Budějovice, 40; Brno, 30; in Slovakia only 5. Although it was the alarming number[66] which motivated Rome to show special patience with the last members of the Jednota, and to exercise special kindness for the returnees, the number who seceded was really not great considering the magnitude of propaganda which had been carried out against the Roman Catholic Church. Most of the propaganda was unjustified, and perhaps now the Czechoslovak Church had to suffer for what she had done.

Motivated by this fear, Dr. Farsky, in the Assembly held on March 8, 1924, in Olomouc in Moravia, declared: "Thus far, and no further with this nonsense! I cannot permit this crisis to continue. I have to stop it!" In fact, the crisis was gradually coming to an end, and favorably for the Prague leaders of the Church. On May 11, 1924, the opponents of Bishop Gorazd called a meeting of the progressive delegates of the Moravian Council of elders of the Church in Přerov in Moravia. At this meeting it was proposed to summon a church general council as soon as possible, to decide whether the Czechoslovak Church was really independent, or whether it was part of the Orthodoxy. Further, it was decided that the organ *Za Pravdou* (For the Truth) should not carry in its subtitle the words "An Organ of the Diocese" for the simple reason that it had become the personal property of Bishop Gorazd. Many of the bishop's opponents were very outspoken, especially his former friend, Professor Alois Spisar from Kroměříž, teacher Hrabánek, owner of the paper, Mr. Zlámal, and the director of the printing shop. Mr. Polešovský, of Olomouc, attacked Gorazd's uncompromising point of view which, he said, made any reconciliation impossible.

This assembly revealed that Orthodoxy was not as strong as had been previously thought in Moravia, that it was now under attack from many sides. Bishop Gorazd's followers stood up for the defense: "Do not believe these false prophets who want to continue the work of destruction!"[67] However, it was a case of "too late with too little" and the present defiance from his previously dedicated friends, like Professor Alois Spisar and others, was very bad news for Bishop Gorazd. Furthermore, the final and decisive opposition against the Orthodox orientation in Moravia had originated in Olomouc. It was again Bishop Gorazd's former friend, Mr. Polešovský, headmaster of the teacher's grammar school, who left the Moravian Diocesan Council and refused to be its chairman. He was responsible for winning two big communities, Olomouc and Řepčín, to his side, and they all agitated against the Orthodox oriented Diocesan Council, shouting: "We do not want to be Orthodox!" and "We do not pay for the Orthodox." Finally, they forced the election of a new Council of Elders to take over the leadership. By now, the Orthodox were in trouble, but even yet they were not ready to surrender. Instead, they organized still one more attack against the progressives. On June 20, 1924, clerical followers of Gorazd, published a protest against Dr. Farsky's articles in *Český Zápas*,[68] in which Farsky had tried to make the Bible coincide with modern life so as to create new interest in the Bible. One article aroused great anger among the twenty clergymen, because in it Dr. Farsky expressed the hypothesis that Jesus probably was not dead after the crucifixion; thus his "resurrection" would not be so incredible. This rationalistic explanation of the resurrection was vigorously protested because it would blasphemously present Jesus and the apostles as deceivers.[69]

Dr. Farsky later published this Biblical exegesis and religious interpretation in book form, titled: *Naše Postyla. Sbírka Prostých Výkladů a Úvah k Evandělíu Ježíšovu.* (Our Postyla. The Collection of Simple Interpretations and Recollections of the Gospels of Jesus) (Prague, 1925). In it he only reiterates the rationalistic interpretation of many questions which had been already treated in the *Czechoslovak Catechism*, and in his Biblical exegetical works, titled *Stvoření* (Creation), published in 1920. By now it was evident that the modernistic theses were going to stay with the progressives in the Czechoslovak Church, and that

---

op. cit., p. 135. This "hypnotic influence" is referred to as the "influence of a strong Roman Catholic tradition."

[66] Josef Doležal, *Český Kněz* (Prague, 1931), p. 77 ff. and *passim*.

[67] *Za Pravdou* no. 20 of 1924.

[68] The names of these clergymen as identified by Urban, *op. cit.*, p. 136 under the note on p. 136. The two most important were Rev. Dr. M. Haškovec of Brno and Rev. Dr. Zdeněk of Brno.

[69] Dr. Karel Farský, *Naše Postyla* (Prague, 1925), p. 230 ff. Idem, *Stvoření* (Výklad k biblickému líčení vzniku světa v duchu církve československé) *Creation* (Exegesis concerning Biblical narration about its origin of the world in the spirit of the Czechoslovak Church) (Prague, 1920), *passim*.

they would be taken as the principal doctrinal tenets of a new national church.

Despite all his efforts, Gorazd's position became more and more insecure. This became obvious when Dr. Farsky was elected bishop of the "new" Prague diocese in June, 1924, thereby becoming also patriarch of the entire Czechoslovak Church. The election was carried out in the following way:

First of all, it was decided that each "new church" diocese would nominate two candidates. On February 9, (1924) the Prague diocesan Council elected Dr. Farsky in first position and Professor Spisar from Kroměříž in second position. Both the East Bohemian diocese (Gustav Procházka's residence was in Turnov), and the Silesian diocese put Dr. Farsky in the first place. Professor Kalous (East Bohemian diocese) and Martin Zandu (Silesian diocese) were put in second place. Only the Moravian diocese proposed Bishop Gorazd for first place and Professor Alois Tuháček for second place. Then the second phase of the election began. All the religious communities of the Prague Diocese had till April 10 to elect three candidates out of the number of candidates proposed, and inform the Diocesan Council of the result. The Central Council announced that Dr. Farsky had been elected by the majority. In second place was Professor Alois Spisar, and in third place, Professor F. Kalous.

In June, the final elections were held at a plenary meeting of all the religious communities. In the Prague diocese this was the result: Out of 42 recognized religious communities, 40 participated in the election. Dr. Farsky received the unanimous votes of 37 communities, and nearly all of 3 more. In the Moravian and Silesian dioceses, it can be said that out of about 110 communities, 95 participated. Dr. Farsky won in 83 communities, was favored in 7 others, and had a small majority in 5 more. Thus, in Moravia and Silesia, a total of 94 communities which had state approval, voted either unanimously or in great majority for Dr. Farsky.[70]

This impressive victory was too big to be ignored. It gave Dr. Farsky a complete mandate for the leadership of the Czechoslovak Church and, furthermore, it was a confirmation that his modernistic theses would determine the final direction of the Czechoslovak Church. This, of course, was unfortunate for the Orthodox. Even traditional Moravia, where Bishop Gorazd had been born and educated, had worked as a Catholic priest, then as minister, and finally as bishop of the Czechoslovak Church, failed him. Bishop Gorazd considered this election of Dr. Farsky as the appropriate occasion to anounce his resignation as bishop of the Czechoslovak Church, and make his formal exodus. In fact, he had no other choice.

At the meeting of the Moravian Diocesan Council, held in Olomouc the following month (July 21, 1924), Bishop Gorazd announced this intention, giving as his reason that Dr. Farsky's election as Patriarch of the entire Czechoslovak Church had determined the trend of the Church, thus making it impossible for him either to exercise his office as a bishop or even to remain in such a church. To avoid any misunderstanding, Bishop Gorazd published the following:

The followers of the radical orientation have let me know unmistakably that I should leave the Czechoslovak Church with the thought that this would stop the quarrels and fights. Now, with a feeling of unshaken and undying love, I depart, having come to the conclusion that any further effort on my part would be a waste of time and energy.[71]

At the same time, another rival of Dr. Farsky, Ministerial Counsellor and writer, Rev. Bohumil Zahradník-Brodský, proclaimed his sympathy with Bishop Gorazd's Orthodox orientation which, in his view, meant the fulfillment of Czech reformation in the spirit of Sts. Cyril and Methodius, as well as of Hus. To keep this relationship with the Orthodox Church alive, would mean to follow the legacies of many Slavic thinkers like Sladkovský, Barák, Mrštík, and others.[72] The emphatic sympathy of this influential man was a great consolation to the bishop, but it was too late to stop the drive of the progressives into the inner sanctuaries of thought, life, and organization of the national church, the church to which all had been so dedicated. Dr. Farsky was in his glory and his countenance glowed in anticipation of further power.

Then came a disclosure, only partly true, but slanted so as to be devastating in its implications against the bishop. Sometime earlier, Bishop Gorazd had written a very confidential letter to Dr. Farsky, informing him of the bishop's planned resignation if events continued as they were going. Now, however, when Dr. Farsky considered the time propitious, he disregarded the claims of decency, informed the Central Council of the Czechoslovak Church, as well as the Moravian Council at Olomouc, of the letter's existence, leading them to suppose that the bishop had turned over the "office" to him, as of July 21, 1924. Simultaneously, all the counsellors and clergymen in Moravia were asked to sign an oath of allegiance to the Czechoslovak Church, declaring that they would obey all future decisions of the Church Councils.

This petition caused great distress among the Orthodox-oriented clergymen. In fact, on that same day, July 21, Dr. Farsky personally had gone to Olomouc to get the records (agenda) from the Diocesan Council, but was refused. This unexpected action by

---

[70] These statistics are taken from the organ of Czech Dioceses, *Český Zápas* 7, 14, 21, and 29.

[71] *Za Pravdou* no. 30 of July 25, 1924, which has a complete text and a detailed account about the event.

[72] *Za Pravdou* no. 30 of July 31, 1924, which contains a complete text. This is only author's excerpt and interpretation of it.

which Dr. Farsky revealed not only his unusual character, but also his determination to crush his opponents by any available means, was quickly challenged by Bishop Gorazd, who categorically denied that he had intended for some time, to withdraw himself completely, explaining that this was only Dr. Farsky's wrong assumption; and he asked all his followers to hold to the Orthodox orientation.

It is interesting to note that the Moravian Diocesan Council at Olomouc, although it supported Bishop Gorazd's ideas, surprisingly elected, on that same July 21, 1924, Rev. Alois Ševčík of Brno as Gorazd's successor. Perhaps this was for the purpose of a possible reconciliation, to make it more acceptable to the opposition; but it really became a further embarrassment for Gorazd, and was too late to effect any conciliation. Instead of helping, it aggravated the situation.

However, the Central Council of the Czechoslovak Church in Prague, at its meeting on August 7, 1924, did not acknowledge the election of Ševčík as Gorazd's successor but, instead, asked that the Moravian Diocesan Council be dissolved, giving two reasons: (1) The Moravian Diocesan Council had neglected its duty of defending the property rights of the Czechoslovak Church when the Chudobín religious community joined the Prague Orthodox Church; (2) the same Diocesan Council had wrongly allowed the former diocesan organ *Za Pravdou* to become Bishop Gorazd's private property. These two cases,[73] it was said, were sufficient evidence of the inability of the Moravian Diocesan Council to administer church matters properly. One note of interest has to do with the just-mentioned church community in Chudobín, near Litovel, which was under the pastoral care of Father J. Žídek. He always had been of the Orthodox orientation; and, in May of 1924, both pastor and flock changed to the *Československá Obec Pravoslavná* (Czechoslovak Orthodox Church) in protest to the liberal trends then predominating in the Czechoslovak Church. The fact that this community changed three times, i.e., from the Roman Catholic to the Czechoslovak Church and from this to the Orthodox Church, puts the Czechoslovak Church claim to the proprietary rights of this community in doubt. Even legal aspects were accommodated according to conveniences of the times.

When the Czechoslovak Church insisted on property claims against the Roman Catholic Church it was considered legal, but when the Orthodox Church began acting the same way towards the Czechoslovak Church, it was considered illegal. Suddenly, the Czechoslovak Church became very "legalistic." Reflecting on all of this, Bishop Gorazd gathered an assembly of about 307 confidential followers of the Orthodox orientation at Olomouc on August 10, 1924. The principal point of their program was complete separation from the progressives of the Czechoslovak Church. The petition to leave the Czechoslovak Church and join the Czechoslovak Orthodox Church in Prague was debated and accepted. The statutes (regulations) of the Czechoslovak Orthodox Church in Prague, and the Church laws and doctrinal tenets of the Orthodox Church in general were accepted *en bloc*. This was the Bishop's final farewell to the Czechoslovak Church, and it was the beginning of independence for those of Orthodox orientation in a new moral, social, legal entity under the name of Czechoslovak Orthodox Church.

This separation was bound to happen because of the diametrically opposed views of these two groups. While one group, i.e., of the Orthodox orientation was for a church based on tradition, the other (progressive) group was for a church without tradition at all. Coming originally from the Roman Catholic Church, one with full apostolic tradition which they rejected, the progressives also had to reject the Orthodox traditions, in order to express their reform, protest, and revolt more emphatically and dramatically. Their fall into heresy, so abundantly manifested and so adamantly attested to, had to end in schism, a double schism: (a) a Catholic-Czechoslovak schism, and (b) a Czechoslovak-Orthodox schism. This constituted clear evidence that the Czechoslovak schism should not be counted as merely politically or culturally or socially inspired as were some others like the Great Eastern Schism (1054). It must be considered as a real church schism, with a direct interaction between heresy and schism, since both gave preference to protest and revolt before reform.

IV. AN INDEPENDENT AND NATIONAL CHURCH

By this time, the two opposing ideas had caused such a violent separation, that there were both priests and people in each of the hostile camps. Those of the Orthodox persuasion were bitterly opposed by the advocates of evolutionary progressivism.[1] The fol-

---

[73] These practices for which the Central Council of the Czechoslovak Church in Prague blamed the Moravian Diocesan Council, were practically general procedures whenever there has been some transfer or change of any Catholic priest to the Czechoslovak Church. They simply seized these Catholic churches, until laws stopped this widespread original practice of the Czechoslovak Church. It is interesting to note that by now they did not like these procedures when this happened to them.

[1] Ervin R. Goodenough, "On Extricating Religionswissenschaft from Theology" *Ways of Understanding Religion*, ed. Walter H. Capps (New York, Macmillan, 1942), pp. 281–289; A. Wenzl, *Wissenschaft und Weltanschauung* (Herder Freiburg, 1949) *passim*; W. Dilthey, "Weltanschauunglehre," *Gesammelte Schriften* VIII (St. Go., 1962), *passim*; cf. Heinz Robert Schlette, "The Problem of Ideology and Christian Belief," *Concilium* 6 (Paulist Press, 1965): pp. 107–129; C. Söhngen, "Weltanschauung," *Lexikon für Theologie und Kirche* (Verlag Herder Freiburg, 1965), pp. 1027–1029; Josef Kubalík, *Dějiny náboženství* (History of Religion) (Praha, 1955).

lowers of tradition were being attacked by those determined to exclude tradition. The theologians who looked for Christian foundations in the supernatural were in conflict with those who favored an untrammelled world-view of scientific religion. Proponents of a spiritual faith found themselves besieged by critics who insisted that mere human reason was sufficiently reliable. The struggle between minds went on regardless of an uneasy hope for peace.

Almost immediately after those of the Orthodox orientation had opted for separation, the question of property ownership came up. On the principle that the best defense is a good offense, the Moravian Czechoslovak Diocesan Assembly met at Brno on August 25, 1924, to determine the official future by preferential vote: Orthodox or National. At the outset, a new set of council members was installed. Father Alois Ševčík, originally picked by Bishop Gorazd to head the Moravian (Orthodox) diocese, was simply replaced by Josef Rostislav Stejskal, one of the National Church founders, a follower of Father Farsky. The Orthodox were "out" and the National Church was "in." To the satisfaction of the progressives, the Moravian Czechoslovak diocese was now firmly in their camp, with only a few adaptations needed for uniformity. The transition was, thus, conveniently accomplished by making Father Stejskal a member of the Czechoslovak "hierarchy."

Born on April 27, 1894, at Hostkovice in the district of Olomouc, Josef Stejskal studied at the Slavic Gymnasium in Olomouc (1906–1914), and was graduated from the theological faculty at Olomouc in 1918. On July 5 of that same year, he was ordained to the Catholic priesthood by Leo Cardinal Skrbenský, and assigned to a parish in the predominantly German area. He became an active member of the Jednota, then of the Club of Reform Priests and, on January 8, 1920, an apostate. Later he became a minister at Vacenovice, Grykov, and Olomouc. A year and a half later, he went to Paris, became a graduate student in Protestant theology and, in 1923, was made a doctor of theology. Upon his return home, he worked as a minister in Moravia and, on August 25, 1924, was elected Moravia's Czechoslovak bishop. He was a good administrator but published only one work of importance, his doctoral thesis:[2] *Les Proces de Jean Hus. Etude Historique at Dogmatique* (Paris, 1923). He was one of the directors of Blahoslav Association which provided religious books under the Central Committee of the Czechoslovak Church in Prague. His literary contributions were varied but his best work was in his Church's legal stabilization. His outlook was progressive but his activities showed moderation. All in all, he continued to live as a tolerant religious Moravian. He died in 1940.

The appointment of Stejskal to replace Ševčík changed the whole course of thinking and action in Moravia, and put an end to any possible cooperation between the Orthodox and the national church; those Orthodox who persisted as such, simply severed their connection with the nationals.

The total impact on Moravia was not surprising, although some of the clergy who had accused Farsky of blasphemy on June 12, 1924, would later also repudiate Bishop Gorazd. Nevertheless, the Orthodox were able to set up fourteen parishes: eleven in Moravia with an enrollment of 6,116 members; and three in Bohemia (Prague, Tabor, and Sviňov) with a total of 3,300, although by 1930, this number had fallen off by about one-third.[3]

Bishop Gorazd realized, at least after his experience in America, that no agreement with the nationalists was possible. For this reason, as far back as February, 1923, he had confidentially told Mr. Sawat and Dr. M. Červinka that, as things were going, he would have to leave the rebel nationals and set up some order in the local Orthodox organization.[4] The reasons, multitudinous and complex, upon which he had based his decision, along with its delay in fulfillment, only he could have known. As the only validly consecrated (non-Roman) bishop in the country, he had hoped for some rapprochement and, for this reason, had remained officially in the Czechoslovak Church. Now, with the exodus of the Orthodox on August 10, 1924, the national church set about to guarantee the separation, and formulate a new constitution. This was accomplished at the (First) Church Council, held on August 29 and 30 (1924) at Prague-Smíchov, in spite of several Farsky enemies, who had formed a small bloc. In attendance at the assembly were Bishops J. R. Stejskal of the Moravian diocese, Ferdinand Stibor of the Silesian diocese and G. A. Procházka of East Bohemia. This was a "working" council, intended to occupy itself with doctrinal stabilization. As a result of their labors, the Constitution came into existence, and Farsky prevailed to the extent of having the national church declare itself anti-Roman, anti-Orthodox, and pro-Unitarian.

The first paragraph of the resultant Constitution declared:

Those Christians who strive to fulfill the demands of contemporary morals, and live in accordance with the advances of science, and in the spirit of Christ as shown in the Bible and in ancient tradition as preserved in the Czechoslovak nation, and as derived through the Hussite

---

[2] This J. R. Stejskal's dissertation was not very original, and it underwent severe criticism, by Professor Otakar Odložilík of Charles IV University, who published its long review in *Časopis Matice Moravské* 48 (Brno, 1924): pp. 277–280.

[3] These statistics are taken from Frant. Cinek, *K Náboženské Otázce v Prvních Letech Naší Samostatnosti* (Olomouc, 1926), pp. 233 ff. and *passim*.

[4] Vladimir Grigorič, *Pravoslavná Cirkev ve Státě Československém* (2nd ed., Prague, 1928), p. 63 ff. and *passim*.

movement and Czech Brethren, are members of the Czechoslovak Church.

As will be noticed, stress is placed first on "contemporary morals" in accord "with modern science." Only then is reference made to the spirit of Christ, and even that is restricted to Czech history.

The accepted doctrinal resolution retained only a belief in monotheism.

The Czechoslovak Church sees her mission, not to return to the early Christian centuries but to the Christianity of the Gospels themselves, to build up a religion conformable to the cultural and moral standards of contemporary men in general, and of the Czechs in particular.

Besides these traditions, the Czechoslovak Church intends to continue, and bring to conclusion, those articles of faith which our first Reformation left untouched.

Yet even those articles of faith are to be subjected to careful scrutiny, and then rewritten so as to be acceptable even to those who have turned away from religion, or who have seen in religion nothing but the left-overs of an inferior culture, from the past.

The only common basis we share with other Christian churches will be the idea and definition of God. We publicly and solemnly declare that we believe in a personal God, the same God who was confessed by the first Christians, and by our own ancestors.

Mainly, we want a Christianity that does not get its ideas and religious testimony from the past but from the present. The Catholic Church emphasized ecclesiastical tradition, and Protestantism relied on the Bible as its principal source of truth; but we regard human living and human experience and human need as well as the Gospel of Christ, as our source.

Our Christianity is not and must not become a mere religious theory, but a practical manifestation. Not faith, but life, should be our Christianity.

The aim of our Christianity, the ultimate goal of our national church, must be our moral and natural perfection, and the betterment of our nation. The completion of our religious program will be love for God and love for neighbor.[6]

Thus, the creed was cut down, and the beliefs *sine qua non* for both the Catholics and the Orthodox, were discarded. The Divinity of Christ, faith in the trinitarian concept of God, faith in the Church as an instrument of salvation, all disappeared. By this act, the leaders admitted that they were negotiating the cheapest price for human living; but what they offered was actually religious decay, a backward step to the *lares* and *penates* of ancient paganism. Compared to the national church's earlier statements, her Council of 1924 now emptied her of all Christian creed and tradition.

Having failed in several attempts to secure episcopal consecration from some source with apostolic succession, the new church was confronted no longer with the necessity of making this decision. A policy was adopted whereby priestly ordination and episcopal consecration were to be conferred simply by the imposition of hands. Thus, the principle of the sacramental character was abandoned. This adoption came about only after some study and was finally described in a special resolution as follows:

> Since we do not accept the traditional doctrine as to the mechanical effectiveness of the sacraments (efficacy *ex opere operato*), either as to priestly or episcopal ordination, we are convinced that the Czechoslovak Church is sufficiently endowed as to be able, by the imposition of hands, and the prayers of her clerical and lay elders, to mediate the grace and power of the Holy Spirit for our future ministers; and we are firmly convinced that if God does not give His grace through these ordainers, nobody else in the world can give it, regardless of the loftiness of his hierarchical dignity, or ancient origin.[7]

In this democratic establishment, clerical dignity was not to depend upon apostolic succession but upon the direct grace of God, once the candidates had prepared themselves by a required professional, general and theological education.

Thus, there arose an interesting relationship between the "constitutional episcopalianism of the Czechoslovak Church" and its democratic framework. Lifetime tenure for a bishop came to depend upon popular referendum in the concerned diocese; or, in the case of a patriarch, upon a vote of the entire membership. The Constitution of the Czechoslovak Church referred to a new kind of ecclesiastical organization which would select whatever it considered best from both the episcopal and the congregational establishments.

By accepting election to the episcopacy on this principle, and recognizing at the same time, the wide administrative autonomy within the individual religious communities, the Constitution produced a modified congregational system. At the same time, in the spirit of constitutional episcopalianism, by admitting the superiority of the diocese over the smaller parish communities, and that of the supreme ecclesiastical establishment over the diocese, the goals of the particular place and those of the entire Church, were harmonized. The supreme unit mitigates the particularism of the individual localities, while still preserving their legal consciousness that they are the fundamental units from which the church organism was formed. Of course, the Constitution bolsters this relationship by mentioning numerous ties with their common, diocesan goals, all of which are integrated in the higher harmonious system of the entire Church.

The Czechoslovak Church claims to have in her diocesan assemblies and Church Council the legally

---

[5] F. Siegmund-Schulttze, "Die Kirchen der Tschechoslowakei," *Ekklesia* 5, 20 (Leipzig, 1937): p. 178 ff.

[6] Josef Doležal, *op. cit.*, pp. 72–74; this is author's translation from the Czech text, given hereby; whole text is to be found in: *Zpráva o I. Řádném Sněmu Církve Československé Konaném ve Dnech 29–30 Srpna 1924 v Praze-Smíchově* (Prague, 1924). It is a report from Council's proceedings.

[7] *Zpráva o I. Řádném Sněmu Církve Československé Konaném ve Dnech 29–30 Srpna 1924 v Praze-Smíchově* (Prague, 1924) 1 Chapter: p. 50 ff.

constituted organs by which she can manifest the common will of the whole people in matters of faith, morals, discipline, and all other details of ecclesiastical and diocesan agenda. The church Constitution further insists that the elected supervisory offices (Central Council and Diocesan Council) along with the leadership of the supreme representatives of spiritual jurisdiction (patriarch and bishops) do represent dynamically, in their very persons, the basic aspirations of the Church. Such supervisory and spiritual powers combine to represent not only formally (before the general public), but materially and actually, the ideological effectiveness of the entire Church.[8]

However, it must be said that the special Resolution of August 1924, indicating the manner of ordaining ministers and bishops, had been conditioned by circumstances. Faced with the impossibility of securing apostolic succession from some traditional church, there was no other choice except a "self-making ordination" which looked to the direct influence of the Holy Spirit, without any sacramental agency. Dr. Farsky and the rest of those chosen to be bishops, took their episcopal titles after being "ordained" in 1924 according to the manner established in this Resolution.[9] Thereupon, Dr. Farsky received the title of patriarch on the basis of his being bishop of Prague, the capital of the republic.

Since, in the traditional sense, a patriarch had first to be a bishop, and a bishop's dignity could be effected only by consecration, it would appear to be inherently contradictory to speak of a bishop who was without this sacramental character. In this case, the gap was even wider because in every traditional Christian church, the title bishop or patriarch goes hand in hand with the dignity and power connected with it; whereas, in the Czechoslovak Church where election replaces consecration, dignity is bestowed by popular mandate, and power is represented by the office, with no other source except the people. Theologically, it is difficult to interpret this satisfactorily unless we accept the hypothesis, as is the case with some Protestant churches, that baptism is the only sacramental source out of which a universal priesthood originates. Perhaps this could be argued in the Czechoslovak case as well. At any rate, on January 5, 1925, all of the men chosen for the bishopric were ordained in Prague at St. Nicholas' Church, and Dr. Farsky then assumed for himself the title of patriarch, on the premise of his being bishop of West Bohemia, with residence in Prague. By this historic ceremony, the ecclesiastical system of the national church was completed.

However, a further anomaly called for explanation. Originally, on September 15, 1920, this Church, as the national church, had received government recognition by virtue of Law #542 which, however, applied only to Bohemia and Moravia-Silesia; it was not until 1925 (Law #123) that it became recognized also in Slovakia and Ruthenia. Only then did it become, in truth, the national church, although it still had to wait for the coming of Czechs from outside Slovakia in sufficient numbers and with enough imported Czech teachers and government officials to set up the new religious affiliation.[10]

There seems to have been another very practical reason for the new church holding on to the old titles of bishop and patriarch, inasmuch as, by maintaining the outward semblance of these offices, there would continue to be a medium for carrying on the rights accorded during the old Austrian regime. The old-time legal classification of religious denominations into "recognized," "accepted," "non-recognized" and "prohibited" was, thereby, maintained. The only new government acts which bore directly on the status of churches, were the Laws #122 of 1926, and the Cabinet Decree #124 of 1928. "Recognized" or "accepted" churches and religious societies were divided into so-called "congrua"[11] churches, in which the state paid the clergy salaries and pensions; and the "dotation" churches, where the state paid the bishops a lump sum which they were to distribute at their discretion. The "accepted" churches of Slovakia had a broad legal right to special subsidies from the old Law #20 of 1848, valid in Hungary. The conditions of these special grants had never been clearly defined.

Concerning freedom of public expression, the "recognized" churches and religious societies did not need special permission for religious functions conducted "in the usual manner." They were also protected by law against slander (Criminal Code #111), blasphemy, and disruption of their ceremonies (Criminal Code #112).

Although the supervision of education was declared solely within the domain of the republic, churches were guaranteed direct participation in religious instruction in public schools, and had also the right to establish denominational schools.[12]

---

[8] This interpretation is by F. M. Hník, *Duchovní Ideály Československé Církve* (Prague, 1924), pp. 181–183.

[9] M. Spinka, *op. cit.*, p. 297.

[10] Rudolf Babula, *Církev Československá a Slovensko. Vznik Církve Československej, Jej Vyvcj, Základy, Učenie, Bohoslužba, Organizacia, Hospodárstvo a. i. vo Světle Pravdy* (The Czechoslovak Church and Slovakia. Origin, Development, Foundations, Doctrine, Worship, Organization, Economics and Others in the Light of Truth) (Neusohl, 1930), *passim*.

[11] Alois Kudrnovský, "Kongrua Katolického Duchovenstva" (Congress of Catholic Clergy) ČKD 80 (105) (1940): pp. 161–191, 233–270, 313–361, 393–400. Here is a detailed treatment of the entire problem concerning state subsidies of all churches. Treatment covers all aspects: historical, legal, and theological.

[12] Vratislav Bušek, J. Hendrych, K. Laštovka, and V. Mueller, *Československé Církevní Zákony* (Prague, 1931), *passim*: idem, *Czechoslovakia* (New York, 1957), pp. 135–136; Frant. Bednář, *Sbírka Zákonů a Nařízení ve Věcech Náboženských a Církevních v Republice Československé* (Collection of Laws and Regulations in Religious and Ecclesiastical Matters in the Czechoslovak Republic) (Prague, 1929), *passim*.

With the republic's legal framework, all churches had great opportunities for the free exercise of religious expression, but the national church, already heavily subsidized by the government, was the first to enjoy this fully free atmosphere. The irony of the situation was that while the Catholic Church had always been in the forefront of the struggle for church rights against state exploitation, it was now the national and smaller churches which began to enjoy the first fruits. Father Farsky was a skilled "operator" with the proper "know-how" for gaining every available advantage for the new church. By his firm use of power, he liquidated every opposition, inside and outside the Church, and was able to concentrate all his efforts to secure a "uniformity" of thought and living. As patriarch, he placed his Church under the shield of legality for which he had a well-developed sense, as can be seen from his book, *Stát a Církev: Poměr Státu Českého k Církvi od Prvopočátku až do Roku 1924* (State and Church: Relationship of the Czech State to the Roman Catholic Church from the Beginnings Till the Year 1924) (Prague, 1924). Furthermore, he was adamant defending his Church's liberal views, as can be seen in another booklet: *Náboženství v Národě Československém* (Religion in the Czechoslovak Nation) (Prague, 1924). He insisted on uniform performance of the Liturgy according to the rules he had expressed in a manual: *Liturgie (Mše) pro Církev Československou* (The Liturgy for the Czechoslovak Church)[13] (3rd ed. Prague, 1925). He even embarked on a defensive apologetic in his *Stručné Informace v Náboženských Názorech, Úkolech a Organisaci Církve Československé* (Brief Information Concerning Religious Tenets, Mission and Organization of the Czechoslovak Church) 2nd ed. (Prague, 1929). As a chronic free-thinker, he sailed his ship so far into nationalist waters, that it was problematical whether it should be included among Christian societies.[14] He used all of the available liberal media to promote his free-thinking Church before the Czech forum and eventually was able to state that his Church "represented the type of Christianity from which, by removing the great burden of church life in Christianity, one could expect a considerable contribution for alleviating today's crisis in the Christian world."[15] He even patronized the *Fifth World Congress for Christian Freedom*,[16] held in Prague on September 4–9, 1927 to manifest his free-thinking interest and concern.

Since he had long been anti-Catholic, and later, also anti-Orthodox, it was easy to blame him for encouraging anti-Catholic propaganda, directed especially against his erstwhile friend, Archbishop Kordač. There is indirect evidence that he was influential in bringing about the elimination of certain Catholic holy days from the calendar. A bill in 1925 officially removed three holy days dedicated to Mary: February 2, March 25, and September 8, as well as that of the great St. John Nepomucene. To replace the three "Mary" days, three "commemoration" days were introduced, designed for national appeal: October 28 (Independence Day), July 6 (Burning of John Hus), and May 1 (Labor Day). For Slovakia only, a provincial holy day was proclaimed to honor Sts. Cyril and Method. That year, the anniversary of Hus's death was celebrated solemnly with official church attendance by government authorities.[17] The Vatican took action. The nuncio, Mons. Francis Marmaggi, sent a note of protest, and the Vatican recalled the nuncio from Prague on May 18, 1925.[18] After that, the government, at the demand of the Socialists and Communists, issued new bills inimical to the life and rights of the Catholic Church.

The tension between Catholics and the government increased and was supported by Socialists and liberals generally. However, the results of the general election in November, 1925, caused a great change in internal policy, because the People's Catholic party was able to gain three seats in the national cabinet. This was a warning for the socialists. That same year, Francis Nosek became minister of the interior; Mons. J. Šrámek, minister of mail and Dr. John Dolanský, minister of food. In 1926 the cabinet of non-socialist parties was inaugurated under the leadership of Prime Minister Antonín Švehla, and it was evident that the Catholics could not be ignored. Relations became moderated and the Ministry of Foreign Affairs, under the influence of the distinguished historian, Dr. Kamil Krofta, began negotiations with the Holy See. The Vatican secretary of state, Mons. Ciriaci[19] displayed patience in maintaining equity on both sides, and promised the Vatican would continue her policy of fairness toward Czechoslovakia.

On February 13, 1927, Pope Pius XI sent a letter to all the (Catholic) bishops of Czechoslovakia[20] and a copy of the same letter to those of Yugoslavia, giving

---

[13] It is interesting to note that this liturgy was translated into the German language, to be used by the German members in their language. See *Die Liturgie der Čechoslovakischen Kirche. Verdeutscht von Franz Pokorný. Cf.* Rudolf Otto, "Die Liturgie der Tschechoslowakischen Kirche," *Die Christliche Welt*, ed. Jg. 42, No. 6 (1928): pp. 249–254.

[14] Karl Geyer, "Tschechisches Neuheidentum," *Die Junge Front* 7 (Fridek, 1936): pp. 114–117; J. B. Kozák -Žilka-Maxa-Hajn, *Naše Pokrokovost a Řím* (Our Progress and Rome) (Prague, 1925), *passim*.

[15] *Český Zápas* of June 5, 1927, where a whole text of his speech is given.

[16] "Zum & Weltkongress fuer Christliche Freiheit in Prag 4–9 September 1927," in *Die Christliche Welt* 41, 19 (1927): pp. 658–660.

[17] S. Harrison Thomson, *Czechoslovakia in European History* Princeton Univ. Press, 1953), p. 324 ff.

[18] J. Schmidlin, *op. cit.* 4: p. 133.

[19] *Ibid.*

[20] *AAS* XIX: pp. 93–96.

instructions in favor of "unionism" as preached centuries before by Sts. Cyril and Method. At the same time he gave due regard to the decisions of the Congresses in Velehrad. The letter was intended to create a friendly atmosphere toward the Czechoslovak Republic and modify the tension created by the presence of the national church.

By the end of the year (1927), the government had permitted the holiday in honor of Hus. Thereupon, the Vatican mitigated its stand and the pope, in a letter *Rerum Orientalium*[21] of September 7, 1928, recalled the work of Sts. Cyril and Method, and the cooperation by the Slavs. This letter clarified the Vatican's position and, once an acceptable *modus vivendi* was agreed upon, normal, friendly relations were established between the Holy See and the Republic. The *modus vivendi* was signed by Cardinal Gasparri and Dr. Eduard Beneš at the Vatican on February 2, 1928.[22] The aftermath of all this was general stabilization of the religious situation throughout the country.

We have offered this outline as a fair appraisal of both sides to the conflict: on the one hand, were the broad demands of the liberals, the instigators, and protagonists of anti-Catholic trends, together with the Evangelical and Czech Brethren churches, who were promoters of the Hussite traditions; and, on the other hand, those of the Catholics, who were trying to capitalize on national feeling, by pointing to the advantages of the old Cyrillmethodian heritage. Dr. Farsky continued to serve as patriarch until he died, in 1927, unreconciled to the Catholic Church. Even in death, he was regarded as a symbol of that protest and revolt, which was to become an obvious stigma to the Czechoslovak Church. Endowed with intellectual ability and a dynamic capacity for work, he could have done great things in a spiritual way if he had allowed grace and humility to become fused with his natural talents. Even so, one dubious achievement must go to his credit: long before Harvey Cox[23] and his followers had ever dreamed of a "secular city" Farský had managed to fit all kinds of modernism into his Church.[24] Perhaps it was the most distinct characteristic of his legacy that he could be styled the "high priest" of modern nationalists, progressives, modernists, secularists, and liberals, so that even Voltaire would have been proud of him. Leaving the final judgment to God, one can only surmise that he was driven by what may be called intellectual pride.

As patriarch he was succeeded by Dr. Gustav A. Procházka (1928–1942), under whom the Church, theologically speaking, was even more oriented in the direction of modernism, and became a member of the International Association for Liberal Christianity and Religious Freedom,[25] to which the American Unitarians and other radically modernist churches belong. After studying in a theological seminary in Litoměřice, Procházka had been ordained to the Catholic priesthood. While a curate, he became inclined towards modernism and later, while pastor in Jenišovice near Turnov in Bohemia, became an apostate, taking his whole congregation with him to the new church. He had been very active in the Jednota, later in the Club of Reformist Priests, and was among the early founders of the Czechoslovak Church in 1920. When the government decided that the rectory and church building he occupied must remain the property of the Catholic Church, he erected, in protest, another building for his national parish next door to the old one. This temperamental action well characterized his nature.[26]

To stabilize church doctrine, Procházka convoked a synod at Prague on March 28–30, 1931, in which another new creed was formulated, and certain Presbyterian elements were included in the Constitution. This synod was well attended by Czechoslovak ministers and representatives of all non-Catholic churches. In the new creed, which had been worked on since 1927, God was professed as the personal Creator of the world; but the consubstantial divinity of Christ was repudiated. Instead, the new text only said "by his model life and death, he united man in himself to God." Under the influence of such a shallow religion of enlightenment, the three equally legitimate sources of Christian faith were said to be the Bible, tradition, and the present (and future) state of human culture. The doctrine of original sin was rejected; baptism was regarded as a symbolic expression of the intention "to free the child by education from the consequences of the sins of earlier men"; confirmation was looked upon as a conforming to moral order and discipline; the Eucharist as a memorial of Christ whereby God becomes present in us: and penance as the independent return from ways of sin, in which the priestly absolution was meaningless. Any teaching about indulgences and extreme unction

---

[21] *AAS* XX: pp. 277–288.

[22] Eduard Beneš, "Exposé Ministra Dra Beneše o *Modu Vivendi* Mezi Československem a Vatikánem," *Zahraniční Politika* 7: pp. 200–203; Schmidlin, *op. cit.* 4: p. 133. For the text of *Modus Vivendi, cf. AAS* XX: pp. 65–66. *Cf.* Alfred Fuchs, *Z Boje o Modus Vivendi*, (Prague, 1934); Giannini Amedeo, *II "Modus Vivendi" fra la S. Sede et la Cechoslovacchia* (Rome, 1928), *passim*; Frant Kop, *Modus Vivendi:Nynější Stav*; *Jeho Provedení* (Prague, Orbis, 1937).

[23] Harvey Cox, *The Secular City* (New York, Macmillan, 1966), pp. 92–95. *Cf. idem*, "Secular Holiness: Loss or Gain of Christian Identity?" *Christian Action and Openness to the World* (Villanova Univ. Press, 1970), pp. 53–63.

[24] See for *modernism* and its shapes Bernard M. G. Reardom, *Roman Catholic Modernism* (Stanford Univ. Press, California, 1972), pp. 9–236. For modernism viewed in official stand of the Catholic Church, as expressed in a papal encyclical *Pascendi* of September 8, 1907, see *ibid.*, pp. 237–248, where the substance of modernistic tenets is well formulated.

[25] M. Spinka, *op. cit.*, p. 298.

[26] Ferdinand Prášek *Vznik Československé Církve a Patriarcha G. A. Procházka* (Prague, 1932), *passim*.

was condemned; matrimony was declared dissoluble in certain circumstances, and the sacramental value of holy orders was denied. The individual's rational knowledge was put above church doctrine so that "even when the Church has formulated her teachings clearly and definitely, no one may be charged with heresy because of his opinions." [27]

The Constitution bound all church members, whether clerical or lay, by a personal pledge to further educational work on behalf of the Church's followers, in the spirit of Christ. According to its second article, concerning the responsibilities of members,

The Church expects from each member a participation in the work for achieving this goal, and obliges everyone to follow, in his life, the principles of the Czechoslovak Church, so that he will educate his children in this spirit; also, if it is possible, he will take part in church assemblies, will contribute toward the expense of church administration, and faithfully, seriously and objectively discharge all the offices, dignities or functions entrusted to him."[28]

This forceful calling upon the responsibilities of members in behalf of their Church, clearly reveals how the ties of church membership were becoming stricter as time went on. In fact, an examination of all the new interrelationships, as they appear in this Constitution, clearly shows that the original broad area of personal religious freedom had been reduced considerably with the simultaneous imposition of new church rules and regulations. It would seem that gradually there was a widening discrepancy between the thinking which was becoming more liberal, and the religious practice which was becoming more traditional, in imitation of other Christian churches.

In this perspective, we can see that Patriarch Procházka not only codified all the modernistic theses of his predecessor, Dr. Farský, but expanded them so radically as to give unlimited scope to reason, and very little to faith. The devastating onward trend of this radical thought now led to a still newer secular schism called the "new Catholic Church," [29] whose doctrinal tenets are rather confused. It is interesting to note that, out of the radical views which he had inherited, Dr. Procházka gradually developed his own. His first work, *Křestănský Humanism a Československá Církev* (Christian Humanism and the Czechoslovak Church) (Prague, 1932), reveals his emphasis on humanistic ideals rather than on theological doctrine.

He debated the issue with Professor J. L. Hromádka in his *V Boji za Pravdy: Připomínsky k Hromádkovým Kritikám Církve Československé* (In the Struggle for Truth) in the *Křestănské Revue* of 1932 (Prague, 1933), in which he refuted the objections Hromádka had made to the modernistic tenets; he also contributed a defensive study: "*Die Tschechoslowakische National Kirche*" in a symposium *Die Kirchen der Tschechoslovakei* (Leipzig, 1937), pp. 175–185, and also made several other journalistic contributions.

In his writings, Procházka does not reveal any special theological competence, but excelled rather as an administrator and organizer. Under him, the Czechoslovak Church grew to 270 congregations, about 300 clergymen and, by 1930, a membership close to 800,000. In contrast to his predecessor, Dr. Farský, who was in his heyday at the beginning of the republic, and could exploit the weaknesses of the Catholic Church to the advantage of his Church's nationalism, Dr. Procházka was hindered by the constantly increasing influence, stability and respect which the Catholic Church was beginning to enjoy.

Soon, his Church's activity, growth, and influence became considerably reduced and put under state control. Perhaps it was this which prompted him to re-orient the activities of his Church towards ecumenical contacts abroad, so as to rescue her from the isolation and ostracism to which her liberal tenets had brought her. The basic guidelines which the patriarch had formulated for the relationship abroad, continued to reveal numerous difficulties with which his Church had been plagued, e.g., in Stockholm (1925), Lausanne (1927), and Arnheim (1930); and with which it will surely be challenged in the future. Nevertheless, the Stockholm Conference gave some encouragement, not because of its doctrinal theses (which were sadly wanting) but because of its social and general religious concern; and this emphasis was resented by many. However, the patriarch expressed his appreciation at the International Conference on Youth, held in July, 1932, at Černohorské Kúpele in Slovakia, in these words:

Back in 1925, the Czechoslovak Church joyfully greeted the action of the great archbishop [Nathan Söderblom of Uppsala] who first welcomed her to an international forum, and into rapport with the world Christian churches. The course of her ideology was now confirmed. It began from the principle that Christianity's value, its relevance and importance, is in its practical application. Not

---

[27] Konrad Algermissen, *Christian Denominations* (translation by J. W. Grundner) (H. Louis, B. Herder Book Co., 1957), p. 304. "Procházka's Credo!: whole text is to be found in *Zpráva o I. Řádném Sněmu Církve Československé, Konaném ve Dnech 28–30 Března, 1931 v Praze-Dejvicích* (Prague, 1931). This is a report of all proceedings and texts.

[28] Quoted by F. M. Hník, *op. cit.*, pp. 171–172.

[29] Head of this Church became Rev. Antonin Kezniček, who originally was ordained a Catholic priest in 1924, and under the influence of modernism, he apostatized to the Czechoslovak Church in 1925 after he got married, and soon after, from frustration, he led the separation of certain numbers of followers to establish a new Catholic Church. There is little information about the doctrinal tenets of this Church, but from all indications it is close to and similar to the Liberal Catholic Church, founded in 1917 by the English Old Catholic Bishop Wedgewood as a modern theosophic of the ancient gnosis under the guise of Catholic sacramental actions. Cf. Algermissen, *op. cit.*, pp. 363–364; William J. Whalen, *Separated Brethren* (Milwaukee, Bruce Co., 1957), pp. 210–212, "The Liberal Catholics"; J. Kubalík, "Nejnovější Sekty po Světové Válce v Naší Vlasti" (Newest Sects after World War in our Country); *ČKD* 80 (105) (1940): pp. 276–284, 372–376.

doctrinal principles, not dogmas frequently outmoded, but the application of Jesus's principles in daily life. Christianity should be as a seed which grows and comes to penetrate the whole of political, economic, social, and cultural life. In this lies our mission. If, in the past, Christian churches had penetrated political life by the principles of Christ, instead of being themselves politicized, either because of their desire for power or influence or wealth, they would not have failed to discharge their mission of becoming messengers of Christ's Gospel, even though they had been firmly convinced of their dogmatic authenticity. In the social and economic development of mankind, if the churches had made the Gospel's program practical, and had taken care that it was being fulfilled, the great masses of working people could never have been alienated from Christianity. The churches should have been the vigilant protectors of justice in the spirit of Christ. Indeed, the Gospel should have been announced to the poor; and not only announced, but used for their help and protection... .The Stockholm Conference humbly confesses before the whole world this guilt of the Christian churches. The Universal Christian Council for Life and Work regards its job correctly. If, up to the present there has been no hope for unification in their faith and doctrine and the field of practical Christianity, such union is now not only possible, but successful.[30]

It was through this social emphasis and ethical concern that the Czechoslovak Church found her way into the world Christian bodies with whom she could share her ideals. For this purpose, she engaged in a detailed study of social Christianity's problems and reorganized her theological commission of the Central Council by adding a department to study Christian life and order. Coordination of this work was put in charge of Dr. F. M. Hník, professor on the Hus faculty, who was largely responsible for its success. Its permanent member was Bishop J. R. Stejskal, as representative for the Czechoslovak Church. Doubts were expressed as to whether that Church, because of the direction its doctrines were taking, should take part in ecumenical work within the framework of a World Conference for Faith and Order at Lausanne, and whether she should be officially represented in the latter's Council. The problem was rendered more delicate because the Czechoslovak Church had just finished formulating (in the Synod of 1931) many aspects of her Christian doctrine differently from what was traditional. Furthermore, just the year before (1930), she had entered the World Association for Liberal Christianity and Religious Freedom as one of its co-founders. There was certainly a crucial determining factor as to whether she should be welcomed or merely tolerated in this World Conference for Faith and Order; the World Conference accepted the trinitarian formula according to the Nicene Creed[31] as the basis for their ecumenical efforts; whereas, the Czechoslovak Church had distinctly excluded this creed from her doctrine, in favor of a broader, more liberal statement. It was due to precisely this external expression that she would play such a prominent role in the International Association for Liberal Christianity and Religious Freedom, especially in its Congress held August 14–19, 1934, in Kodan, and later be associated with the Modern Churchmen's Union[32] in England, and always enjoy friendly contact with English and American Unitarian bodies. At the same time, she was at a real disadvantage in the World Christian bodies because they were based on traditional theology. Could she be recognized as an equal and legal member in assemblies so widely different? Only later, when Christian humanism became popular in ecumenical endeavors, could she find a proper setting for a full, dynamic cooperation with other Christian bodies.

The year 1935 was very important for Czechoslovak Catholics because a Catholic Congress was to be held in Prague and, for the first time, Catholic strength was evidenced in St. Wenceslaus' Square. More than a million Catholics came from all over the republic to honor Jesus Christ, the king and, with the presence of John Cardinal Verdier of Paris, sent by the Vatican as its special apostolic delegate, the political importance of the Congress became evident.

The official anti-Catholic policy broke down and T. G. Masaryk's antithesis, "Reformation-Counter Reformation," was shown to be ineffective, now that Catholics of the whole republic came to be incorporated into the life of the nation. President Masaryk, himself, in the face of this tremendous spiritual demonstration of dynamic Catholic solidarity, indirectly expressed the abandonment of his famous antithesis, and announced a new and less unfriendly aphorism: "Catholics will have as many rights as they will be able to defend." Yet any such antithesis is bad for a national program. Patriarch Procházka, listening to the president, had also to fall in line and restrain himself in his public expressions, for now his Church was losing momentum.

The Catholics, nevertheless, took up Masaryk's new slogan at the first Catholic Congress in Prague in 1935, and began to use it to their own advantage. Fortunately, the motto worked out beneficially for all concerned and was satisfactory to those of whatever shade or tendency of revision: antithesis, action, or reaction.[33]

Later, the rise of Nazism and especially the establishment of the Protectorate of Bohemia and Moravia (on March 15, 1939) proved a great humiliation for the

---

[30] This lecture appeared in *Český Zápas* 15: pp. 249–257; quoted by F. M. Hník, *op. cit.*, pp. 280–281.

[31] Definition, accepted in plenary assembly on August 20, 1927, reads: "We, representatives of many Christian Bodies from all over the world, united by the common confession of faith in *Jesus Christ, Son of God, our Lord and Savior*, and in the faith, *that the Holy Spirit is with us*, are assembled here in order that we consult about matters which are common to us and which divide us." *Cf.* F. M. Hník, *op. cit.*, p. 287.

[32] See statutes of this union in F. M. Hník, *op. cit.*, p. 296.

[33] *Acta et Monumenta Primi Congressus Catholicorum Republicae Cecoslovakae* (Prague, 1936); Josef Doležal, *Politická Cesta Českého Katolicismu 1918–1928* (Prague, 1928), *passim*.

Czechs who had always been a freedom-loving people, and for whom patriotism meant simply to belong to the nation. Now, the heroic stand of the Catholic priests began to stand out sharply; the people began to open their eyes and see, revealed beneath the mask of deceit, the nakedness of the so-called progress. Many of the prominent adherents of "progress" who had proclaimed themselves patriots, now bowed their heads before the German authorities, but not so the Catholic priests and bishops, who withstood the invader and turned out to be intensely patriotic and faithful. Throughout World War II (1938–1945) none of them were collaborators, even among the Czechs and Moravians. "Immediately after the German invasion, Catholic churches were filled with believers who came to seek the only spiritual consolation which remained." [34] The people felt again that the Catholic priests were trustworthy protectors in national affairs despite the insidious attacks upon them by the progressives and liberals of the first Czechoslovak Republic (1918–1938); and the Czechoslovak Church came to lose its attractiveness in spite of its emphasis on national sentiment which had been successfully exploited in the past.

Historically impressive was the fact that Karel Cardinal Kašpar, archbishop of Prague, never made a courtesy call upon the Reichsprotektor, although representatives of all the non-Catholic churches (including Patriarch Procházka) visited him. When reproached for this by German officials, the cardinal replied: "An ecclesiastical prince, cardinal of the Church, accepts visits of foreigners in his palace." [35] While proceeding cautiously, he gave no approval to the German authorities of occupation. The gap between the general population and Catholic priests began to disappear and, regardless of how distasteful it was to some of their erstwhile enemies, Catholic priests now had to be counted among the patriots. The fact that Mons. Jan Šrámek was the prime minister of the government in exile, living in London, that many priests, nuns, and laymen had become victims of the general persecution while the Protectorate of Bohemia and Moravia (1939–1945) existed, inspired national confidence in the Catholic leaders. Fulfilling their national and pastoral duties, Catholic priests regained the nation for the Church. The number of apostasies diminished. Instead of the old *Los von Rom* (Away from Rome), the cry became *Zurück nach Rom* (Back to Rome). The change came about as a result of persecution and national humiliation. The heroic stand by the pope, hierarchy, priests, and people brought about a great change of mind and was an indication of what was to come. The Catholic Church, along with her leader in the Vatican, was being harmonized with the national development. Indeed, the national Czechoslovak Church lost its *raison d'être* when, at the suggestion of the Germans, it changed its political constellation and its name to become the *Czecho-Moravian Church*.[36] At this point some even suggested that it be called simply the Hus Church, to avoid the embarrassment of having to change its name as political circumstance might demand; the name of Hus would at least be a discernible description, befitting a "historical Christian church, more acceptable in the international forum."

The Czechoslovak Church even began to collaborate with Ludwig Mueller, Reichsbischof of the all-German National Evangelical Church in Berlin;[37] and Patriarch Procházta was under pressure to follow the pattern of the German national church by making several concessions, and by his assurance that his church would support the German regime, although the invaders were hated by the Czech people. Before he died, in Prague in 1942, he was severely criticized for some failures of his Church. One of them had to do with doctrine;[38] another was concerned with national appeal;[39] another with the falling-off of the new Czech-Moravian Church's membership due to a crisis of trust on the part of the Czech and Moravian people—all of these brought a saddening eclipse to his own reputation.

The sobering years of World War II caused a setback to the whole progressive and liberalist program,[40]

---

[34] *Two years of German Oppression in Czechoslovakia*, p. 69 ff.
[35] L. Nemec, *Church and State in Czechoslovakia* (New York, 1955), p. 158 ff.
[36] *Two Years of German Oppression*, 78 ff. Cf. J. Kubalík, "Náboženská Společnost Českomoravská Církví Husovou?" (Is a Religious Czecho-Moravian Society a Hus Church?), ČKD 81 (106) (1941): pp. 217–223.
[37] The religious counterpart of Nazism, the "German Christians" with varying degrees of enthusiasm called for a "positive, virile, Aryan Christianity." Their candidate for Reich's bishop, Chaplain Ludwig Mueller, received Hitler's endorsement as against the German Evangelical Federation. In July, 1933, this Federation was legally replaced by a "German Evangelical Church," a centralized body to be "co-ordinated" by Mueller. But a "New Reformation Movement" of twenty-five hundred Lutheran ministers objected to the anti-Semitism of the new church, and were upheld in their stand by Protestant ecumenical groups. Later, "German Christian" demands for rewriting the Bible and removal of the cross provoked a "Pastors' Evangelical League" led by Martin Niemöller. Its leaders were arrested or exiled and all Protestant opposition forced underground by 1938. Finally, the Reichsbischof was supplanted by a lay minister of religion, Hans Kerrl, who demanded a "Nordic Christianity" while Rosenberg campaigned for a "National Reich Church" with a thirty-point program involving pure paganism or pantheism. Cf. Newman C. Eberhardt, *A Summary of Catholic History* (2 v., St. Louis, Herder Book, 1962) 2: p. 729.
[38] Joseph Kubalík, "Věrouka Náboženské Společnosti Českomoravské" (Doctrine of the Religious Czecho-Moravian Association), ČKD 82 (107) (1942): pp. 292–298.
[39] J Kubalík, "Nepravdivá Mystika v Boji o Duši Českého Člověka" (False Mystique in a Struggle for the Soul of Czech Man), ČKD 85 (110) (1945): pp. 142–150.
[40] J. B. Kozák-F. Žilka-Maxa Hajn, *Naše Pokrokovost a Řím* (Our Progress and Rome) (Prague, 1925), *passim*. Cf. J. Kozák, *O Otázce Náboženské* (Concerning the Religious Question) (Kdyně, 1922), *passim*.

so that the description of Viktor Dyk, the Czech poet, was justified when he styled this church's movement as "progress to the point of stupidity." [41]

Procházta's successor, Dr. Francis Kovář (1942–1961), became patriarch under difficult and deteriorating conditions. Having been connected with the Hus faculty in Prague, he soon engaged himself in writing popular journalistic contributions and articles for various learned and professional journals. He also wrote several books in which he gradually expressed the development of his thought. His first work, called *Církev Pravoslavná a Římská: Několik Kapitol k Poznání Obou Církví* (The Church, Orthodox and Roman: Several Chapters Concerning Knowledge of Both Churches) (Prague, 1920) revealed a tendency toward Orthodoxy. Later, he followed Dr. Farsky's progressive line in *Naše Dílo: Sborník Prací Číslo První* (Our Work: A Collection of Works, #1) (Prague, 1928). Still later, he expressed his views in *Deset Let Československé Církve 1920–1930* (Ten Years of the Czechoslovak Church 1920–1930) (Prague, 1930); *Die Tschechoslowkische Kirche*, published in the *Prager Rundschau* 5 (1935): pp. 171–185; and, finally, he professed liberal theological modernism and progressivism in *Náš Poměr ke Katolictví* (Our Relationship to Catholicism) (Prague, 1936); and even wrote panegyrics on his predecessor as a teacher and thinker in *Dr. Charles Farský, the First Patriarch of the Czechoslovak Church* (Prague, Orbor, 1937). One can see from some of his works that he was a rather practical man, an administrator with a deep sense of legal balance and pastoral caution. Perhaps one thing he learned quickly from his predecessor was that if their Church was to be revitalized and accepted as the national church, it must regain its ability to appeal to the people nationally.

Since it was clear from 1943, when agreement with Russia was reached,[42] that Communist orientation would follow the end of the war, Patriarch Kovář decided to follow the Communist trend and thereby repair the Church's reputation which had been compromised by its cooperation with the Nazis during the war years (1939–1945). Concurrent with the main campaign against the Catholic Church, the Czechoslovak Communist regime gradually undermined the autonomy of the non-Catholic churches as well. The Czecho-Moravian Church, which again had become known again as the Czechoslovak Church, was the first to be brought under the new regime's control, although it had been virtually in Communist hands since the end of World War II. In 1945, immediately after the war, the representatives, including the patriarch, were accused of having collaborated with the Germans; and the Church was placed under the temporary administration of a Central Action Committee, composed mainly of Communists.[43] With reference to the patriarch's collaboration with the Nazis, the Central Council of the Czechoslovak Church recommended (in 1946) the then widely held opinion that "bishops" should be elected for seven years and not, as previously, for life.

As had been decided in the Constitution of the Church and, especially, after the Communist putch of 1948, the Committee placed the nationalist church in the service of the Communist regime. In addition to this, a great reduction in the country's population made for a numerical weakness of the Church and, as a result, the traditional dependence on the state for financial support, placed the non-Catholic churches, especially the national church, in a difficult position. Furthermore, one of the Communist regime's main strategies in bringing the Church into submission was to play on her latest hostility against the strong, ideologically dynamic and well-organized Catholic Church. The twin facts of her liberal doctrine and congregational structure enabled the Communists to contrive noisier "mass pressures from below with greater ease and effectiveness" in the name of the people than could have been used against the Catholic Church.

In the opinion of some, the tragedy was compounded by a willing and generous offer of the Protestant theologian and bearer of the Order of the Czechoslovak Republic in recognition of his "struggle for peace," Professor Josef Luke Hromádka (1889–1970).[44] He offered to carry out a Christian-Marxist dialog at the cost of sacrificing religious influence and jeopardizing the very existence of the churches.

In all justice, it most be said that Hromádka, a man of considerable theological influence, and experience in Czechoslovak circles, at home and abroad, gave leftist orientation to non-Catholic churches; this provided for most people the needed justification for accepting the communistic mission.

Professor Bohdan Chudoba has critically analyzed the "stages in the Czech Protestant tragedy" in which the leading role was played by J. F. Hromádka, dean

---

[41] Jan Drábek, *Z Časů Nedlouho Zašlých* (From Times not Long Past) (Rome, 1967), pp. 202–231; Hanuš jelínek, *Viktor Dyk* (Prague, Czech Academy of Art and Sciences, 1932), *passim*. For the views of Viktor Dyk see F. M. Hník, *op. cit.*, pp. 39, 63–67, 73, 75–80. He was very influential, especially in national matters, and his judgment had respect and authority among liberals.

[42] Hubert Ripka, *The Soviet-Czechoslovak Treaty* (London, Czechoslovak Ministry of Foreign Affairs, Infor. Service, 1943). Cf. *Smlouva Mezi Československem a Sovětským Svazem* (Prague-Orbis, Ministerstvo Informaci, 1945), where whole text is to be found.

[43] Vratislav Bušek and Nicholas Spulber, *Czechoslovakia* (New York, Fred A. Praeger, 1957), p. 151.

[44] Bohdan Chudoba, "Czech Protestants and Communism," *America* (Nov. 12, 1949), pp. 149–151. For a positive evaluation of Hromádka's thought, see F. M. Hník, *op. cit.*, pp. 36, 46, 131–134, 139–140, 163 and *passim*. This was, of course, Hromádka from the time of the First Czechoslovak Republic (1918–1938) with his great authority, influence, and integrity, before he was affected by communism.

of the Hus faculty in Prague. In this theological thesis, *We Need a New Mission*, Hromádka brought his church ideologically into a position favorable to Communism, and induced people "to cooperate with the Communists toward social works."[45]

As early as World War II, while living in the United States (1939–1945), Hromádka had inclined toward this synthesis. Even in his earlier work, *Masaryk as European* (Prague, 1936), he had betrayed a leaning in this direction. In 1941, in his study, *The Modern Trends in European Protestant Theology*, Hromádka proclaimed the aim of unifying not only all Christian churches, but all political factors when he said, "We are living in a terrific crisis. However, this crisis is a great challenge for us. If we theologians are faithful to the divine truth, we might some day be credited with having brought good news and a remedy to unhappy humanity."[46] In 1943 he explained the philosophy of Emmanual Rádl,[47] and in the year 1945, after analyzing Dostojewski, T. G. Masaryk, and E. Rádl, he said prophetically:

We cannot go back! We cannot save civilization by conservative caution or by reactionary devices. We cannot impose our abstract formulas and blue prints on the events of current history. Behind history, the Risen Lord is doing His work. What does it mean that the vast areas of Russia and the hundreds of millions of the Soviet people have found themselves on the side of the Allies? What does it mean that the spiritual and moral motifs of Russian history have been released by revolution and war, and are shaping the days to come? What does it mean that the liberal and democratic world has undergone a trial by blood and sweat?"[48]

Later, serving as a member of the Communist regime's Central Action Committee, Hromádka declared before a gathering of the Czech Brethren in Prague on December 8, 1947:

[Today] . . . all problems of any material importance, be they spiritual or ecclesiastical, moral or cultural, are so closely linked with political and social happenings, that no one can escape being drawn into politics. Today, none of us can claim to know religion or the tasks of theology well, unless we pass through the red-hot furnace of political and social happenings that are shaking the world. . . . The Communists are the dynamic force of political and social changes. . . . That is why it is not only wrong, but downright dangerous to set up any combination of forces without the Communists. . . ."[49]

From these several statements one can clearly see that Hromádka's collaboration with Communists was planned, deliberate, and ideological. His influence affected some of the more liberal priests, greatly undermined Catholic opposition, and even disoriented the progressive circles, especially around the Hus faculty and the Charles IV University in Prague.

It would seem that Professor Hromádka simply failed to discern a fundamental contradiction between Christianity and Communism, while deliberately assuming the task of bridging the gap between them. Many members of the Evangelical Church of Czech Brethren did not approve his extravagant overtures; but the Czechoslovak Church embraced his views unreservedly and applied them pragmatically, or at least used them to justify their collaboration. Mindful of their guilt from the Nazi era, and with the pressing demand for forming a new Constitution (in 1948), many of the Church leaders were driven into the Communist embrace. Indeed, Dr. F. Linhart, a colleague of Professor Hromádka, was active in the formation of the Communist-sponsored Association of Christian Societies, which published a Declaration calling dialectical materialism an explanation of the teachings of Christ.[50] On May 9, 1948, following formal acceptance by the National Assembly, held in the famous Vladislav Hall in Hradčany Castle, the new Constitution[51] was proclaimed, with the explanation that a vote for the new Constitution would mean "to give the country a new Constitution adapted to the people's democratic character; a Constitution leading to socialism,[52] that, furthermore, this Constitution referred to the best traditions in the history of the Czech and Slovak nations and Hussitism."[53] The Czechoslovak Church was easily lured by this rhetorical propaganda.

The Constitution was promulgated on June 9, 1948, in the official code, issue 42, number 150.[54] It is based upon the old Constitution of February 29, 1920 number 121, Coll.,[55] but in the spirit of a "people's democratic institution."

This new Constitution introduced several new concepts.[56] In economic matters (paragraph 4, pp. 146–

---

[45] Joseph L. Hromádka, *Between East and West*, cited in Chudoba, *op. cit.*, p. 151. R. H. Markham, *Communists Crush Churches in Eastern Europe*, 16. *Time*, p. 60, No. 13 (Sept. 29, 1952), p. 52.

[46] Joseph L. Hromádka, "The Modern Trends in European Protestant Theology," in *The Univ. of Pennsylvania Bicentennial Conference, Religion and the Modern World*, pp. 21–25.

[47] Joseph L. Hromádka, *Don Quijote České Filosofie, Emanuel Rádl 1873–1942*.

[48] Joseph L. Hromádka, *Doom and Resurrection*, p. 121. Cf. *The Red and the Black*, p. 28: "Hromádka's Protestants." Hromadka's point of view regarding the Communists is here well expressed.

[49] *The Red and the Black* (New York, Free Europe, 1953), p. 28.

[50] *The Red and the Black. The Church in the Communist State* (New York, The National Committee for a Free Europe, 1953), p. 28.

[51] Vratislav Bušek, "The Czechoslovak Constitutions of 1920, 1948, and 1960," *The Czechoslovak Contribution to World Culture*, ed. M. Rechcígl (The Hague, Mouton & Co., 1964), pp. 396–404.

[52] *Ústava Ze Dne 9 Května 1948* (Constitution of May 9, 1948). Cf. *Lidová Demokracie* of April 15, 1948, pp. 1–2

[53] *La Documentation Catholique* 46 (1949), 1051 Col 1178. C . *Lidová Demokracie* (May 11, 1948), p. 1.

[54] Albert Flory, "La Constitution Tschecoslovaque," *La DC* 46 (1949), 1051 Col. pp. 1178–1179.

[55] This Constitution was compiled by Alfred Meisner, Social Democrat. See *The Constitution of the Czechoslovak Republic*, a reprint of the English version published in Prague, 1920, by the Société de L'effort de la Tschecoslovaquie.

[56] *Constitution of May 9, 1948*, p. 81.

164) the former order was reversed in favor of a socialistic thesis, and the cultural and educational systems were put under state control; whereas personal property rights were restricted (paragraph 9): personal freedom was limited by the conditions of the law (paragraph 2); and ecclesiastical matters were regulated as follows:

Par. 13 1) Only state schools are recognized and admitted.
   2) Elementary school education is to be uniform, obligatory, free.
   3) Particulars and exceptions are to be as fixed by law.
Par. 14 1) All education and teaching must be accommodated to and in accordance with the results of scientific research, and not be out of harmony with the people's democratic regime.
   2) In the carrying-out of all education and teaching, and also in the supervision of it, only the state is authorized to exert any influence.
Par. 15 1) Freedom of conscience is guaranteed.
   2) Faith and conviction may be a disadvantage for some, but cannot be taken as a reason for refusing to fulfill the duties of citizens as fixed by law.
Par. 16 1) Everybody is entitled to avow, in private as well as in public, any religious faith, or to be without confession at all.
   2) All religionists and atheists are equal before the law.
Par. 17 1) Everybody is free to practice his religion, or to be without confession. Its practice, however, must not be discordant with public order or with good morals. It is not advisable to misuse this right for non-religious purposes.
   2) Nobody can be forced, either directly or indirectly, to take part in religious acts.
Par. 18 1) Freedom of speech is guaranteed.
   2) Everybody can, within the limits fixed by the law, express his opinions in word, in writing, by picture, or in any other way. The exercise of this right must not be to the disadvantage of anyone.
Par. 21 1) Freedom of press is guaranteed, preliminary censorship of the press is not admitted on principle.
   2) The law will regulate who is authorized to edit and print newspapers and periodicals, and the conditions under which this may be done; especially regarding this last clause, profit alone should not be a motive.
   3) The law will regulate regarding the freedom of science and arts, and the protection of valuable works, the editing and publication of matters of a non-periodical nature, especially of books, music, and reproductions of creative works.
Par. 22 1) The right of reproduction or publication of politically performed attractions is also of importance, and export of films is reserved for the Slavs.
   2) Transmission of broadcasting and of television is the exclusive right of the state.
   3) Execution of these rights is regulated by the law, which will also fix any exceptions.
Par. 24 1) The right to hold meetings and establish associations is guaranteed so far as they are not a menace to the people's democratic institutions and to the public order. Execution of these rights is regulated by law.[57]

Even though the Communists, wishing to safeguard their international reputation, tried to maintain a semblance of religious freedom, it soon became evident that it was very limited in comparison with the religious freedom which had been expressed by the old Constitution of the Republic of February 29, 1920. The Communists did not respect even this minimum guaranteed by their new Constitution, as can be seen unmistakably.

President Eduard Beneš refused to sign the new Constitution and, on June 9, 1948, submitted his resignation in protest. This protest should have been evidence that the Constitution, in spite of the oratory, did not guarantee religious freedom; but evidently it did not bother the leaders of Czechoslovak Church because their church would now be favored over the Catholic Church.

Three months earlier, but immediately after the Communist take over in February 25, 1948, Patriarch Kovář had reassured President Gottwald of the Church's support. About a year later, the General Synod of the Czechoslovak Church, meeting in Prague on February 20–22, 1949, sent this message to President Gottwald: "We solemnly affirm our determination to give full moral support to our people in their efforts for the building of a socialist society in this country. We condemn all reactionary tendencies, and we are determined not to let them be established within the organism of the Church."[58] This, of course, is indisputable evidence of the Czechoslovak Church's surrender to the Czechoslovak Communist regime.

In this, the Czechoslovak Church followed the model of the Czech Brethren, although the latter's membership was almost a traditional heritage of the National Socialist party. In the Czechoslovak Church, only Bishop Tabach resisted; while Dr. Kovář, the patriarch of the entire church, in his comment on the new ecclesiastical laws of October 14, 1949, introduced by the Communist regime, openly declared:

It is possible to live in accordance with the spirit of Jesus only under the condition that we endeavor to nullify all class privileges, and concentrate our efforts on attaining social justice. But there is only one way to attain social justice, and that is the way of socialism. Therefore, our Church has decided, according to its best lights, to support this ideology."[59]

---

[57] This English translation is from *Digest-Index of Eastern European Law*, "Czechoslovakia: Church and Religion," ed. by Vladimir Gsovski (Washington, D.C., Law Library of Congress, 1951), *passim*.

[58] *Prague Newsletter, 22 February, 1949*, Quoted by Barron and Waddams, *Communism and the Churches* (London, S.C.M. Press, Ltd., 1949), p. 52. It was reported by J. Hutchison Cockburn, *Religious Freedom in Eastern Europe* (Richmond, Virginia, John Knox Press, 1953), p. 72.

[59] *Nové Církevní Zákony* (The New Church Laws) (Prague,

The patriarch evidently used social emphasis and ethical concern, as reflected in the Church's tenets and offered her cooperation willingly and deliberately, as being in ideological accord with the official doctrinal stand.

In fact, the Instruction of the Central Action Committee of the Communist party in Prague, containing secret information for the party's secretaries said, among other things: "The Czechoslovak Church and the Evangelical Church will be proclaimed as 'national' churches. The properties of the Roman Catholic Church will be confiscated and assigned, in case of need, in favor of these 'national' churches." [60] Furthermore, there was another embarrassing document, circulated secretly in Slovakia in the summer of 1948, in which the Central Action Committee of the National Front insisted on a basic plan of action against the Roman Catholic Church. Paragraph #5 read: "Close cooperation with the Czechoslovak (National) Church should be emphasized. Participation of its bishops in state ceremonies, and their reception with great honors, should be encouraged." Paragraph #6 called upon the officials "to emphasize the present disunity of the people, as much as possible, and to stress the need for unity. In the first phase, the Czechoslovak (National) Church should be used as a unifying factor; in later phases, other means could be employed, namely, cooperation with the Orthodox Church." [61]

These obviously unflattering documents reveal that there was planned, not imposed, collaboration with the Communists.

A special workshop held in the building of the State Office for Church Affairs in Prague from January 9 to February 1, 1951, was headed: "Aims of the Vatican Policy and Means of Frustrating Them" and, among other things, it said: "Where there are few Catholics, the church (building) will be disposed of and given to another religion. The preferred churches will be the Orthodox Church, because it is amenable to socialism; and the Czechoslovak Church, because it is flexible in any direction." [62]

The description of the Orthodox and the Czechoslovak national churches as "preferred" instruments of Communist aims, constitutes a poor tribute to both of these churches. The view concerning the Czechoslovak Church is readily understood in the light of a statement of February 1, 1950, made by the patriarch: For us and our Church, these laws mean an end to the discrimination from which our Church suffered during the first republic and under the occupation. The people's government found a just solution to the problem of the standing of the various churches, so that no church can complain that its present position in the republic is worse than it was before, when the Church did not enjoy equality.[63]

Such a servile stand brought its own rewards. For example, the Cabinet Decree No. 112 of July 14, 1950, Coll. abolished all Roman Catholic theological schools, with the exception of two: Prague and Bratislava; while at the same time, it established three evangelical schools: two in Prague, and one in Bratislava, and created a new Orthodox school in Prague.[64] This may serve as a typical example of the communistic state's favoritism towards "flexible" churches. The Czechoslovak Church was repeatedly favored in all matters, while the Roman Catholic Church was persecuted beyond measure. Patriarch Kovář declared on several occasions that the Communists were fighting the Catholic hierarchy only to protect the people from clerical oppression. While all the Roman Catholic bishops, together with the heroic archbishop of Prague, Josef Cardinal Beran (1888–1971), were suffering, silenced, jailed, tortured, and persecuted, Patriarch Kovář was appearing in all public Communistic festivities as a churchman, apparently giving his blessing to all their actions. There is much documented evidence elsewhere, of this kind of collaboration. Suffice it to say that, before his death in 1961, Patriarch Dr. Francis Kovář, by his collaboration with the Communists, outdid his predecessor, Patriarch Procházda, who in his day had collaborated with the Germans. Each, it must be argued, fulfilled his mission which, according to their church Constitution, was "for the benefit of the Czechoslovak nation." Patriarch Kovář evidently saw the Czechoslovak Church in terms of so-called "political ecclesiology," [65] in his case, "Communist ecclesiology," [66] where the state is the master, always to be obeyed, even at the cost of the Church's own ideology.

His successor, Miroslav Novák, took over the patriarchate in 1961, under rather confused circumstances, and on the eve of an ecumenical era launched by Pope John XXIII in 1962. Not involved in scholarly interests, Novák contributed little to literary or theological lore. Besides his public addresses and popular journalistic articles, he published several

---

State Bureau for Church Affairs, 1949). *Cf.* J. B. Kozák, *The Future of Czechoslovakia* (Washington, 1944), pp. 46, 49, 62.

[60] This document in *CML* archives in Rome. It was reprinted in Czech journals *Katolík* and *Národ* and translated into English in L. Nemec, *Church and State* (New York, 1955), p. 253.

[61] Whole text of this circular may be found in Theodoric J. Zubek, *The Church of Silence in Slovakia* (Whiting, Ind. Lach, 1956), pp. 50–51.

[62] This document in Czech is in the Cyrillomethodian League (*CML*) archives in London and its English translation is provided by author and can be found in L. Nemec, *op. cit.*, pp. 370–371.

[63] *The Tablet*, February 11, 1950, p. 116.

[64] Gsovski-Kocvara-Nosek, "Czechoslovakia: Church and Religion," *Digest- Index of Eastern European Laws* (Washington, D.C., 1951), p. 21.

[65] Bernard F. Donahue, "Political Ecclesiology," *Theological Studies* **33** (June, 1972): pp. 294–306.

[66] L. Nemec, "The Communist Ecclesiology During the Church-State Relationship in Czechoslovakia, 1945–1967," *Proc. Amer. Philos. Soc.* **112**, 4 (1968): pp. 245–275. *Cf.* Josef Petula, *Christian Political Theology. A Marxian Guide* (Maryknoll, New York, Orodis Books, 1972), pp. 169–229.

booklets and, to date, one study, in *Die Christliche Welt 44 No. 2 (1957):* pp. 88–90. He enjoys a reputation of being a rather practical organizer and skilled public speaker. The fact that as early as 1948 he ordained women as ministers on what was, supposedly, the first such occasion in Europe, reveals that he was a reform-minded churchman.[67] He expended much effort in building up church structures and increasing church membership. In the official census of 1963, there were listed about 750,000 members in 345 parishes and 5 dioceses: Prague, Pilsen, Hradec Králové, Brno, and Moravská Ostrava.

Novák was also preoccupied with looking to the education of ministers. Candidates were trained in the Hus-Czechoslovak Theological Faculty in Prague.[68] That faculty, in 1964, had about 30 students and 8 professors. Patriarch Novák attempted to staff the faculty with some better trained professors who, together with their Protestant colleagues, were engaged in publishing learned studies and works. Since the end of World War II in 1945, there have been concentrated efforts to make the theology of his Church more acceptable in a traditional way, as can be seen in an interesting treatise written by one of its professors, Zdeněk Trtík, *Christology in the Spirit of the Czechoslovak Church* (Prague, 1951) which gives us a new insight into its doctrinal make-up. Through the Church's principal organ, *Náboženská Revue*, a useful journal existing since 1930, efforts have been made to promote public relations and advance religious views.

More practical was *Idea*, a journal for religious instruction in the Church. The periodical *Svoboda Svědomí*, served the clergy, and *Husova Liga* was a newspaper designed for laymen. During wartime, some of these were temporarily interrupted, some were stopped and later reactivated. All in all, these attempts brought a certain respectability which was needed for better contacts with other churches abroad. Since 1920, the official weekly, had been *Český Zápas* (Czech Fight). In addition to these publicity outlets, there were propaganda and information items published in the papers of every diocese. In general, it can be said, that their Church had adequate communication media, which were not restricted even during the harsh Communist rule (1950–1960) largely because the Church was patronized by the state. To be in the good graces of the Communist state was of great practical advantage especially when the Church's encounter with the state was difficult.

This period of relative quiet came to an abrupt when, on June 12, 1960, after ten years of lies, trickery and treachery, the real face of Czechoslovak Communism was revealed to the largely uninformed world. On that date, a national organ, *Svobodné Slovo*, published the entire text of the new Constitution entitled: *Ústava Československé Socialistické Republiky* (Constitution of the Czechoslovak Socialist Republic).[69] This document unveiled what had been kept hidden under the cloak of propaganda. Once more, the Czechoslovak Communists were exposed as being in direct opposition to human liberty and dignity. Further evidence was given to prove that the intentions, purposes, and goals of the Communists of the 1960's were the same as those formulated by Marx, Engels, Lenin, and Krushchev. It was damning testimony against the wishful thinking and exaggerated hopes of those liberals who had sought for coexistence, based on the same tolerance for the evil which they, mistakenly, had concluded would be minimized by the influence of a free democratic world.

The Constitution of 1960 is very laconic on religious freedom and prefers to omit any specific consideration of the religious human being as such. The Church is not mentioned, and even though religious freedom is included within the framework of human rights, it seems to be regarded as an annoying disturbance to the socialist atmosphere. In Art. II, Sec. 32, Par. 1, religious freedom is treated thus: "Freedom of religion is guaranteed. Anyone may profess any religious belief, or be affiliated with any denomination, and take part in any form of worship as long as it does not violate the law." Par. 2 continues: "Religious faith or conviction is no reason for anyone failing to fulfill a civic obligation imposed on him by law." In comparison with the provisions of the earlier Constitutions of 1920 and 1948, this is short shrift indeed, and evidences rather the tone and influence of the Soviet Constitution of 1936.

The newly formulated "freedom of religion" clause appears to be in direct contradiction to the mission of the socialist state, since Art. 1, Sec. 18, Par. 1, states that the "entire cultural policy of Czechoslovakia and the development of education and schools are conducted on a scientific basis according to Marx-Leninism, and in close conjunction with the life of the

---

[67] *Nové Církevní Zákony* (New Church Laws), p. 39; *The Red and the Black*, p. 28; L. Nemec, *Church and State* (New York, 1955), p. 189.

[68] J. Krajcar, "Czechoslovak Church," *The New Catholic Encyclopedia* (4 v., New York, McGraw Hill Co., 1966), pp. 588–589.

[69] *Ústava Československé Socialistické Republiky* (Prague, *Svobodné Slovo*, July 12, 1960). This is a special offprint prepared in booklet form to serve as an official communication to bring its text to the people. *Cf.* Ludvik Němec, "Nová Československá Ústava Hrobem Všech Lidských Práv" (The New Czechoslovak Constitution, a Tomb of Human Liberties), *Katolík* (Chicago, Sept. 23, 1960), pp. 1–2,8. For other aspects of this constitution see Josef Kalvoda "Czechoslovakia's Socialist Constitution," *Amer. Slavic and East European Rev* (April, 1961), pp. 220–336; *idem.*, "Czechoslovakia's Socialist Constitution," *Congressional Record* (Washington, D.C., June 14, 1961); a juridical analysis was elaborated by Professor Wier in Vienna; Dr. Skilling analyzed it in *Jour. of Politics* (summer, 1962).

workingman." In Par. 2, we read: "Based on a scientific world-view, scientific advances are fully employed in the society of workingmen for the regulation of society, and in planning future progress."

A consideration of the formulation of the so-called guarantee of religious freedom and of the mission of the socialist state, shows them to be in direct conflict and, as a result, "freedom of religion" automatically disappears, because the citizen is not free to oppose the Communist line. It is noteworthy that the new Constitution specifies only the freedom of religion of the individual, and makes no mention of such freedom as pertaining to "organized" religion. The omission of the term "churches" from the Constitution as formulated by the Communist legislators, appears to be deliberate. No doubt, it was done to avoid any unpleasantness from the people who would evince strong religious sentiments and ecclesiastical loyalty, and who were instinctively aware of the practical difficulties involved in bridging the gap between communism and religion. In the face of this Constitution and its double-talk, one can see that the Czechoslovak Church, because of its privileged position, was in a better position to deal with the Communist state than any other church.

It was in the 1960's that the way to the ecumenical Areopagus opened again for the Czechoslovak Christian. From its beginning in the Czech Reformation, Czech theology has been "ecumenical-minded." In 1961, however, the first All Christian Peace Assembly met in Prague, and made that city one of the very centers of ecumenical activity. Thereafter, Czechoslovak ecumenical contacts developed intensively and extensively so that the minority churches with small theological faculties were overwhelmed. At the same time, active cooperation of the Evangelical Church of Czech Brethren with the World Council of Churches began to increase considerably. At New Delhi, in 1961, Dr. J. F. Lochman of the Comenius Faculty in Prague, became a member of the working committee on Church and Society. Later, ecumenical confrontations at the World Conference on Church and Society in Geneva (1966), and the Upsala assembly (1968), became an enduring challenge to religious and theological ideas of the Czech churches. It was during this period, and due to Hromádka's followers, that representatives of the Czechoslovak Church took advantage of these ecumenical contacts. Perhaps they felt guilty on account of the past, with its cheap adaptation and base compromise; and now the ecumenical contacts gave them some kind of justification for collaborating with Marxists as well.

Since 1967, democratization has opened up new possibilities of Christian participation in the Communist society. Christians have begun to be recognized as responsible members of Czechoslovak society. Public meetings of Christians and Marxists have been organized in the universities and churches, sometimes in the largest halls available in Czech cities. The first such public dialogue at Prague, in April, 1968, attracted more than three thousand people who responded passionately to an intensive exchange of ideas, and played a new role in socialist society.

When the Communists, under the influence of J. L. Hromádka, allowed some ecumenical contacts, especially association with the World Council of Churches, with headquarters in Geneva, Patriarch Novák took further advantage of the situation and, strictly for pragmatic reasons, tried to get into contact with other churches and gain some degree of credibility for his church. One must keep in mind that the Czechoslovak Church had been isolated in her own country and, because of her tainted past, was considered by other denominations to be lacking in religious earnestness. Now, because of her teaching, her proposed membership in the World Council of Churches was kept pending and even objected to for quite some time. As a result of this ostracism by other religious bodies, there had been a revival of discussion inside the Czechoslovak Church, as to whether or not the official title should be expanded, or revamped as the "Hussite Church."[70] (*Husitská Církev*). Many favored the change and many opposed it.

Finally on October 16–17, 1971, the highest organ of the Czechoslovak Church, the (sixth) Church Council convened. It confirmed the fundamentals of faith and various proposals for the future activities of the Church, and reelected Patriarch Novák for a second term. The title of the Church was changed to *Československá Husitská Církev* (Czechoslovak Hussite Church). It is important to note here that this sixth Church Council was attended by several Czechoslovak Communist officials, representatives of non-Catholic churches. The newly reelected patriarch, in the Comunique of this newly-named Hussite Church, exhorted the faithful to work in political circles and give intense support to all candidates of the National Front of the Communist Regime.[71]

This advice is characteristic enough to reveal how their Church always and everywhere had to politicize, willingly or under pressure. Interestingly, it must be noted, that in this ecumenical era, the former archenemies, the Roman Catholic and the Hussite Churches, came together in 1969 to celebrate memorial days of Sts. Cyril and Method and of John Hus. One can sense the opportunism for which Patriarch Novák is well known, and see the accommodation and flexibility of his Church. The Czechoslovak Church can be so flexible only because she never had a basic set of rights about which to worry. Nevertheless, even in

---

[70] *Nový Život* (Rome) **23**, 3 (March, 1971): p. 69.
[71] *Nový Život* (New Life) (Rome) **23**, 12 (December, 1971): p. 245; Rudolf Urban, *Die Tschechoslowakische Hussitische Kirche* (Marburg/Lahn: Verlag j. g. Herder Institut 1974), *passim*.

the "tranquility of the graveyard," [72] to use Friedrich Schiller's expression, there should be basic principles for which any church, and any being, should be concerned. In this sense it is to be hoped that all who believe in the need for a Christian-Marxist dialogue (either in the manner cooperation of R. Garaudy[73] or as a means to the world's renewal in the spirit of Vatican II),[74] will see that these principles ought not to be jeopardized or compromised, and must be accepted as a minimum[75] or there would be no church structure at all. Moreover, because of the dangers inherent in a constantly growing secularization, no one should expect these basic principles to be abandoned.

The fact that a Christian-Marxist dialogue was held in April of 1967 at Marianské Lázně (Marienbad)[76] seems to indicate that the Communists are at least open to this method of communication. If such a dialogue is to give rise for hope of success, some minimum expression of the Church's position would have to be accepted. If a dialogue is not to deteriorate into a monologue, there should be talking between partners who are equal and free.

The present emphasis on Christian humanism[77] may point to a way which the Communists might pass from "anathema to dialogue." A little modification of their atheistic humanism[78] could provide the basis for such a mutual encounter. With only a modest change in their philosophy, the dignity of man could again appear and their "robot" be reinstalled as the "image of God" or at least as a free human being. The recent thaw in the cultural atmosphere, so decidedly reflected in the manifesto[79] of the Czech and Slovak intellectuals, has kindled a spark of hope for the emergence of the Czech free man who might well be the forerunner of a "free religious man." The subsequent reprisals[80] against the authors of this manifesto are a regrettable testimonial to the unwillingness of recent Czechoslovak governments to concede even a small amount of the cultural freedom which was sought but never granted.

That the national church fully collaborated with Communists all these years without having to even try for a dialogue, is evidence that her ecclesiology was excessively political and contrary to the Biblical injunction to give to Caesar what belongs to him "but to God, what is God's." Caesar was not to get everything.[81]

In one way, since the national church concerns herself mostly with ethical and humanistic matters, she may be better adapted than any other church, to meet the Communists on common ground. (Strictly speaking, to meet on such a common ground, there would be no need for a church at all, since any organization with philanthropic motives[82] could serve as well.) A church, however, would have to represent at the same time, the "Kingdom of God" and should do so in accord with Christ's statement that "My

---

[72] The original term, *Ruhe Eines Kirchhofs* (The Tranquility of a Graveyard) has grown to mean more than its words literally express since Friedrich Schiller formulated them in his *Don Carlos*. It means that in a dictatorship—whenever and wherever—people have no more to say than the dead in their graves. *Cf.* for this interpretation, Franz Glaser, "Tranquility of a Graveyard in Czechoslovakia," *Central Europe Journal* **20**, 4 (April, 1972): pp. 138–140.

[73] Roger Garaudy, "Christian-Marxist Dialogue," *Jour. Ecumenical Studies* **4**, 2 (spring, 1967): pp. 207–222; Markus Barth, "Developing Dialogue between Marxists and Christians," *Jour. Ecumenical Studies* **4**, 3 (summer, 1967): pp. 385–405; Oliva Blanchette, S. J., *Initiative in History: A Christian-Marxist Exchange* (Cambridge, Mass.). An occasional paper by the Church Society for College Work, 1967), pp. 1–27; here is a detailed account of the dialogue, held at Harvard Divinity School in 1967, sponsored by the Church Society for College Work in the United States; *cf.* Bernard Häring, *Road to Renewal* (New York, Doubleday, 1967), *passim*.

[74] Pope Paul VI's *Decree on Ecumenism* of November 21, 1964; see its English translation in Walter M. Abbott, ed. *The Documents of Vatican II* (Herder and Herder, 1966), pp. 341–366; *cf.* Pope Paul VI's *Declaration on the Relationship of the Church to non-Christian Religions* of October 28, 1965; see its English translation in *op. cit.*, pp. 660–668; *cf.* Pope Paul VI's *Pastoral Constitution on the Church in the Modern World* of Dec. 7, 1965; see its English translation in *op. cit.*, pp. 199–308.

[75] Nels F. S. Ferrer, "The Church, Communism or Christ-Community," *Jour. Religious Thought* **22**, 1 (Washington, D.C., 1965–1966): pp. 51–71.

[76] "Juxtaposition at Marienbad," *Herder Correspondence* **4**, 9 (September, 1967): pp. 267–271; Jar. Karat, "Žádají od Křestanů: Toleranci a Lidové Fronty" (They Ask from Christians: Tolerance and "People's Fronts"), *Demokracie v Exile* **10**, 3 Munich, June, 1967): pp. 7–8; a very interesting book on this subject is Milan Machovec, *Marxismus und Dialektische Theologie* (Zurich, EVZ-Verlak, 1965); it is a translation of a Czech original (Prague, 1961). This dialogue was sponsored by Paulus-Gesellschaft, directed by Father Erich Kellner of Germany and by the Sociological Institute of the Czechoslovak Academy of Sciences in Prague, directed by Dr. Erika Kadlecová, with the approval of the government and ecclesiastical authorities.

[77] Karl Rahner, "Christian Humanism," *Jour. Ecumenical Studies* **4**, 3 (summer, 1967) pp. 369–384.

[78] Henri De Lubac, *The Drama of Atheist Humanism* (Cleveland and New York, The World Publishing Co., 1963), pp. 188–213; *cf.* "Marxist Sociology of Religion," *Herder Correspondence* **4**, 2 (February, 1967): pp. 57–60; Olaf Klohr, *Religion and Atheism* Today (Jena, 1966); H. Lilje, *Atheismus-Humanismus-Christentum* (Hamburg, 1962).

[79] This manifesto was first published in the London *Sunday Times* of September 13, 1967, and subsequently in the *New York Times* of September 17, 1967, and other important organs in various countries. The authenticity of this manifesto was verified by the Jesuit philosopher Martin D'Arcy, whose proclamation in this regard was also published.

[80] Richard Eder, "Some Interesting Happenings in Prague," *New York Times Magazine* (November 12, 1967), Sect. 6, 32, pp. 92–98, pp. 104–109; "Režím Tordě Zakročil Proti Odbojným Spisovatelům (Regime Took Hard Steps Against Rebellious Writers)," *České Slovo* (Journal of the Czechoslovak Exiles, Munich, Germany) **13**, 10 (November, 1967): p. 3, here is a detailed account concerning the affair involving the manifesto.

[81] Cr. Jacques Maritain, *The Things That Are Not Caesar's* (London, Sheed and Ward, 1939).

[82] Frant. M. Hník, *The Philanthropic Motive in Christianity: Analysis of the Realtionship Between Theology and Social Service* (Oxford, B. Blackwell, 1938), *passim*; idem, *Duchovní Ideály Československé Církve* (Prague, 1934), *passim*.

kingdom is not of this world." [83] Eventually, there would have to be at least a little "more" than mere humanism and, for the present at least, discussion of that little "more" would seem scarcely acceptable to the Communists. Thus, at first glance, collaboration by any church with Communists might seem to be out of place, if the church were still to hold out for that little "more."

Nevertheless, in the furor of immediate action, the long-range purpose of the Communists and their Marxist ideology should not be ignored. Extirpation of religion remains their ultimate goal. The Marxist dogma that the "abolition of religion as an illusionary happiness of the people, is a requisite for their real happiness" is still the guiding maxim for Communist policy. However, the plan for exterminating religion had to be carried out cautiously and slowly; first, because the churches had to be converted so as to be become ready instruments of state policy; secondly, because of Lenin's advice that direct assault would only lead to greater religious resistance.

Anti-religious campaigns insinuated into youth movements, and the education of the youth in Marxist-Leninist principles, are the chief means of creating an atheistic atmosphere. When the expression "freedom of religion" is restricted to mean mere ritual observances,[84] and when even these external signs of religion are gradually removed by government edict, defense of the faith becomes outlawed, while antireligious propaganda is encouraged. Under these conditions, it is almost impossible for any church to counteract atheism, which is an integral part of communism. Yet, as soon as certain churches did begin to collaborate, the Christian-Marxist dialogue produced a special impact in bringing about a change in critique and attitude. In recent years, the old antagonisms of Christianity and communism, e.g., labelling communism as intrinsically evil and atheistic in character, have been gradually modified on both sides. Some kind of new platform of discussion should be attempted, in a try for a gradual symbiosis.

However, while the world needs the Church,[85] (what kind of world would there be if there were *no* church?), it is also true that the Church needs the world; for a church without the world would be no Church at all. It may not be out of reason to suggest that perhaps the collaboration by the Czechoslovak Church with communism was justifiable, on the premise that a changing church should accompany or follow a changing world! Could the early collaboration of the Czechoslovak Church be styled as moving forward with the times when communism was the issue of the day? If it be true that most liberal Christians are "dormant" Christians[86] might not the Czechoslovak Church be called a "dormant church" with dormant visions and vistas? as a church presently best suited to fulfill this peculiar modern mission?

It might be looked upon as part of Divine Providence, that the green shoots of man's belief in God should inevitably grow and flourish, should staunchly refuse to be crushed out of existence by the Communist hammer, or cut down by the Stalinist sickle. If this is true, any church should still strive to have the Kingdom of God[87] permeate and enliven the world's mental atmosphere, rather than be absorbed by a deadening worldliness. Unfortunately, the Czechoslovak Church had been totally conditioned and made ready for absorption into the Communist state. First, by heresy, she cut herself away from the supernatural doctrine of service; then, by schism, from the very life of spirituality. Now she remains, and seemingly will remain, a dried-out branch, fallen from the Tree of Christ.

---

[83] W. Charles Lowry, *Communism and Christ* (New York, Harper & Britton, 1953); Nikolaus Lobkowicz, *Marxismus-Leninismus in der ČSR: Die Tschechoslowakische Philosophie Seit 1945* (Dordrecht, Holland, 1962), *passim*.

[84] Alexander Heidler, "Vztah Církve a náboženských organisací ke společenským problémům současnosti" (The relationship of the Churches and of the Religious Organization to the contemporary problems of the society) *Studie* **2** (Rome, 1972): pp. 796–800.

[85] J. M. Lochman, "Radical Secularity and Radical Grace" *Theological Crossings*, ed. Alan Geyer-Jean Peerman (Grand Rapids, Michigan, William B. Eerdmans Publishing Co., 1971), pp. 65–74.

[86] This term was expressed by Professors Charles Glock and Rodney Stark, sociologists of the University of California, in their article, "Will Ethics be the Death of Christianity?" in *Christian News*. *Cf.* Paul H. Hallett, "Dormant Christians," *The National Register* (July 21, 1968), p. 7.

[87] Richard P. McBrien, *Church: The Continuing Quest*. (New York: Newman Press 1970) pp. 67–85, "Church and Kingdom," especially p. 85.

INDEX

Abbo, J. A., 4, 5, 6
Abbott, W. M., 5, 8
Agnes of Bohemia, 10, *passim*
Algermissen, K., 65
Allmen, von, J. J., 52
America, 60, *passim*
American Episcopal Church, 46
American Methodist Church, 51
American Unitarians, 64
Anglican Church, 56
Anglicus Constantine, 26
Anti-Semitism, 67
Apostate, 5, 40, 35, 60 *passim*
Apostolic Succession, 33, 39, 51, 52, 53, 59, 61, 62; doctrinal tenets of, 52
Apostolic institution, 53, *passim*
Arnheim Conference, 65, 61
Association of Christian Societies, 69
Atheistic Humanism, 74
Attwater, D., 39

Baar, J., 14
Babula, R., 62
Barth, K., 6
Bartoš, F. M., 10, 27, 39
Bauer, K., 36, 54
Bauer, W., 3
Bednář, F., 26, 62
Benedict XV, 18, 19, 45
Beneš, E., 11, 20, 21, 45, 64, 70
Beran, Cardinal Josef, 71
Betz, H. D., 3
Biblical Heresy, 4
Bidlo, J., 39
Bochle, F., 9
Boháč, A., 34, 35
Borgongini-Duca, 45
Brno, 59, 60
Bulgakov, S., 43
Bušek, V., 22, 25, 46, 62, 69

Calvin, 6
Capps, W. H., 59
Catholic Congress (1935), 66
Cegielka, F. A., 7
Census (of Feb. 1921), 45
Census of 1963, 72
Central Action Committee of the Communist Party, 71
Central Action Comittee of Government, 69
Central Action Committee of the National Front, 71
Černohorské Kúpele, 65
Cerreti, 45
Červinka, M., 60
Československa Husitska Cirkev, 73
Český Misal, 16, 24
Český Zápas, journal, 34, 37, 38, 44, *passim*, 63, 72
Chalupecký Václav, 33
Charles IV University, 69
Charlot, J., 3
Chelčický, P., 6

Chelodi, J., 5
Christian Humanism, 66, 74
Christian-Marxist Dialogue, 68, 74
Chudobín, 59
Church Constitution, 62
Church Council, 60
Church of Sinners, 4
CIC, 4, 5
Cinek, F., 14, 37, 40, 43, 44, 46, 47, 48, 54, 60
Ciriaci, P., 63
Club of Reformist Priests of the Union of Czechoslovak Clergy, 9. 16, 18, 60, 64, *passim;* excommunication of, 18
Cockburn, H. J., 70
Comenius Faculty in Prague, 73
Communist Ecclesiology, 71
Communist Orientation, 68
Communist Policy, 75
Communist putch, 68
Communist State, 73, 75
Congar, Y., 52
Congregational System, 61
Congrua Church, 62
Constitution of Czechoslovak Church, 60–61
Constitution of the Czechoslovak Socialist Republic (June 12, 1960), 72
Constitution of Feb. 29, 1920, 45
Constitution of May 9, 1948, 69; religious and ecclesiastical matters regulated by, 70
Constitution of the Republic of Feb. 29, 1920, 4; religious freedom, 21; religious laws, 21
Constitutional Episcopalianism of the Czechoslovak Church, 61
Coronata, 5
Council (VI) of Church in 1971, 73
Counter-Reformation, 6, 10
Cox, H., 64
Cozens, M. L., 3
Creed of the Czechoslovak Church, 64–65
Cristiani, L., 1
Crvčanin, attaché of the delegation of Yugoslavia, 27, 28, 29, 38, 53
Cyrillomethodian heritage, 33, 37, 39; unionism, 41, 42, 64
Cyrillomethodian League, 71
Cyrillomethodian tradition, 48, 58
Czech Brethren, 64
Czech Church, 8, 10, *passim*
Czech liturgy, 15, 16
Czech schism, 7
Czecho-Moravian Church, 67, 68
Czechoslovak Catechism, 46, 48, 49, 50, 51, 55, 56, 57; doctrinal content of, 47; condemnation of by Bishop Gorazd, 50
Czechoslovak heresy and schism, 3, 6, 7, 10, 18, 21
Czechoslovak Orthodox Church, 59
Czechoslovak-Orthodox schism, 38
Czechoslovak patriarchate, 12
Czechoslovak Republic, 9, 10, 11, 12, 19, 21, 67; census of, 34

Czechoslovak Church, 6, 7, 8, 9, 12, 13, 17, 18, 20, 60, 61 and *passim;* emergence of, 21, 22, 24, 25; ecclesiology, 34, 36; first congress of, 30, 32, 34; census of, 33–34; statutes of, 33; and Hromádka, 69; Central Action Committee of, 68, 69; growth of, 65; dioceses of: Prague, Pilsen, Hradec Kralové, Brno and Moravská Ostrava, 72; Moravian Diocese of, 49; statistics of clerical membership, 57

D'Arcy, M., 74
Declaration of Washington (October 18, 1918), 11
De Lubac, H., 60, 74
Denis, E., 25
Devotio moderna, 10, 12
Dialectical ideology, 7, 8
Dialectical thinking, 7
Dilthey, W., 59
Dimitrij, Patriarch of Belgrade, 43
Dlouhý-Pokorný, E., 17, 18, 45, and *passim*
Dobrovský, J., 40
Dolan, J. P., 3
Dolanský, J., 63
Doležal, J., 14, 17, 18, 36, 57, 61, 66, and *passim*
Donahue, B. F., 30, 71
Dostojewski, 69
Dotation Church, 62, 63
Drábek, J., 42, 68
Dvořák, F. X., 14, 20
Dvornik, F., 3, 9, 10
Dyk, V., 68

Eberhardt, N. C., 67
Ecclesia semper Reformanda, 1
Ecclesiastical System of National Church, 62 and *passim*
Ecumenical Areopagus, 73
Ecumenical contacts, 65, 66, 75
Ecumenical Councils, 40, 41, 44, 45, 53 and *passim*
Eidos of heresy, 4
Engels, 7
Episcopal Church of the United States, 34
Episcopal ordination by imposition of hands, 61
Ernest of Pardubic, 10
Ethos of Christianity, 9
Ethos of truth, 4
Evangelical Church of Czech Brethren, 10, 12, 40, 69, 73, and *passim*
Farský, Karel, 9, 12, 13, 14, 15, 16, 17, 21, 22, 24, 25, 26, 27, 28, 38, 39, 40; as bishop, 40, 43, 44, 46, 48; as patriarch, 43, 49, 50, 51, 56, 60, 62, 63, 64, 65, 68

Fincke, E., 52
Freemasonry, 51
Free thinking, 63 and *passim*
Fuchs, Alfred, 64

76

INDEX

Garaudy, R., 74
Gasparri, Cardinal, 19, 64
General election in Nov. 1925, 63
Geneva, 73
German National Evangelical Church, 67
Geyer, Karl, 63
Giannini, Amedeo, 64
Glaser, Franz, 74
Glock, Charles, 75
Goodenough, Ervin R., 59
Gordillo, Maurice, 40
Gottwald, Klement, president, 70
Grigorič, Vladimír, 49, 50, 60
Grovanin, 34
Grykov, 60
Gsovski, Vladimir, 70
Guiton, Jean, 3
Günther, Anton, Rev., 26

Habrman, A., minister of education, 25
Habsburg monarchy, 10 and *passim*
Hannon, Jerome B., 4, 5
Hanuš, Josef, 30, 35
Hardon, John A., 8
Häring, Bernard, 74
Haynes, Carleton J. H., 10
Hegel, 7
Heidler, Alexander, 75
Heraclitus, 7
Heresy, 1, 4, 5, 6, 75, and *passim;* as species of unbelief, 4, 5; material, 5 and *passim;* personal, 5; cryptogamic, 4; crypto-heretically structured world, 4; heretical authenticity, 6
Heydrich, Reinhard, 42
Hitchcock, James, 5
Hlinka, Andrej, 21
Hník, Francis M., 6, 7, 11, 15, 25, 30, 33, 34, 36, 41, 62, 63, 65, 66, 68, 69, 74
Hoc, Josef, 17
Holba, Fr., 17
Holotíková Zdeňka, 44
Hradčany Castle, 69
Hromádka, Josef Luke, theology of, 68–69, 6, 42, 65, 73, and *passim*
Hronek, Josef, 47
Hudal, Alois, 26
Humanistic ideas, 65
Hurban, Mořic, 42
Hus, John, 6, 9, 12, 15, 48, 60, 73, and *passim*
Hus Church, 67
Hus Czechoslovak Theological Faculty, 69, 72
Husova Liga, 72
Hussite Church, 73
Hussite tradition, 64, *passim*
Hussitism, 69, *passim*
Huyn, archbishop of Prague, 15
Hyma, Albert F., 10

Idea, journal, 72
Intellectualism, 7, 8
International Conference on Youth, 65
Internationalism, 7 and *passim*

Jastrebov, 34
Javierre, Antonio, 52
Jednota, 8, 9, 10, 12, 13, 15, 16, 17, 18, 19; liquidation of, 19, 20, 64, *passim*
Jenišovice, 56, 64
John XXIII, 71
John of Jenstein, archbishop of Prague, 10
St. John Nepomucene, 10
Journal of Ecumenical Studies, 74

Kadlecová, Erika, 74
Kalous, Francis, 46, 48, 49, 50, 58
Kalvoda, Josef, 72
Kašpar, Cardinal Karel, 47, 67
Kellner, Erich, 74
Kerrl, Hans, 67
Kezníček, Antonín, 65
Khrushchev, 72
Kodan, 66
Koester, Helmut, 3
Kohn, Theodor, archbishop of Olomouc, 42
Kolísek, Alois, 40
Komenský's Ksaft, 24
Konečný, Jan, 48
Kop, Francis, 64
Kopal-Stěhovský, Paul, 26, 51, *passim*
Kordač, Francis, archbishop of Prague, 9, 11, 12, 13, 15, 19, 21, 35, 60, 63, and *passim*
Kovář, Francis, Patriarch of Czechoslovak Church, 27; biography of, 68; support of Communists, 70, 71, *passim*
Kozák, J. B., 63, 67, 71
Krajcar, J., 72
Kramář, Karel, 12, 21, 22
Krásl, Francis, 10
Krejčí, Francis, 35
Krofta, Kamil, 63
Krojher, F., 9, 21, 35, and *passim*
Kroměříž, 41, 42, 43
Kubalík, Josef, 17, 59, 65, 67
Kubíček, Emanuel, 47
Kudrnovský, Alois, 62
Küng, Hans, 52

Lausanne Conference, 65, 66
Lease, Gary, 4
Lenin, 7
Liberal Catholic Church, 65
Linhart, Francis, 69
Liscova, Míla, 35
Litoměřice, 64; Seminary of, 13, 18
Liturgy of Czechoslovak Church, 63 and *passim*
Lobkowicz Nikolaus, 75
Lochman, J. F., 73, 75
Los von Rom, 10, 12, 35, 67
Lowry, Charles W., 75
Luther, Martin, 6

McBrien, Richard P., 6, 75
Machovec, Milan, 74
Magisterium, 4; ordinary, 5; universal, 5
Maguire, E., 1, 2
Maltzew, Alexios, 27
Mareš, F., 25
Marianské Lázně, 74
Marmaggi, Francis, 45, 63
Marx, 7, 72
Marxism-Leninism, 72, 75
Marxist ideology, 75, *passim*
Masaryk, T. G., 11, 12, 21, 34, 45, 66, 69
Meisner, Alfred, 21, 69

Meyendorff, John, 26
Micara Clemens, Cardinal, 45
Modern Churchmen's Union, 66
Modernism 10, 64, and *passim*
Modernistic theses, 65
Modus vivendi of 1928, 64
Mueller Ludwig, bishop, 67
Murray, J. Courtney, 11

Náboženská Revue, 72
National Catholic Czechoslovak Church, 46
National Church, 7, 48, 50, 56, 59–75, 60, 62, 64, 68, 71, 72, 74, and *passim*
National Front, 73
National Reich Church, 67
Nationalism 7, 8, 10, *passim*
Nemec, Ludvik, 7, 9, 10, 20, 25, 33, 35, 67, 71, 72
Neuman, Augustin, 4, 35
New Catholic Church, 65
New Delhi Conference, 73
New ecclesiastical laws of October 14, 1949, 70–71
Nicene-Constantinopolitan Creed, 40, 41, 44, 45, 48, 49, 53, 66, and *passim*
Niemöller, Martin, 67
Nosek, Francis, 63
Novák, Francis X., 9, 63
Novák, Miroslav, Patriarch, 71, 72, 73, and *passim*
Novotný, Václav, 10
Nový Život, 8, 72, 73

Odložilík, Otakar, 11, 27, 60
Old Catholic Church, 26
Olomouc, 40, 59, 60; Assembly in, 40, 57
Orthodox Church, 8, 71, and *passim*
Orthodox orientation, 60
Ottaviani, Alaphridus, 12
Otto, Rudolf, 63

Palcát, journal, 55
Panslavistic propaganda, 8
Pardubice, 45
Pařík, Rudolf, Rev., 41, 43, 48, 51, 55, 56
Patriotism, 7, 8, 67, and *passim*
Paul VI, Pope, 8, 74
Paulová Milada, 27
Paulus Gesellschaft, 74
Pavlík Matěj, 12, 28, 30, 31, 40, 41, and *passim*
Pavlík-Gorazd, bishop, 41–42, 43, 44, 45, 46, 48, 55, 56, 58, 59; journey to America, 46, 50, 60
Pekař, Josef, 10
Perman, Dagmar, 10
Perutka, Th., 14
Petula, Josef, 71
Pharisees, 4
Pius XI, 28 and *passim*
Pius XII, 5
Pluralistic world, 4
Podlaha, Antonín, bishop of Prague, 22, 47
Polešovský, A., 49
Political ecclesiology, 71
Pospischil, Victor, 28
Prager, Tagblatt, 35
Prášek, Ferdinand, 11, 64

Právo Národa (The Right of Nation), leading organ of the Church, 12, 16, 21, 22
Pravoslavný Směr, journal of Orthodox Church, 55, 56
Premoli, Orazio M., 27, 45
Přerov, 51, 52, 57; Assembly in, 54; Moravian Council of Elders, 56 and *passim*
Procházka, Gustav A., Patriarch of Czechoslovak Church, 11, 17, 50, 60, 66, 67, 68, 64–65, and *passim*
Progress, 10, 11, 68 and *passim*
Progressivism, 59
Prokeš, Jaroslav, 11
Protectorate of Bohemia and Moravia, 66, 67

Ráček, Blažej, S. J., 17, 35
Rádl, Emanuel, 69
Rahner, Karl, 4, 6, 74
Reardom, Bernard M. G., 64
Rechcígl, M., Jr., 9
Reformation, 6 and *passim*
Reichsprotektor, 67
Religionswissenschaft, 7, 30, 37, 48, 59, and *passim*
Religious freedom, principle of, 5, 32, 39
Religious freedom, 73, passim
Remmers, Johannes, 52
Renaissance, 6
Říčan, R., 39
Ripka, Hubert, 68
Rouček, Joseph J., 46
Russian Orthodox Church, 34
Ruthenia, 7

Sacraments: ex opere operato, 25, 61; ex opere operantis, 25 and *passim*,
Sacred canons, 5
Sadducees, 4
St. Adalbert, 10, *passim*
St. Cyril and St. Methodius, 9, 33, 39, 41, 42, 43, 46, 47, 63, 64, 73, and *passim*
St. Nicholas Church in Prague, 22, 44, 46, 62
St. Paul, 1, 3, 5
St. Procopius, 10
St. Wenceslaus, 9
St. Wenceslaus' Square, 66
Šanda, Adalbert, 14
Sawat, 60
Schiller, Friedrich, 74
Schism, 1, 4, 5, 6, 9, 18, 75, and *passim*; schismatic, 18, 51; double schism, 59; Czechoslovak-Orthodox schism, 40–59

Schlette, Heinz Robert, 59
Schlink, E., 52
Schmemann, Alexander, 24
Schmidlin, Joseph, 45, 63
Scholasticism, 6
Schulttze, Siegmund F., 61
Secular city, 64
Self-making ordination, 62
Separation of Church and State, 11
Serbian Orthodox Church, 30, 32, 37, 38, 40, 41, 44, 46, 48, 52, 53; Episcopal Conference of, 40, 46, 48; Serbian Patriarch, 28, 35; Synod of, 36–37, 39
Ševčík, Alois, 17, 28, 54, 59, 60
Ševčík, Frank, 17
Skilling, Gordon, 72
Skrbenský, Leo, Cardinal, archbishop of Prague, 15, 60
Slovakia, 7, *passim*
Smith, Keating, Rev., 28, 46
Sobor, memorandum of, 28–29, 41, 44
Sobornost, 52
Söderblom, Nathan, 65
Söhngen, C., 59
Sokol, a gymnastic organization, 23
Šorm, Antonín, 23, 24
Soviet Constitution, 1936, 72
Spinka, Matthew, 43, 62, 64
Spisar, Alois, biography of, 42–43, 46, 57
Šrámek, Jan, 19, 35, 63, 67
Stark, Rodney, 75
Šťastný, Vladislav, 40
Statečný, Karel, 48
Stauracz, Franz, 35
Stejskal, Josef Rostislav, 10, 66; as bishop, 60; biography, 60–61
Stibor, Ferdinand, Rev., 15, 51, 52; as bishop, 55, 56, 60
Stloukal, Karel, 11
Stockholm Conference, 65, 66
Stojan, Antonin Cyril, archbishop of Olomouc, 19, 40
Strakoš, Jan, 10
Sturzo, Luigi, 7
Sušil, Francis, 40
Šusta, Josef, 25
Švehla, Antonín, 11, 63
Svoboda Svědomí, 72 and *passim*
Sýkora, Jan Ladislav, Biblical scholar in Prague, 13
Synod of March 18–30, 1931, 64

Tabach, bishop, 70
Thomson, S. Harrison, 11, 63
Thurian, M., 52

Trtík, Zdeněk, 72
Tuháček, Alois, 24, 30, 38, 43, 58
Turner, H. E. W., 3

Uniformity of the Church, 63
Union of Czech Brethren, 26, *passim*
Unionism 64, *passim*
Unionistic Congresses at Velehrad, 40, 42
Universal Church, 7 and *passim*
Universal priesthood, 62
Upsala assembly, 73
Urban, Rudolf, 12, 13, 14, 15, 16, 17, 19, 28, 32, 36, 39, 48, 54, 56
Urbánek, Rudolf, 27
Utraquist Church, 26 and *passim*

Vacenice, 60
Vajs, Josef, 10
Vašica, Josef, 10
Vatican I, 4, 19
Vatican II, 8 and *passim*
Veblen, Thorstein, 8
Velehrad, 19, 40; Congresses of, 64 and *passim*
Verdier, Cardinal, John, 66
Vladislav Hall in Prague, 69
Vlastimil Tusar, prime minister, 11, 12
Volná myšlenka, 34, *passim*
Voltaire, 64
Vrchovecký, Josef, 34
Vychodil, Jan, 40
Vyskočil, J. K., 10

Wach, Joachim, 8
Waldensians, 39
Weltanschauung, 48, 59, *passim*
Wenzl, A., 59
Whalen, William J., 65
Winter, Edward, 10
Women ministers, 72
World Association for Liberal Christianity and Religious Freedom, 66
World Conference of Faith and Order, 66
World Congress for Christian Freedom, 63
World Council of Churches, 66, 73, 74, *passim*
World War II, 67, 68, 72, *passim*

Za Pravdou, 30, 40, 58, *passim*
Začek, Joseph F., 7
Zahradník-Brodský, Bohumil, 14, 15, 16, 26, 43, 58
Žídek, J., 59
Žilka, Francis, 56
Zubek, Theodoric J., 42, 72
Zwingli, 6

RAYMOND H. FOGLER LIBRARY

Q
11
P6
n.s.
v.65
pt.1

JUL 22 1975